The
Newgate
Novel
1830-1847

THE NEWGATE NOVEL,

1830-1847

Bulwer, Ainsworth, Dickens, &
Thackeray

BY KEITH HOLLINGSWORTH
Wayne State University

With illustrations by George Cruikshank,
Hablot K. Browne, & W. M. Thackeray

81138

Detroit   Wayne State University Press   1963

Grateful acknowledgment is made to the
FORD FOUNDATION for financial
assistance in the publication of this book

TO RUTH

CONTENTS

ILLUSTRATIONS

PREFACE

This work began as and probably remains a book for persons interested in the history of fiction and in English literature of the nineteenth century. Friendly optimists have insisted, however, that since it has to do with taste, literary morals, and social history it may speak to a wider audience. For the sake of the reader whose special interest is not English literature, I have inserted an occasional explanatory phrase. I hope that the scholar who finds it superfluous will not object.

No one can acknowledge all his obligations, but it is a pleasure to mention some that can be specified. I am indebted to the Victoria and Albert Museum, South Kensington, and in particular to the former Keeper of the Library, Mr. A. W. Wheen, for permission to quote from the unpublished correspondence between Edward Lytton Bulwer and John Forster. These letters, in the Forster Collection of the Museum, were first made known to me by J. Lee Harlan, who also lent his photostats and assisted in transcription; I am glad to be able to make record of his generous assistance. I am indebted to Jerome H. Buckley for helpful and sympathetic advice. To Susanne Howe Nobbe I am more grateful than I can say, not only for advice but for encouragement which spanned a period of extraordinary interruptions.

K. H.

I

THE NEWGATE THEME

In a manner curious and now foreign to us, Newgate prison and the gallows, the ultimate enforcers of the law, hovered in the imagination of Englishmen in the eighteenth century. Witches, ghosts, and devils had not lost their diminishing sway, but they shared it with these human instruments of terror. The twentieth century has provided spectacles of horror, inescapable and vast, but these older symbols of punishment and death were intimate, comprehensible, and known to everyone. In these days, when the penalty of death has withdrawn to privacy, there is no one object like the gallows which familiarly and constantly presents to the eye the final power of the law.

It was the theory of officialdom that seeing criminals in the last extremity would frighten spectators away from evil courses. If it failed to do so, a lack of demonstrations was not to blame; hangings were to be seen at least eight times a year in London, though country dwellers had fewer advantages. For generations the executions were at Tyburn, outside the city; the criminal's ride there was a lively occasion for the crowd, especially if the man had some notoriety, and sometimes it required special precautions against escapes. In 1783 the authorities ended the riotous processions ("Tyburn itself is not safe from the fury of innovation," said Dr. Johnson) and had the gallows set up in the street outside Newgate. Here too, though the space was limited, huge crowds gathered; twenty-eight persons were crushed to death in a panicked throng in 1806.[1] If the weather allowed, many came the night before, and the street was filled long before daybreak. Some were able to avoid inconvenience. Tenants with windows or roofs near the scene rented space to those who could pay for their pleasures. Tavern keepers profited. Gay young men held supper parties the night before and breakfasts after the execution. No doubt manners were much softened by the

3

eighteen-fifties, but at that late time a room with a good window still brought twenty guineas. It was the custom of the governor of Newgate to entertain his friends well: they saw the executions from good official places near the gallows, breakfasted leisurely with their host, and went out to see the bodies cut down when he gave the order.[2]

The spectators were people of all conditions. Besides the simple curiosity-seekers and the roisterers, there were a few men of leisure; the wit, George Selwyn, to name one enthusiast, was notoriously devoted to executions. The crowd in the street included vulgarians of the middle class and large numbers of commonplace city dwellers whose bleak lives demanded excitement. The street children were there of themselves, and others were brought by their elders for a fright or a treat.[3] The underworld turned out in force, for social and business purposes: friends met friends in the festive crowd, prostitutes made new connections, and pickpockets found their work at its easiest. Ballad mongers and all hawkers had a good market; if a criminal of the day was notable the broadside sellers had already a tale of his life, and would soon have an account of his last words, probably fictional.

Mounting the platform before all these, the hardy criminal might be encouraged by calls from his supporters, with a "Bravo!" from his mother or his moll if he seemed ready to die game. The still current ballad of Sam Hall suggests the tone of these occasions:

> "I saw Nellie in the crowd,
>   And I hollered,—right out loud—
>   'Say Nellie, ain't you proud—
>   Damn your eyes.' "[4]

Though the doomed man was sometimes visibly near to collapse, he usually showed stiffness and courage or even a feverish gaiety. There was an opportunity for him to speak last words to the clergyman and officials on the platform—and to address the spectators if he wished. This was a moment of glory, drama on a grand scale, a part to be played once and never repeated. Time after time, the same expansive urge which had made some man seek distinction above his competitors—as a highway robber, perhaps—caused him to exploit marvelously the little range of the gallows stage. He received religious consolation if he was open to it; he was blindfolded, and the trap was sprung. The body—or, it might be, the row of bodies—swung for a time from the crossbar, and within some two hours was cut down. It went to relatives, if there were any to claim it; but bodies of murderers were hung in chains or given to a hospital for dissection.

As in other theatres, the audience too had acted in this drama. Their starved lives contained little that was dramatic, and they would rather be cruel than never be in a play. But their public experience of vicarious death made them a little crueller than they were. The spectacle came too often, and the fated ones seemed too oddly chosen. It had some little ceremony, but often it was deprived of meaning, and this—to add nothing else—was enough to make it wrong.

The criminal and his activities—and consequently Newgate and the gallows—were heard of everywhere. As for the newspapers, besides exploiting extraordinary crimes, they regularly carried columns of "Accidents and Offences," with a generous allotment of space. Even so enlightened a weekly as the *Examiner* did so, presumably as a routine duty. It is amusing, therefore, to see what happened when a country paper, in 1818, got into the hands of a real enthusiast for crime. When Thomas DeQuincey edited the *Westmorland Gazette*, he dispensed with editorial matter, neglected Lord Lowther's political interest, and almost did away with news:

> Instead there were long reports of the assizes in Yorkshire, Hertford, Salisbury, Wilts, and Winchester. Indeed, during his entire editorship, the assize news formed not only a prominent, but frequently an all absorbing, portion of available space. DeQuincey's fascination . . . appeared . . . in the careful selection of peculiarly mysterious and revolting cases. His prepossession necessitated frequent apologies for the omission of really important news and communications.[5]

It is significant that such editing should have been considered tolerable for sixteen months. The dominance of interest in crime is also to be seen in the *Annual Register*, which set out to record the important happenings of each year. Along with accounts of political and diplomatic events, acts of parliament, and other useful matters, it included summaries of numerous criminal cases, to the distress of later historians, who wish the space had been otherwise occupied.

For those who could not afford newspapers or who wanted nothing but a report of the latest murder, broadsides were sold in the city streets. Besides those which were written as news, there was a large production of ballads, true confessions, and "last dying words." Confessions were a specialty of the Ordinary (the chaplain) of Newgate, a perquisite of his office; he was in the most favorable position to obtain them and published his authentic versions within twenty-four hours after each execution. The ballad publishers, who dealt not solely but largely in crime, were located at Seven Dials, a circus in a wretched neighborhood of Holborn; the chief of them in the nineteenth century, James Catnach (who died in 1841), kept four or more presses busy and had criers always out with his wares.[6]

If a criminal's deeds or his trial or his behavior at the gallows proved interesting, his fame would pass beyond the newspapers and the patterers' broadsheets; there would be pamphlets and chapbooks, and perhaps later he would be included in some one of the collections of criminal biography—ultimately called Newgate Calendars—which appeared from the early decades of the eighteenth century onward. Crown Calendar or Calendar was the name of the court document officially listing persons imprisoned for trial at the assizes. The primary right to the name of Newgate Calendar for a book of criminal lives seems to belong to a work of 1773, *The Newgate Calendar, or, Malefactors' Bloody Register.* In five volumes, it was the largest that had yet appeared. Three years later, the Ordinary of Newgate, John Villette, produced a similar collection, *Annals of Newgate.* The two were unrivalled in the market for more than thirty years.

Among the many criminal reputations which sprang up and flourished for a time, a handful survived for generations. Certain murderers and Jonathan Wild, who was both criminal and informer, were remembered as infamous; the highway robber, on the other hand, belonged to the elite of the profession and seemed a little like Robin Hood to the city crowds, to whom he did no harm. Claude Duval, Dick Turpin, and several others became the centers of attractive legend; they shone brightly in the thoughts of boys, and stirred the imagination of men who lived in narrow rooms and dirty alleys. Turpin and Jack Sheppard, for particular reasons, were the folk heroes of poor city boys in the middle of the nineteenth century.

The stories did not stir ragged boys only; the affairs of bloody criminals entered also into reverie and dream in comfortable homes. Perhaps boys' imaginations tend easily to the Gothic; at any rate, the punishments meant to terrify evildoers frightened the innocent as well. Servants told tales of the gallows, parents used them to caution naughty children, and the boys themselves sought a delicious chill from accounts of horrifying murders. For many, all this was enjoyment, but some—sensitive beyond the ordinary—carried into manhood the memory of their fears. Serjeant William Ballantine, eminent barrister, as a boy was tender enough to fear damnation for sleeping in church. When he was filled with tales of violence by a well-meaning nurse, he often grew nearly frantic in his lonely bedroom at the top of the house, in terror of murder. "Unheard and unpitied, I many a time cried myself to sleep. . . . Such memories remain—perhaps, also, their consequences." [7] A great and good man of an earlier generation had equally vivid memories:

> The prints, which I found in the lives of the martyrs and the Newgate Calendar, have cost me many sleepless nights. My dreams too were disturbed by the hideous images which haunted my imagination by day. I thought myself present at executions, murders, and scenes of blood; and I have often lain in bed agitated by my terrors, equally afraid of remaining awake in the dark, and of falling asleep to encounter the horrors of my dreams. [8]

This was Samuel Romilly, who later set himself to diminish the terrors of other men's dreams.

On the other hand, images so powerful in private sometimes demanded to have their terrors eased in public. The ultimate threat of the law, like other austere powers, was often treated in jest, as one can see in the work of Thomas Hood and a host of forgotten humorists. Most of the jokes about hanging were commonplace, but probably the dullest of puns had a little liveliness when its subject was so frequent an actuality. The very word hangman had its euphemism, as if it named a deity. The original Jack Ketch, of the time of Charles II, was known for clumsiness and barbarity; his name was given to every hangman after him, and the unpleasant syllables became humorous.

Some of the ballads sought a gruesome tone: an Irish importation, "The Night before Larry was Stretched," has had a long popularity, and so has "Sam Hall," already quoted, which celebrates some unknown recalcitrant, bitter to the last. "Sam Hall" was a successful night-club song in the eighteen-thirties.[9]

Trials and executions excited, of course, the grisly appetite of souvenir hunters. These persons as a class are timeless, but the restraints upon them, tangible and intangible, were slighter a hundred and fifty years ago than at present. The universal feeling for mementoes, which signifies their aid to the imagination, is very close to the foundations of magic: the hangman's rope, cut into small pieces, was always eagerly bought. The nineteenth century, however, deplored this primitive lust:

> The landlord upon whose premises a murder is committed, is now-a-days a made man. The place becomes a show—the neighborhood as the scene of a fair. The barn in which Maria Marten was murdered by Corder, was sold in toothpicks: the hedge through which the body of Mr. Weare was dragged, was purchased by the inch. Bishop's house bids fair to go off in tobacco-stoppers and snuff-boxes; and the well will be drained—if one lady has not already finished it at a draught—at the rate of a guinea a quart. . . . If a Bishop will commit a murder for £12, which seems the average market price, the owner of a paltry tenement might find it worth while to entice a ruffian to make it the scene of a tragedy, for the sale of the planks and timbers in toothpicks, at a crown each. . . . Some of the newspapers make murder so much their staple of interest, and such large profits of it, that we have for some time apprehended that, in the event of a scarcity of subjects, the proprietors would find their account in killing their own mutton, i. e. committing their own murders.[10]

This pervasive curiosity was not limited to the masses, hungry for sensation. The collector of a famous library, the third Duke of Roxburghe, collected also the portraits of criminals, and other men had at times the same fancy.[11] Persons of means and influence fre-

quently arranged for admittance to see notable criminals imprisoned in Newgate.

It was another sort of curiosity which drove John Howard to
see the interior of every prison in England, to its darkest, dirtiest
cells, occupied by persons forgotten by everyone else. His seventeen-
year obsession, ended only by his death in 1790, set a new humanitarian example; and Elizabeth Fry's efforts, in the second decade of
the nineteenth century, set another. The eighteenth-century writers
on law and punishment—Beccaria, Bentham, and the rest—were
not the first to speak of their subject with passion or conviction; but
they wrote for a public which was every year larger and more concerned, and they gave their age something really new—a sense of
confidence that old custom could be changed for the better. They
brought light. Criminal law and capital punishment, as well as
prisons, became popular subjects in England and on the Continent;
the earlier writers about them were followed, in the nineteenth century, by a few professional students and hosts of amateur observers
and publicists.

So obtrusive in life, the theme of Newgate and the gallows
could not fail to show itself in all the popular arts. One element of
it was the life of those who lived outside the law; this had entered
into the drama in a tradition which included such various plays as
Bartholomew Fair (1614), the *Jovial Crew* (1641), and the *Squire
of Alsatia* (1688). The lives of beggars, wandering gypsies, and
thieves likewise formed the material of a number of ballad operas
in the seventeenth and early eighteenth centuries. These works
reached a climax of manner in the gaiety of the *Beggar's Opera*
(1728), which used the underworld for humor and topical satire.
Its assimilation of incongruities was so successful that it lived on,
quite independent of its connections with contemporary politics,
to become the most famous of English operas and to become the
inspiration of an independent new work in the twentieth century.
Its light-hearted way of dealing with crime and punishment aroused
a recurring discussion about the tone in which these subjects might
be spoken of publicly. The argument began with a rebuke from a
well-known clergyman in the opera's first season; it included, many
years later, complaints from several judges; and it had not quite

ended with the earlier part of the twentieth century.[12] The old controversy reached a new peak of intensity in the eighteen-thirties,
when the *Beggar's Opera* had exerted its influence in a new form,
through a popular novelist.

Though law and morality suffered transposition to a new key
in the most famous opera, they kept their simple character in the
most famous domestic tragedy of the eighteenth century, written a
few years later. Disgrace, imprisonment, and death loomed before
George Barnwell, and through him warned generations of apprentices against evil courses. Those who approved one treatment of the
theme were not always ready to approve the other. The satire in the
Beggar's Opera, said Martin Madan, a clergyman concerned about
law enforcement,

> is quite lost upon the lower class of people, and little of the piece
> may be supposed to remain on their minds, but the *mischief* of it:
> . . . it is hardly to be doubted, that many a wretched youth . . .
> has been determined upon the most flagitious courses, from a
> *noble ardour,* which has been kindled in his imagination, to imi-
> tate the illustrious hero of the *Beggar's Opera.* . . .
>
> How different a performance is the *George Barnwell* of Lillo
> . . . its hero led forth to public ignominy and death—exhibiting
> a striking lesson to all beholders, and an awful caution against the
> first solicitations of vice.[13]

There was a play far more popular, however, than the *London
Merchant* or the *Beggar's Opera.* It had an older stage history, and
it played to more varied audiences, especially to children and the
crowds of the streets and fairs. This universally attractive piece,
Punch and Judy, was also a Newgate drama; by symbolic action as
well as humor, it exorcised the menace of the gallows. (The reper-
toire of the same puppet showmen might contain, of course, particularized representations of notorious contemporary crimes.) In the
standard versions of the first half of the nineteenth century, Punch
is a part of everybody, an irresponsible Id: he throws the baby from
a window, and kills in turn his wife Judy, the dog Toby, and frequently a servant. Jack Ketch (sometimes called Mr. Graball) takes
Punch to Newgate, sets up the gallows, and calls him to come out
and be hanged. But the indestructible Punch is too wily for that.

He must be shown what he is to do; and when Jack Ketch sticks his own head in the noose, Punch hangs the hangman. He completes his triumph by killing the Devil, who has come to claim him.[14] This happy inversion of reality, though not invented in England, was completely at home there; this Newgate drama of the hangman hanged was played in innumerable streets, at uncounted fairs and markets, where no other theatre was. In later days, however the puppets might attract, the fable could not have the same value it had when its audiences were so well acquainted with Jack Ketch.

To speak of another art, the most popular of English painters used the prison and the gallows for the same didactic purpose as had George Lillo. The familiar pair of terrors waited for the idle in Hogarth's pictures of the Idle and Industrious Apprentices, done in 1747. Besides his far-reaching effect upon illustration and caricature, Hogarth (like Gay) was directly used by a nineteenth-century author: his apprentices reappeared in a novel of the eighteen-thirties, *Jack Sheppard*.

Among writers, dramatists were not the only ones to touch the criminal theme. There are the occasional poems, such as "Newgate's Garland," by Gay or by Swift,[15] and the more numerous occasional essays. James Boswell furnishes one of the best examples. His absorption was such that he was "never absent" from executions, and he seems to have desired his friends to share his interest, once persuading Sir Joshua Reynolds to attend. He liked to speculate on how his own behavior might compare with that of the felons on the scaffold.[16] Such an enthusiasm for executions would have been embarrassing to Boswell if he had been born a hundred years later.

With nineteenth-century writers, the criminal theme appeared in forms various and subtle: the obsessive brooding of DeQuincey, the meditation of Alexander Smith in "A Lark's Flight," the dramatic monologue of Tennyson's "Rizpah," the persistent exploration of Browning's *The Ring and the Book*, and many, many more.

Among novelists, the theme begins with the first professional and does not end. Defoe moved with ease between journalistic pamphlets on notorious criminals and picaresque accounts of fictional rogues; Newgate scenes (and of course debtors' prisons) figured in numerous eighteenth-century novels, major and minor; and Field-

ing took for the material of a satire the career of the most despised
of criminals, regretted by no one when he came to the gallows. Certain nineteenth-century novelists could point to *Jonathan Wild*
(1743) as an ancestor of their works, while their critics, in reply,
cited it as the great exemplar—the model to show how the criminal
might healthily be dealt with in fiction.

Probably the most interesting novel in the last decade of the
eighteenth century had no scenes in Newgate and no hanging, but
it belongs to our theme and strikes the note of a new age. Like
later dramatizations of the sense of guilt by Dostoevsky and Franz
Kafka, William Godwin's *Caleb Williams* (1794) owed much to
the tensions of its author's personality and something to the contemporary world. Godwin had intellectually rejected, in *Political
Justice*, the world's highest authorities, church and state; his next
work was a fiction of accusation, imprisonment, pursuit, and out-
lawry, with the gallows and the jail waiting just off the scene. "I
bent myself," he said,

> to the conception of a series of adventures of flight and pursuit;
> the fugitive in perpetual apprehension of being overwhelmed by
> the worst calamities, and the pursuer, by his ingenuity and re-
> sources, keeping his victim in a state of the most fearful alarm.

Godwin read, among other things, "a tremendous compilation,
entitled *God's Revenge Against Murder*, where the beam of the eye
of Omniscience was represented as perpetually pursuing the guilty,
and laying open his most hidden retreats to the light of day." [17]
But his novel secularized this theme: his guiltless victim was pursued by a determined opponent who could draw upon the legal resources of a state prejudiced in favor of aristocracy. While writing
Caleb Williams Godwin was "extremely conversant" with the
Newgate Calendar and the lives of the pirates. This kind of history
must have enhanced his sense that punishment was everywhere;
the England shown in it matched the landscape of his mind. The
book, however, mapped the psyche more than it attacked the puni-
tive laws. Nearly forty years later, Godwin remembered distinctly
the heightened state of mind in which he wrote his first novel, and
he said, in a phrase modern in its implications, that he had been
"exploring the entrails of mind and motive."

A few years later, Godwin's friend, Thomas Holcroft, touched the Newgate theme in *Memoirs of Bryan Perdue* (1805), a novel avowedly directed to the reform of the criminal law. It was the first to announce such a purpose, and there was no other for twenty-five years. The author's conviction did not inspire his pallid narrative, but he spoke the language of humanitarian enthusiasm. He mentioned, by chance, two favorite figures from criminal history who were to be taken up by later novelists:

> Oh, that the guilty might be sent, like patients afflicted with dangerous disease, to hospitable mansions, that might be humanely constructed for their reception, and their reform!
>
> How many men of enterprise and high faculty would then be preserved! What might the mind of Jack Shepherd [sic] have achieved. . . . he gloried in vice: alas! it was only because such was the stimulus that had been given him. . . . How inestimable might have been the labors of Eugene Aram, that man of extraordinary attainments and stupendous faculties! . . . How easily are minds like these destroyed! but by whom shall they be restored? [18]

In the ensuing apostrophe to kings and legislators, Holcroft called upon them to "study how life may be preserved and vice corrected. . . . Deal not in human blood!"

The legislators of that generation were not ready to listen. But within less than forty years, the ancient criminal law was readjusted to the society which had long been in advance of it. Before the arrival of the mid-century, a milder law presided over a milder people, the prison and the penitentiary were replacing the gallows and the convict ship, and confinement was confusedly but hopefully being thought of as reformation for the criminal. When hanging was no longer the promiscuous threat of the law, the simple Newgate-and-gallows theme lost its insistence and retreated to a suitable minor position in literature.

This book is an account of what happened—what the writers did and what the response was—during the decades before 1850 when fiction, under modern conditions of publication, consciously and deliberately took up the criminal as subject. During the critical decade of the eighteen-twenties, when reform of the parliament and reform of the criminal law were equally overdue, the Newgate

theme was everywhere, and it occurred in a few novels without
drawing particular notice to itself. Between 1830 and 1847, however, a series of novels having criminals as prominent characters
aroused widespread attention. Contemptuous critics at the time
called them Newgate fiction, and later writers have grouped them
under the label of the Newgate novel. The name has had general
currency among those who study the period, though it is not usually
found in histories or literary handbooks, and it is a convenient historical term. It can be misleading to the casual reader because it
suggests a type or a school with internal qualities giving it a unitary
character, whereas the external reasons for the grouping are the
more substantial ones.

The single element common to the Newgate novels—the use
of a criminal as an important character—does not preclude wide
variation in treatment, and the books differ vastly when looked at
one by one. The criminal may be made the object of a search, so
that the interest is that of the chase; he may be exhibited as a symp-
tom of social evil; or he may be examined ethically and psycho-
logically as a study in motivation. All these types of treatment are
to be found in the Newgate novels, which are early examples of
what later fiction was to do again and again. (The present-day
reader of *Crime and Punishment* or *An American Tragedy* or of
detective novels and murder mysteries can see approaches to their
technical problems in works of the second quarter of the nineteenth
century.) What firmly draws the Newgate novels together is that
most of them met strong opposition on the ground of morality or
taste. Other faults might be alleged against them, but the general
objection was that they familiarized their readers with vice and
crime, perhaps to a degree socially dangerous. We are dealing with
a school defined by its contemporary critics.

It is possible to generalize about the novels which were condemned, although doing so makes them sound rather more like a
type than they were. To repeat the sole common feature, a Newgate novel was one in which an important character came (or, if
imaginary, might have come) out of the Newgate Calendar. The
term was not applied to picaresque fictions, in which a wandering
rogue practised bold trickery and exposed the meanness of others
along with his own; nor to Gothic tales, though a Newgate novel

might borrow some Gothic elements; nor to romantic accounts of banditry, even though any of these three types might contain violence and crime. (Picaro, gypsy, highwayman, and ordinary criminal all fall within the province of F. W. Chandler's inclusive work, *The Literature of Roguery*.) In general, the Newgate novel dealt with low life in an English scene; but, because persons with respectable connections sometimes got into criminal history, the word might be used of a novel with a background of upper- or middle-class life. Such a book was not likely to be damned with the accusing name unless it seemed to arouse an unfitting sympathy for the criminal.

The Newgate novels have merit, in varying degrees, or they could hardly have been worth attacking; but none of them (unless we include *Vanity Fair*), is of the highest rank in fiction. Some had enormous popularity, which made them the more feared. The number of them, however, amid the host of novels published in the thirties and forties, is very small: eight or nine titles claim special attention. The most important authors—fewer still—are Bulwer, Ainsworth, Dickens, and Thackeray. The writers' names are well known, but the works, with patent exceptions, are not read. The controversy over them, nevertheless, affected the later writing of each of the four novelists. All the books have some interest, intrinsic or historical: the better ones are worthy of examination for their intellectual or artistic intent, and even the shallowest deserve it for their place in the history of taste. Their very differences, when observed, show how insistent were the feelings of the critics who lumped them together. This critical opposition itself requires a scrutiny of its motives and meaning; at some moments it proves more interesting than the books which aroused it.

The simple fact that controversy developed raises a question. When the Newgate subject was so old and so familiar, why should it attract a new kind of attention, genuinely hostile, after 1830? One answer is that what came to be done had real novelty: the new books were not repetitions. Although *Jonathan Wild* was a narrative about an eighteenth-century gangster, its real subject was the "greatness" of men great in the eyes of the world; the new books found interest in the criminal himself. The other answer is that the times had changed: *Moll Flanders* published as a new book in 1840 would not have been welcomed. The Newgate novels appeared in the era of the Reform Act of 1832, when social change was both swift and deep. The literary war they occasioned gives evidence not only of the reaction against Regency looseness (still common in the decade after 1820, when the Regent had become George IV), but also of a pervasive fear that crude manners and crude morals might flood upward with a rising populace, whose education was a problem still doubtful of solution.[19] The books appeared, too, when the reading public was enlarging; the controversy was aggravated by a perhaps unavoidable confusion about theatre-goers and new readers, and was sharpened when the penny-serial publishers of the forties marked a large body of the new readers for their own. At the same time, the novel itself was an expanding form, seeking new subjects and fumbling for new techniques; the argument which might have produced benefits for fiction failed to do so because of the dearth of enlightened criticism.

The controversy, ostensibly always about propriety or morals, began as a quarrel and too seldom rose above that level. It was obscured from the start by personal and political antagonism, so that one must try to disentangle mere reprisal from opposition born of conviction. It had a definite beginning and, after eighteen years, a definite end. By reason of the activities of the two chief critics, it had two phases, which may be seen as three chronological periods. The first phase was the feud of Maginn and Bulwer, which ended at some time after 1836, when Maginn ceased to be editor of *Fraser's Magazine*. The second phase was that of Thackeray's prominence as lictor, a ten-year vendetta against Bulwer; this may be divided into two periods, one including the correction of Dickens and ending with the defeat of Ainsworth, about 1840, and the other ending with the defeat of Bulwer, in 1847. Oversimplified as it is, this summary in terms of personalities reflects the unfortunate side of an affair in which writers of great ability, who represented divergent modes in fiction, differed about the nature of the artist's social responsibility.

Why the Newgate novels appeared at their own particular moment of history is one of the first questions. A significant part of the answer lies in the history of the criminal law, which is taken up next, in Chapter II, in order that the chronology of the literary account may not be interrupted. Chapter III describes the prominence of crime in life and in print in the eighteen-twenties, when there was no controversy about its literary use. Chapter IV and those after it take up the controversial books, with their variations on the Newgate theme; some of them precede, some follow the accomplishment of legal reform.

II

REFORM IN THE CRIMINAL LAW

As we look at the novels about criminals published between 1830 and 1847, an interesting historical question presents itself: what connection was there between the appearance of such fiction and the condition of the criminal law? A summary sketch of the law will enable us to draw a chronological parallel and will explain in part the presence or absence, in novels, of propaganda for legal reform. In the period under consideration, the eighteen-twenties, -thirties, and -forties, the criminal law and its administration were constantly discussed and were, after numerous efforts, vastly changed. At the beginning of the period, the law was as it had been in the eighteenth century; at the end, it was essentially modern.

The eighteenth-century law was marked by confusion, severity, and uncertainty in its operation. The confusion represented centuries of island history. Anglo-Saxon law was only partly written; even with additions in Norman times, the nation continued to rely upon custom and precedent—that is, common law. From time to time, this was further supplemented by written statutes, shaped by new needs. These were relatively few while social change was slow; they multiplied enormously during the eighteenth century, with the industrial revolution and the rise in population. Successive parliaments then created scores of new offences, many of them "new" only because particular circumstances were enumerated. Old laws, largely superseded, were often left unrepealed. In this state of affairs, Blackstone's *Commentaries on the Laws of England* (1765–69) became invaluable for students; but his volumes gave to the law a seeming consistency which it did not have in fact. The results of the long, undirected transition from common law to statute law horrified Jeremy Bentham, who for decades preached codification, but no one in government undertook an inclusive revision until the eighteen-twenties.

The severity of eighteenth-century law was erratic but extreme. All the common punishments appear heavy to later times, but the chief offence to contemporary—as to modern—feeling arose from the large number of crimes punishable by death. Beyond murder and treason, capital in most ages and countries, the death penalty could be inflicted for burglary, robbery, breaking and entering, arson, and for stealing from a house or vessel to the value of forty shillings; for stealing from a shop to the value of five shillings; and for picking pockets to the value of five shillings. It was a capital offence to steal a horse, a cow, or a sheep (but not a pig or a donkey); to make or utter false coin; to forge almost any sort of paper; to incite to mutiny in army or navy; to show false lights to cause shipwreck; or to return before the end of a term of transportation. All these form a familiar, unhappy legend; others are not so well known. It was a capital offence to cut the bank of sea or river, to drain a fishpond, to be disguised in the Mint, to go about at night disguised or with the face blackened, to steal cloth from bleaching greens, to steal or destroy game, to cut down a tree not one's own, to impersonate a Greenwich pensioner—the list went on and on. The total number of capital offences cannot be given with accuracy. Blackstone's figure of more than one hundred sixty was extremely conservative. This, or the larger estimates later given by others, could easily be multiplied if one took account of the various details in the descriptions of offences.[1]

This amazing body of statutes protected property of all sorts at the expense of life. Sir James Fitzjames Stephen, the nineteenth-century historian of the criminal law, commented that its "extraordinary lenity . . . towards the most atrocious acts of personal violence forms a remarkable contrast to its extraordinary severity with regard to offences against property." [2] The country gentleman, with his game laws, had the most elaborate armor, but other classes had imitated him successfully.

The English nation was never, of course, as harsh in its administration of criminal justice as the statutes might lead one to expect. In earlier times, the expedient for one kind of mitigation was benefit of clergy. By the eighteenth century, this had been renounced (not abolished), and the royal mercy was extended, upon the recommendation of the crown judges, more and more often;

the transportation system made it possible to send the offender out of the country for life. The table in Appendix A shows how death sentences were being carried out in the early years of the nineteenth century: in 1805, for example, three hundred fifty persons were sentenced to death, but sixty-eight were hanged. Besides the remission of death sentences, the growing disposition to clemency showed itself in two other ways: the frequent refusal of injured persons to prosecute for small thefts, and the common practice of juries in finding (when a guilty verdict was necessary) that stolen goods were worth less than the minimum constituting a felony.[3]

If confusion and severity marked the statute law, uncertainty was the chief quality of its operation. The deliberate leniency just described contributed to the uncertainty, but there were other factors. Prosecutors often were unwilling to bring charges because they feared the costs they would incur. A criminal who could afford a clever lawyer might sometimes gain advantage because of the intricacy of the rules governing indictments, the restrictions upon allowable evidence, or the various rigidities of procedure. But the greatest uncertainty was simply that the criminal might not be caught. There were no professional police, in the modern sense; parish constables were unsalaried, and the watchmen, scantily paid, were not much better than Dogberry and Verges. At the end of the eighteenth century, there were perhaps two thousand watchmen in London, but they were governed by some seventy different local bodies; there was no central authority.[4] After 1792 there were salaried magistrates, with constables under their direction, at eight police offices in London, including the previously existing one in Bow Street, where Henry Fielding had presided. In the early eighteen-twenties, the fringes of London and the roads leading to the city were watched by the Horse Patrol. All these forces, however, were not enough for the prevention of crime. As for detection afterward, the chief reliance was upon informers, either regular or casual. Legally fixed sums, running as high as forty pounds, were divided by the court among those who contributed to the conviction of a criminal. The reward system, though a source of corruption, was long regarded as indispensable.

If the criminal was caught and placed on trial, however, the uncertainties remaining were of a different and more limited order, for he was in the grip of an engine designed to convict him. Poor prisoners could not afford legal counsel and often could not have their witnesses at hand. Moreover, the time limit was likely to work against the accused, for no criminal trial could extend beyond one day. The limit was a traditional one, apparently imposed by unwillingness to isolate the jury overnight. Pope did not exaggerate:

> The hungry judges soon the sentence sign,
> And wretches hang that jurymen may dine.

In the nineteenth century, the old custom was no longer binding, but ordinary trials were probably even more hasty. At the Old Bailey, prisoners were kept herded in readiness, and cases were run through with dizzy rapidity. The anonymous author of *Old Bailey Experience* (1830) gave an average time of eight and one-half minutes; a reviewer of the book thought this not quite accurate—he calculated an average of twenty-two.[5] Such haste could not but produce inequities.

Guilty of something less than a felony, the prisoner might be transported for seven years or fourteen; if the former, he might spend much or even all of the term in the hulks, awaiting transport. Guilty of a felony, he heard the death sentence pronounced, even if the judge intended to recommend mercy.[*] If the convicted one was not thus favored, he would be hanged—and murderers had to be hanged within three days—at one of the routine, gruesome spectacles which, in the prevailing opinion, deterred prospective criminals. Almost everyone, reformers and conservatives alike, believed in deterrence. When it was argued that certainty of punishment, not the fear of the gallows, was the most essential factor in deterrence, the conservative had a reply: if certainty is lacking, the more need for the fearful public examples.

---

[*] The recorded sentence was shorter. It drew a comment from the well-known barrister, Joseph Chitty, whose *Practical Treatise on the Criminal Law*, first published in 1816, was a standard text for decades. In this unemotional work, dense with fact, one comes upon an unexpectedly personal remark, more striking in its context than perhaps it will seem when quoted here: "The judgment, as entered on the record, is with a singularly laconic brevity, sus. per col. instead of suspendatur per collum, as if the infliction of capital punishment were a circumstance of trifling moment." Chitty, *Criminal Law*, 3rd American ed. from the 2nd and last London ed. (Springfield, Mass., 1836), I, section 705.

In the eighteenth century, the several efforts to bring about reform in the criminal law were unsuccessful in parliament. In the nineteenth century, ten years of persistence (1808–18) by Sir Samuel Romilly resulted in the repeal of only three seldom-used capital statutes, and the law in 1820 remained substantially what it had been. Public sentiment was changing, but Romilly's most popular measures broke against the bulwark of the House of Lords. Argument came to nothing there. It became evident to many observers that the system of criminal justice was retained because of its place in the psychological structure of governing power, and that it would not be deeply changed until political power had shifted.

Sir James Mackintosh, leader of the legal reform group after the death of Romilly, successfully pressed for the repeal of several capital penalties between 1820 and 1823; as in Romilly's victories, the laws repealed dealt with uncommon crimes or with common ones for which the death penalty had ceased to be carried out. The most extensive debate took place in 1821 over Mackintosh's forgery bill, which ultimately lost. There was much public interest, because the crime was common and the death penalty so often inflicted.

The support given to Mackintosh showed the direction in which events must move. After 1823, when Robert Peel became Home Secretary, the ministry blocked further private members' bills by making legal reform a government project. Peel was energetic, efficient, and committed to moderate revision; the administrative changes he brought about were many and valuable. His term in the Home Office is best remembered for the establishment of the Metropolitan Police, in 1828; this disciplined force, under a single authority, very soon proved itself more effective than the severities of the criminal statutes. The Bow Street runners remained, frequently employed (as before) in private service, until the Metropolitan Police set up its own detective force in 1842. Bow Street men appear sometimes in novels; we meet them in Dickens' *Oliver Twist* and in Bulwer's *Night and Morning*.

The statute revision which Peel directed was aimed at coherence and consolidation; the resulting measures, often called Peel's Acts, were passed in 1827, 1828, and 1830. Obsolete capital statutes were repealed, benefit of clergy was abolished, and the new laws were grouped according to what they dealt with: theft and injury to property, offences against the person, and forgery.[6] This was not the codification Bentham had always demanded, but it was a movement toward order. Reformers were disappointed because the real incidence of capital punishment was so little changed.[7] Nevertheless, all the bills carried easily except the last, dealing with forgery, presented in April 1830. Public interest in forgery was even greater than at the time of the 1821 debate; in the lush years of the twenties, there had been a series of swindlers such as had never before been seen within so short a period. Nevertheless, much of the world of commerce was convinced that capital punishment was not the remedy. Peel's bill, retaining the penalty, passed only because of the intransigence of the Lords. In fact, however, no forger was hanged after the beginning of 1830.

At the end of the third decade of the nineteenth century, therefore, the statutory penalties, only slightly mitigated, were still anachronistic. As the table in Appendix A shows, there were 1,385 death sentences in 1829; seventy-four persons were hanged, of whom thirteen were murderers. Since 1805, the number of death sentences had multiplied fourfold, but the number of executions had increased only a little. Thus the death penalty was still threatened with a frequency that even conservative opinion did not wish to carry out in fact; and, despite greater leniency, it was still carried out in fact with a frequency that liberal opinion found horrifying. Such was the condition of the law at the time Edward Bulwer's *Paul Clifford* appeared, in 1830. The first of the Newgate novels, its serious object was to attack a legal system which was an instrument of class oppression.

In November 1830, Lord Grey led a new government, devoted to reform. The next changes in the criminal law were not delayed until after the reform but were accomplished while the struggle for the vote was going on in parliament. The removal of indiscriminate death penalties was one sort of enfranchisement, symbolically important, but the Lords yielded on this while still holding out against political enfranchisement. In 1832, the death penalty was removed from coining; from most types of forgery; from stealing horses, sheep, and cattle; and from stealing in dwelling-houses.[8] (Burglary, *i.e.*, theft at night, was not affected; nor was the forging of wills and of powers of attorney for handling government securities and the income from them.) The striking result of these acts of 1832 may be seen in the table of figures: in the next year, death sentences and executions suddenly diminished. The repeals had reached common offences.

In the reformed parliament, a royal commission was established to revise the whole of the criminal law. Again, however, some changes were not allowed to wait. An act of 1833 removed the death penalty from larceny accompanied by breaking and entering, if persons were not put in fear; once more the figures for the following year show an impressive change. After this time, it could be said that capital punishment had been withdrawn from the common crimes that by strict definition involved property only. The fear of death was no longer the chief instrument of the criminal law.

An act of 1834 is worth noting because of its literary connections: after this year it was not a capital offence to return illegally from transportation. The situation of the returned convict was later used by several novelists.* Various other acts affected the conditions of trial and execution: after 1834, bodies were not hung in chains, and after 1836 the defendant in a felony trial could be fully represented by counsel. In 1834, the court commonly called the Old Bailey was reconstituted as the Central Criminal Court. In continuous session, with a jurisdiction covering the metropolitan area, the new court did away with the worst evils of the old.

* Returned convicts appear briefly in two novels discussed in this study, *Oliver Twist* (1837) and Bulwer's *Night and Morning* (1841). In the latter, a would-be blackmailer is easily frightened off when he is recognized as a returned convict. The time is after 1834; he is not threatened with death.

Thackeray used the same device in *Pendennis* (1848–50). Blanche Amory's father successfully blackmails Clavering and flees to the Continent when his identity is known. The time may be after 1834. Amory can be threatened with death in England, but it is because he has killed a guard at the time of his escape.

Not until *Great Expectations* (1860–61) did Dickens make full use of the returned convict in hiding, under fear of death. The situation of Abel Magwitch, Pip's benefactor, determines the movement of the last third of the book. It is for returning that he is sentenced to death (though he dies of an illness), and it is this conviction of felony, necessarily followed by forfeiture of the felon's property to the crown, which removes the expected inheritance entirely from Pip's reach.

At several points in the novel, Dickens remarks upon the events as distant in time, but he does not mention that Magwitch's hazard has been impossible for more than a quarter of a century. During his period as a parliamentary reporter, Dickens may perhaps have been present when William Ewart's bill was before the House.

In a report of May 1837, the Royal Commission, which had been at work for over three years and which was to continue until 1845, presented its major recommendations on capital punishment. With the passage of these bills, the death penalty was removed from twenty-one crimes and restricted with regard to ten more. Thereafter it was statutory for the following: high treason; murder and attempted murder resulting in dangerous injury; rape, carnal abuse of girls under ten, and buggery; arson, piracy, and certain other acts, when life was endangered; riot, riotous destruction, and destruction of ships and stores of war; and embezzlement by employees of the Bank of England.[9] Again one sees in the table of figures an extraordinary reduction of death sentences for the following year, 1838. As to executions, the judges and the Home Office anticipated the imminent change in the law, for only eight persons were hanged in 1837. This figure was doubly unique: of the unprecedented number, all were murderers.

Although 1837 thus became the climactic year in the reduction of capital punishment, the reformers were not satisfied. Acts of 1841 removed the death penalty from rape, abuse of children under ten, embezzlement by Bank employees, and the destruction of buildings in riots.[10] No further repeal of capital statutes occurred until 1861.

Near the end of 1841, Wordsworth—not yet the Laureate, but acting the part of national sage—warned his countrymen that they had done enough. He had been disturbed for two years or more, particularly by the fact that total abolition of the death penalty could be soberly talked about, and had written a series of poems, "Sonnets upon the Punishment of Death," to assert that capital punishment for "worst offenders" was both necessary and morally right. They were first published in a general review of his sonnets written by Henry Taylor for the *Quarterly*.[11] The article may be taken to express the general conservative opinion at the time: that the removal of unused statutes had been good, that all the changes so far made were at least acceptable as experiments, but that the stopping point had been reached. For twenty years to come, parliament agreed.

By the latter part of 1841, then, the statute law differed from that of later periods only in assigning the death penalty to certain sexual offences and to violent injury short of murder and in assigning secondary punishments which—though many were soon to be reduced—were still excessively severe. The great change, so long desired, had taken place within less than a decade. An official of the Home Office calculated that if the offences of 1841 had been tried under the statutes of 1831, the number of capital sentences would have been not eighty but 2,712.[12] Much remained to be done, but it is easy to see why contemporaries took pride in what had been achieved. In the whole society, cruelty of all sorts was less and less tolerated; gentler manners prevailed in all classes. The reduction of capital punishment was both a cause and an effect in the change. Executions, still public, had become few. The hangman had been replaced by the uniformed policeman as the visible and familiar representative of the power of the law.

Succeeding chapters will describe the use of the criminal theme in the literature of the twenties and will examine *Paul Clifford* and the novels that came after it. As will appear, Bulwer's book was not merely the first but the only novel to make an open and extended attack on the criminal law. It was quite clear, after the Reform Bill passed, that the desired changes in the law would come; such a writer as Dickens would know that legal reform did not depend upon his writing propaganda novels. What both he and Bulwer did, while society was assessing the relation of the criminal to itself, was to take the criminal seriously as available for fiction. Society decided that, in most instances, the offender was not to be stricken by death from membership in the human race. The novelists examined the criminal as one who, however perverted, must be recognized as belonging to the human family. It was in this way that the novel accompanied and paralleled, rather than determined, the social movement.

III

THE NEWGATE THEME IN THE TWENTIES

In a time like the eighteen-twenties, one might expect to find some use of literature as an instrument of propaganda or some new examination of society showing criminal activity in its relation to the fabric of ordinary life. Strangely, neither of these things appeared in unmistakable form in English until the beginning of the next decade. One finds instead that the huge preoccupation with crime—characteristic of the large new mass of uneducated readers—was fed by newspapers, pamphlets, guides to sporting life, and the theatre; and that writers either casually reflected the general interest or, sharing it themselves, made some opportunistic, unsatisfactory use of criminal stories, which remained quite unassimilated by the imagination.

However, the chief Newgate novelist of the thirties, Bulwer, began his career in this decade, using in two of his books some elements of a contemporary murder and a contemporary forgery; and other writers undertook a like method of gaining sensational new territory for fiction. This use of factual materials was a novelty, distinctly different from the already successful trick of using known persons in society under a disguise of name. The best illustrations of these features of the time—the notoriety of criminal cases, along with the curiously limited use of criminals in fiction—are to be seen in certain actual cases of the twenties and the byways which lead from them. And at the close of the decade, Victor Hugo did, simply and immediately, what no English novelist had yet thought of doing.

The newspapers, daily and weekly, made a specialty of crime news—those with the most fervent interest in politics and public affairs along with the others. Newspaper buyers, moreover, were not the populace, for until 1836 weeklies cost 8½d. and dailies (which existed only in London) 7d.[1] Fashionable novelists of manners noticed what the papers printed. In a romance of 1830, a young reporter describes the drunken veteran of the staff who, getting his materials from the volunteer visitors to Newgate, writes "those execution scenes at the Old Bailey, which, strange to say, are become one of the most popular features of a fashionable newspaper!" The publisher, he says, wants the paper to sell, and, lacking any pretensions to a classical education,

> affects no love of taste—denies allegiance to it, and will pay it no tribute. Hence the alliances he forms with Bow-street runners and the bottle-holders to prize-fighters—the high premiums he will pay any first-rate doer of a "barbarous, cruel, and most inhuman murder"—the smartest getter-up of a racy *crim. con.*, or the first discoverer of gentleman forgers or lady swindlers.[2]

In 1833, young Thackeray, himself essaying journalism, described the relish with which newspaper men greeted a story:

> A good murder is a great godsend. Light be the stones on Thurtell's bones;—he was the best friend the penny-a-line men had for many a day. Corder was good—Cook was good—Burke was good— Bishop and Williams were good—many others, were no doubt, very excellent; but Jack Thurtell was the flower of the flock. He fed some of the best public instructors for months; and when he was turned off, their lamentations were sincere. There are few windfalls like this.[3]

The taste for crime news extended to politically radical papers which were anti-fashionable, one of which—the most outspoken and the most popular in the twenties and early thirties—is especially interesting because of its ownership. It is not an accident, in the larger sense, that such a paper, the *Weekly Dispatch*, was in the hands of the most famous criminal lawyer of the time. James Harmer, from the beginning of his practice in 1799, handled a multitude of criminal defences, including some of the most notorious. He accumulated a large fortune from the *Dispatch*, and his legal business at its height yielded £400 a year; he could well afford the Thames villa which his friends nicknamed Newgate, and he could retire from practice when he became an alderman in 1833.

On several occasions he wrote pamphlets presenting the case

for persons he thought unjustly charged, and indeed was ready to use any instrument of publicity for a client he considered in danger of excessive punishment. His reputation in the underworld was very great,[4] and certainly the machinery of justice bore less heavily on prisoners who could hire a Harmer or a Mr. Jaggers. Obviously no one could be better informed than Harmer on the uncertain operation of the criminal law; and he wished to see it changed. In 1819, he gave impressive testimony before Mackintosh's Select Committee on Capital Punishment, especially upon the evil effects of the rewards offered to informers. Thus Harmer illustrates in a special way the connection between legal reformism and the political unorthodoxy which all conservatives feared. He devoted his life to a queer passion—a well-paid one—for miserable scamps, the most unattractive members of the lower levels, whom nobody could look upon as the good poor; and his political opinions—also well-paid, by means of his paper—were of the far left in contemporary radicalism. (Harmer was solicitor to Samuel Bamford, but the *Dispatch* never became a Chartist paper.) As a newspaper owner, he made himself felt; the circulation claimed before 1836 was 30,000, and in 1840 it was 60,000. These were astonishing figures for the time. Among the "legal," stamped papers of 1830 to 1836, says a historian of Radicalism,

> the greatest power in Ultra-Radical journalism was the *Weekly Dispatch* with political columns which specialized in highly-spiced attacks upon Bishops, Peers, Parsons, the Pension List, and *hoc genus omne*, and with news columns which were never so popular as when tricking out luscious Court accounts of the drunkenness or sexual misbehaviour of the wealthy. . . . What gives [the circulation] figures the more significance is the fact that thousands of these copies went to public-houses and made the favourite reading matter of their customers.[5]

Harmer's activities did not meet with universal approval. Certain of them seem to be represented among the doings of a rascally criminal lawyer named Scampo, in a novel of 1828 by Thomas Gaspey. Unlike Harmer, Mr. Scampo is active in forming bubble schemes and rigging stocks; but he seems intended to suggest Harmer in his chief business of criminal defense and his sideline of journalism. He carries on a rivalry with other visitors in getting the best stories from Newgate prisoners: "Mr. Scampo had a share in a Sunday paper, which depended for its sale, on the P. R. and 'the College'—the prize ring and Newgate, to which he was in the habit of communicating flash intelligence." [6] Even if Scampo is intentionally a fictional composite, his portrait (by a sub-editor of a Tory paper) demonstrates what a more conservative level of society thought of Harmer and his *Weekly Dispatch*.

Equally characteristic of the twenties were the activities of Pierce Egan, the journalist and sporting man. As a reporter, he made himself an authority on boxing and prize fighting; from 1816, he wrote on boxing and racing in the *Weekly Dispatch*; during the twenties, he did pamphlet accounts of several criminals whom he happened to know or simply cultivated; and he later became editor of a sporting newspaper. In 1821, he made himself famous by the serial publication of *Life in London*, a handbook of the interests of the dashing young visitor to the city: boxing, the theatre, prostitutes, street brawling, the debtors' prison, fashionable slang, and "flash," or underworld, language. Society life is not shown; the night life is that of low dives where prosperous rakes and sporting men rub elbows with the underworld. Among other celebrities, the young men see Townshend, the most famous of the Bow Street runners, the favorite of the wealthy.* A scrape brings them to the Bow Street police office, but they go by choice to see Newgate and the condemned yard. With their high spirits and their simple-minded vulgarity, Jerry Hawthorn, Corinthian Tom, and Bob Logic were known to everyone, including King George IV, and they were even more popular when transferred to the stage. There were numerous imitations, and the public appetite was capacious enough to make these popular too.

In a market without photographic magazines, illustrators and print-sellers performed a function now lost to them, the representation of current events. The more elaborate pamphlets or books on notorious crimes often had one or more engraved plates, and there were in the shop windows single prints of notable criminals and the

---

* Twenty years earlier, there was a glimpse of Townshend in a fashionable romance, Thomas Skinner Surr's *A Winter in London*, of 1801.

scenes of their wicked deeds. The occurrence of William Hogarth's name in *Life in London* is a reminder of the lasting popularity of this favorite painter of the English; in the twenties and thirties, one finds his name constantly. Approved by moralists, enjoyed by everyone, and kept available by the print-sellers, he was a lively influence in the arts and was usually called upon as encouragement to a racy realism. He had become the patriarchal ancestor of a whole group of illustrators—and in particular of one genius, George Cruikshank, who had humor and darkness and a distorting individual eye not inherited from Hogarth. Besides the later book-illustrations for which he is best known, George Cruikshank, along with his brother Robert, was chief in the field of occasional pictures—including prize fighters and murderers—after the death of Gillray, in 1815.[7] Cruikshank's manner and tastes have the status of a distinct influence upon literature.

The theatre, always a raffish institution in the view of sober people, did its part in the twenties to satisfy and to stimulate the desire for sensation. The licensed theatres might carry on the dignified tradition, and critical readers might rediscover the lesser Elizabethans; but it was the unlicensed houses which throve by providing lively entertainment for persons of simple tastes. There was a novelty among the offerings of this period: plays based on the affairs of English criminals. Along with the variety already present in the theatre, from Gothic melodrama to *George Barnwell*, the lists of 1815 to 1850 included plays about eighteenth-century criminals (Dick Turpin, Jack Rann or Sixteen-String Jack, Jerry Abershaw, Jack Sheppard, Bamfylde Moore Carew); various dramatic items taking their title or theme ("six degrees of crime") from Hogarth's *Rake's Progress*; and some few that dealt specifically and by name with the here and now. Beginning with the Thornton case, of 1818, the notoriety of which came from its embarrassing revelation that trial by a battle with wooden staves was still a legal method of settling an accusation of murder, the major criminal sensations of the fifteen years after the war reached the stage quickly and with a minimum of dramatic transmutation.[8] The same could not be said of any like span of years before 1815; nor is quite the same thing true of the period immediately following 1830, though the stage of the thirties and forties continued to be inhabited by criminals of other origins. The taking of recent sensational cases into the theatre was the novelty of the twenties.

The use of such contemporary materials, showing a primitive impulse toward realism, came from a time when the living scene was rich with them and a time when the theatre audience was being democratized. Despite the battalions of the poor, more people had more money, and the city-dwellers required amusement. The unlicensed houses—in the theatre, as in everything else, the temper of conservatism was to leave the license law unchanged and let things work themselves out—filled prosperously and were hungry for scripts; they drew voraciously upon history and pirated from the foreign stage and popular fiction. With their new, untutored theatre-goers, they covered a wide range of literacy and decorum. At the bottom were the penny theatres, which now have no names and almost no history, miserable rooms where slum children and their elders were amused by the cheapest of performances. If other theatres were considered vicious by many, these "gaffs," frequented by pickpockets and prostitutes, were regarded by everyone who knew of them as nurseries of evil. They seem to have grown in number as fairs near London and the large towns died out or were forbidden; the performers who had made a living at them moved to the cities. In a world without motion pictures or television, every sort of drama exercised its fascination, whether Douglas Jerrold's *Black Eyed Susan*, at the Surrey, which had a stabbing, a trial, and preparations for an execution, or the low exhibitions where, in the words of a contemporary observer, "the highwayman, the brigand, the pirate, and even the murderer are shown under circumstances of the most favorable view; their crimes being either wholly excused or much palliated." [9]

The twenties had a more than ordinary share of notorious criminal cases, in part because public attention made the most of them. They passed into the popular memory; without so much printing, they would have made folklore. It was the last decade in which the hangman stood guard over so many laws. It is no accident that Thomas Hardy placed in the twenties the rural episode which he recounted in "The Three Strangers"; the hangman figure which lingered in the folk imagination belonged to no later time. Certain notorious cases of the eighteen-twenties permeated the general consciousness and presented themselves as literary material even before any writer of the time had built a whole novel on the career of a criminal.

Although John Thurtell never figured as principal in a Newgate novel, he achieved a greater literary and semi-literary notoriety than any other criminal of the nineteenth century, and he well illustrates the enormous popular appeal of gallows lore in the twenties and thirties. Beyond this appeal, Thurtell's fame came partly by pure chance, for he had the singular fortune to be slightly known to several literary men. Most modern readers will have met him under the name of Tom Turtle in Hazlitt's "The Fight," a lively, open sketch unshadowed by the crime to come, and Thurtell's happiest appearance in print.[10] In spite of this, his later notoriety is hard to account for: the affair was a dismal and commonplace murder, involving no extraordinary persons, no extraordinary feat of detection, and no extraordinary legal tangle at the trial.

John Thurtell, whose father was once mayor of Norwich, included in his experience a period of service in the marines and some business ventures which failed under suspicious circumstances. He became a minor prize-fight promoter—whence his appearance in books about the fancy, such as Pierce Egan's *Boxiana*—and he went to London to enjoy the sporting life. In 1823, he entangled himself with a gambler, William Weare, whose activities may have aggravated Thurtell's perpetual shortage of ready money. Thurtell, using as accomplices William Probert and Joseph Hunt, coldly arranged to do away with Weare. Weare was easily enticed to Probert's little cottage some miles from London and was murdered in a lonely lane at night. Because of an unexpected fault in the plans, Thurtell did the deed alone, but Probert and Hunt later helped him hide the body in a pond. It was a clumsy affair, and the guilty men were quickly found.

This was the event which, in the words of G. M. Trevelyan, "created the most popular interest between the Queen's trial and the Reform Bill."[11] Thurtell's acquaintance among theatrical people and the fancy is part of the explanation, and undoubtedly the newly employed facilities of the London papers built up the notoriety of a very ordinary crime. The mere quantity of material which the papers printed was unprecedented. A penny-a-liner, who sub-mitted unsolicited material at space rates, estimated that he made seventy pounds from the Thurtell case.[12] The modern chronicler of the affair, Eric R. Watson, calls it the first trial by newspaper, "the first in which there was any very serious collision between the Bench and the Press as to the duties of the latter in relation to the detection of crime and its investigation."[13] Thurtell's counsel pro-ceeded against certain publishers, but the papers were not to be discouraged. During the trial at Hertford, they kept express riders to speed their dispatches to London.

Thurtell had reason to object to another form of publicity—a play based on the case, which came to the stage with astonishing rapidity. Presented at the Surrey theatre, it assumed the guilt of the arrested men even before there was an indictment from the grand jury. A competitor opened a similar one on exactly the same night, November 17, at the Coburg.[14] The Surrey performance had su-perior attractions: the manager advertised that he had purchased the chaise in which Thurtell drove Weare to his death and the same bald-faced horse which had been present at the murder. The play was stopped by injunction but was put on again in January 1824, after Thurtell's conviction.[15]

The traditional forms of publication, the ballad and the pam-phlet, were equal to the occasion. James Catnach, king of the ballad publishers, is said to have gathered five hundred pounds in pennies from his series of broadsides on the Thurtell case.[16] As for pam-phlets, the most interesting were two by Pierce Egan, who had previously been acquainted with Thurtell and who interviewed him in prison.

From all accounts of the trial and execution, Hertford became the scene of a macabre festival. Sightseers came from distant parts of England and even Ireland, in such numbers that they could not find accommodation in the town.[17] They gathered on January 9, 1824, for a single execution, Thurtell's; for Hunt was sent to the hulks and Probert had turned king's evidence. Egan estimated that fifteen thousand people attended; the rivalry for roofs and high points was intense. George Borrow was in the crowd; Charles Lamb was not, but he exercised his imagination on the occasion.[18]

As usual, people tried to buy the hangman's rope; but an

under-sheriff, a man of rare virtue, ordered the rope burned. Thurtell's body was taken to Bartholomew's Hospital for dissection, losing a finger to some curiosity-seeker or wen-curer on the way. A famous surgeon performed the dissection before a crowd who, in order to gain admittance, had had only to profess themselves students of anatomy. The demonstration went on for weeks and was duly reported in the newspapers.

Thurtell then passed into a quieter immortality. The old tale stirred again, a year and a half later, when Probert was hanged, ostensibly for horse-stealing;[19] and twenty years later, when gossip went round among theatre-goers that a successful new actress was Thurtell's daughter.* Out-and-out young gentlemen continued to boast of having shaken Thurtell's hand, for the sporting world probably remembered him best.[20] But nobody, as will appear, seemed to forget.

Thurtell was destined, obviously, for the Newgate Calendars. George Borrow, who knew of him from boyhood years in Norwich, was the first to include him in one. His *Celebrated Trials and Remarkable Cases of Criminal Jurisprudence from the Earliest Records to the Year 1825* was published, without the author's name, in March 1825. In closing his volumes with Thurtell, Borrow attempted a vividness he was not inclined to elsewhere in the performance of a routine task.[21] He continued to make use of his recollections of Thurtell. He managed to speak of him in the early pages of *The Zincali*, in 1841; he made use of him again in minor episodes in *Lavengro* and *The Romany Rye*, during the eighteen-fifties. So late as that, he could omit the murderer's name and yet be sure that the character would be recognized.[22]

When one has spoken of the writers who happened to be personally interested in Thurtell, the after-history of his case is only begun. Walter Scott, as Lockhart recorded in his biography, was one of the fascinated contemporaries. Thurtell could not, of course, be omitted from DeQuincey's essay in macabre humor, "On

---

* "And a Madame Anna Millon *has fascinated everybody* by her acting & singing at the little theatre in Oxford Street. Who do you think she is??—The daughter of Thurtell by the sister of Hunt. Fact upon my word." Letter of May 25, 1844, from John Forster to Edward Bulwer Lytton. (Unpublished original in the Forster collection, Victoria and Albert Museum.)

Murder as One of the Fine Arts," published three years after he
was hanged. The most famous by-product of the case was Thurtell's gig, which Carlyle turned into a symbol. A witness at the
trial had seemed—so Carlyle remembered a printed report, not
quite accurately—to say that Thurtell's keeping a gig made him
respectable.[23] From 1830 on, gig, gigman, and gigmanity were a
favorite part of his vocabulary of abuse for the smug materialism
of "respectability." Thurtell continued to have a varied life in
literary allusion; he bobs up everywhere. Interest in the case lasted
into the present century, which has seen, besides Watson's factual
and legal summary, a new account by Thomas Burke in the form
of fiction.[24]

The Thurtell affair demonstrated the unbounded enthusiasm
with which the early nineteenth century publicized its criminals.
A young writer, Edward Lytton Bulwer,* who was always to show
an unusual perception of what readers wanted, contrived to work
over the Thurtell case for his second novel, and *Pelham* became
the sensation of 1828.

Its crime story was not the only reason for its popularity, especially among sophisticated readers. It was a clever book, with
a good deal of topical comment on politics and society; and its
main interest for some readers was certainly the young dandy,
Pelham, who manages to maintain himself as both an aristocrat
and an intellectual. He is a surprisingly lively character, even at
this distance in time. He enjoys travel and his position in a wealthy
caste, but he has a heart and a conscience and a mind for higher
things. At the behest of his uncle, he reads Jeremy Bentham, James
Mill (in the *Encyclopaedia Britannica*), and the political economists; and thenceforth he follows the principles of morality, both
political and private. He presents an intelligible kind of response
to much that interested contemporary readers. The book had a
conventional love story and a few characters drawn from life.[25]

* His full name, Edward George Earle Lytton Bulwer, was usually shortened to
Edward Lytton Bulwer. After 1838 he was a baronet, and ultimately he was the
first Baron Lytton of Knebworth. After 1843, still a baronet, inheriting Knebworth
from his mother, he followed her example and added Lytton to his last name; then,
and for many years after, he was Sir Edward (Lytton) Bulwer-Lytton. Since he
was Bulwer during most of the period dealt with in this book, I avoid Bulwer-
Lytton and continue to call him Bulwer to the end, for the sake of simplicity.

Nevertheless, the chief interest of the novel's slender plot (which may owe something to *Caleb Williams*) hung upon the consequences of a murder: a sympathetic character is wrongly suspected of the deed. In the histories, *Pelham* has not usually been described as a crime novel; but large numbers of readers must have hastened through Bulwer's demonstration of integrity in politics and constancy in affection simply to find out who really killed Sir John Tyrrell.[26] In certain respects, the murder resembles Thurtell's murder of Weare. The principals in the crime are not among the main characters; but Sir Reginald Glanville, Pelham's friend and one of the chief persons of the story, is suspected of committing it. Glanville's explanation to Pelham—a gaudy tale of rape and madness—is that Tyrrell has been responsible for the death of a young mistress whom Glanville dearly loved, and Glanville has made it the business of his life to pursue and ruin Tyrrell, with the aid of a tool, Thornton. Tyrrell is murdered, and the tool has been in a position to extort money from Glanville unmercifully. When the latest demand is resisted, Thornton causes Glanville to be apprehended for the murder. To save him, Pelham sets out to find and prove the real murderer. So it comes about that we have in the latter part of *Pelham* one of the earliest real tales of detection in English literature. Bulwer's pattern—the nonprofessional doing the work of a legal officer in order to clear an innocent friend—has proved to be an enduring one.

He obviously took delight in working out the chief climax of his book. Having hired a stool-pigeon, Pelham plans to go to the hide-out of Thornton's gang to meet a witness-accomplice to the murder. Pelham is given a quick lesson in flash language to enable him to pass the comrades safely, and is conducted blindfolded to the hideaway. The plan succeeds; Pelham gets a confession and even gets the accomplice into his custody, though his life is temporarily in danger when the gang find him out. Thornton, who intended robbery and killed Tyrrell only when he was recognized, is hanged unrepentant. Glanville dies; Pelham marries.

The chief use Bulwer made of Thurtell was to model the hard and stolid Thornton after him.[27] He is a meager and ill-drawn character in the novel, but he must have seemed convincing enough to readers of 1828, who were familiar with this sporting type and whose memories could do the author's creative work for him. Bulwer used other materials currently fashionable. He followed the formula of including both high life and low life; Pelham is no pseudo-gentleman like Egan's Bob Logic, but he enjoys some of the same rakish accomplishments—the acquaintance with shady characters in flash-kens and their underworld slang. When Job Jonson cleverly picks Pelham's pocket, Bulwer cites as authority for the episode James Hardy Vaux, whose *Memoirs* (1819) of swindling and pocket-picking were well known in the eighteen-twenties.[28] Bulwer did not content himself, however, with reading books of roguery. He visited the thieves' quarters of London some few times while writing *Pelham*, and on one of these occasions was pleasantly entertained by a man who had tried to rob him a few years before. Bulwer's son tells us also that Job Jonson, Pelham's clever informer, "had his prototype in a member of the swell-mob known to the author." [29]

In the present context *Pelham* has a particular significance because in it an author introduced the contemporary underworld as a part of his scene and its inhabitants among his characters. Gothic criminals there had been before, and rogues in the chronicle novels, and gentlemanly blackguards and upper-class villains. But what Bulwer did was new. It is of special interest, moreover, because, having found this successful, he continued to use similar materials in other books.

The aspect of *Pelham* which is emphasized here, surely a factor in its immediate popularity, received little attention in print. Of a representative half-dozen reviews, that in the *London Magazine* was the only one to notice the criminal part of the story. It found merit in the scene of Pelham among the London thieves: overwrought, but "done with very vigorous power, both of narrative and description." [30]

In the midst of all else that was in *Pelham*, it is not surprising that most reviewers said nothing of the underworld element. There was in it even a definite and self-conscious theory of fiction, worth remarking because of the author's works to come. Bulwer himself seems to speak, though the words are those of his Tory literary man, Vincent: every good novel has the aim of "increasing our knowledge of the heart," a large end which may be vitiated by "rigorous attention to one isolated moral." The writer must be a realist. And it is not enough for him to have a good heart—he must be a philosopher.

> Before he touches his tale, he should be thoroughly acquainted with the science of morals, and the metaphysical, as well as the more open, operations of the mind. If his knowledge is not deep and clear, his love of the good may only lead him into error.[31]

Such an utterance is that of a young philosopher—a follower of both Godwin and Bentham—trying to arrange a harmony of his opinions and his feelings. Among novelists, Bulwer deserves credit for being the only one to do exactly this, though John Stuart Mill, in whom the conflict was deep and real, was already privately reconciling his Benthamism and his emotional nature. Bulwer had always the fortune to be able to imagine grandeurs beyond his powers of creation. His theories of fiction were to become more explicit as he wrote more novels and replied to the attacks of critics; unfortunately, the novels would always fall short of his aims for them.

The most notorious crime of the eighteen-twenties next to Thurtell's came to light shortly after his; the offender was executed in the same year, 1824. It was of a very different sort, an offence involving forgery. Henry Fauntleroy's case was the first of the several mentioned above which aroused argument about capital punishment between the failure of Mackintosh's forgery bill in 1821 and the debate on Peel's in 1830. The case had also the effect of attracting certain novelists to the use of contemporary events in fiction, in a decade when historical romance was dominant; and of drawing the attention of writers (especially Bulwer) to the psychology of criminal acts.

Henry Fauntleroy, a swindling banker who carried on his enormously complicated system of frauds for ten years before being discovered, represents to perfection some characteristic aspects of the eighteen-twenties. He belonged to a pious and highly respectable dissenting family. He first was cast in the role of earnest, honest, middle-class boy determined to make good, and he succeeded his father as manager of a bank. In time, however, he began to play the part of the vulgar young man of wealth. This outside role did not immediately affect his standing at the bank —perhaps he was not conspicuous among the young men whose fathers had come into money during the war. In some crisis of his affairs in 1814, he committed his first forgery. His private memorandum made at the time blamed the Bank of England for his troubles; it was a popular defence.[32]

Since he had everything about the bank in his charge, the beginning was easy. Large numbers of his depositors held government securities, the income from which was paid directly into their bank accounts. His method was to make a power of attorney, forging the signatures of the client and witnesses, which would allow him to dispose of securities for the owner. Having removed them from the Bank of England and sold them through his own broker, he used the proceeds as he pleased, saving only enough to pay to the unsuspecting "owner" the proper amount of interest at the proper times. Simple enough in one case, when repeated variously—as it was in the next ten years—the trick became burdensome. By 1824, extending his system unbelievably, Fauntleroy had stolen some £400,000 in government securities and was required to find £16,000 of new money in a year to keep up the payments on them. The end had to come, even in those easygoing days. Executors of an estate visited the Bank of England and found only a fraction of a fund of £46,000; for some reason Fauntleroy had not been able to cover the loss. He was arrested on Friday, September 10, 1824; his house suspended payment on Monday and went into bankruptcy a few days later.

Many people were ruined by the failure of the bank, the clients ranging from wealthy persons to local tradesmen. The owners of the securities were in the best position, since the Bank of England was required by law to make good such losses, but the complexity of the transactions was such that final settlements were not completed until twenty-six years later.

The public tumult was in keeping with the size of the frauds. People talked of Fauntleroy incessantly, and the newspapers were filled with truth and legend about him. This too became a trial by newspaper, but with no judicial objection. He was universally despised and condemned, at least until the time of the trial. He was convicted, of course—but sentiment thereafter became more favorable. Although he was the sole author of the forgeries, the public naturally found it hard to believe that his partners were as ignorant and as negligent as they appeared.

Besides the frauds, a great deal of information about Fauntleroy's private life became public at the time of the trial. His wife had separated from him, taking their infant son. He kept a succession of expensive mistresses, the best known being Mary Bertram, "Mrs. Bang," the Corinthian Kate of *Life in London*.[33] By 1816 he had a fine house at Hampton-on-Thames, where he gave gay parties on Saturday nights, though he never failed to be at the bank on Monday mornings. Later he took a splendid house in Brighton. The notorious Mrs. Bang was replaced by a young girl, Maria Forbes, who bore him two children, and whom he took care of to the extent of £6,000, a London house, and an annuity. (His wife received trifling amounts, if anything, and in her later years was taken care of by their son.) As his financial affairs grew more complicated and more dangerous, his need of diversion became incessant; but his reputation as a man about town did not prejudice his business position. On the contrary, he was reputed to be a very rich man.

When so scandalous a personal story accompanied the largest banking fraud in history, it is not surprising that there was a festival of publicity. Much of it was sensational gossip, but so notorious a case could not fail to become a test of public sentiment on capital punishment. Here was a kind of forgery which surely the law aimed at. In such a case, ought the criminal to be put to death? Two of the most important daily papers, the *Morning Chronicle* and *Morning Herald* thought he ought not; others of the same opinion were the *New Times*, the *Examiner*, the *Sunday Times*, and *Bell's Weekly Messenger*. Fauntleroy's attorney, James Harmer, who had defended Joseph Hunt, took advantage of every circumstance to arouse sympathy for his client. After the death sentence, he appealed, of course, for a royal reprieve; and he carried on a campaign for sympathy for Fauntleroy in the *Weekly Dispatch*. As a result of such efforts, the formal plea for mercy was accompanied by a petition of 25,000 names.[34] But the plea was refused, and Fauntleroy's execution was set for November 30.

From beginning to end, the case fed the newspapers and

broadside printers—though apparently not the theatres [35]—with incidental curiosities. People had early become familiar with the picture that slightly resembled Napoleon's, showing the hair combed straight to the forehead; Fauntleroy seems to have dramatized himself as a Napoleon of commerce. There was a rumor that he had committed suicide; and another, better justified, that the friends who had constant access to him were planning his escape. Fauntleroy's estranged but faithful wife came to see him in prison; but current gossip was far more interested in the visits of Maria Forbes, who sent him each day some delicacy from her kitchen. Her final and famous contribution was a pigeon pie. During the last days she brought the two children, eighteen months and three years old, to see him; they were dressed in black, like herself. One Edmund Angelini was widely publicized when he pressed a request to be allowed to take Fauntleroy's place on the scaffold. The mass in the streets outside Newgate was said to be more than one hundred thousand persons—the largest yet known. Restaurants opposite the scaffold charged their patrons a pound each for their places.

The Napoleon of forgers, serene in his last days, was composed before the throng of spectators. For some reason, the fall arranged was only eighteen inches; the crowd did not see the helpers under the platform who seized his legs to make sure the process did not fail.

Charles Lamb used the Fauntleroy case as the spring-board for an essay printed a few months later, "The Last Peach." [36] The novelists did not get to it so soon, but within six years it had been put to use by several of them. The first was Bulwer, with *The Disowned*, his third novel, published in October 1828. The book was hastily got up to follow in the wake of the successful *Pelham*, published five months previously; quite justly, it is now unread, but at the time it made a greater appeal to the lending-library public,[37] for it had a fine collection of aristocratic names and a plot that got under way with less delay. It has some interest here as a contemporary document and as an embodiment of the ideas which interested Bulwer in this early stage of his career. The ideological hero of the book, one Algernon Mordaunt, is a Byronic lonely genius, a benevolent liberal aristocrat—the dramatized

Bulwer whom Bulwer so much enjoyed. His function is to exemplify and utter noble sentiments and to influence the young hero of the principal plot. The time is given as the eighteenth century, but the important materials of the book are all of Bulwer's age.

Only one part of the story need be recounted. The Fauntleroy character is juxtaposed as an unworthy contrast to Mordaunt, who has lost his estate through no fault of his own and who now appears as an impoverished writer, Glendower, struggling energetically to support his wife and child. Glendower-Mordaunt, who shuns contact with wealthy friends, is sought out by an old acquaintance, Crauford, a prosperous financier. Like Fauntleroy as a youth, Crauford has a reputation for virtue; his acquaintances all regard him as a very model of rectitude. Pretending to be moved by the purest friendship, he persists in his visits in spite of Glendower's efforts to keep him away. In reality, however, Crauford is engaged in gigantic (but unexplained) frauds; Glendower's ability and known integrity would make him an ideal instrument for the swindler in a coming emergency. Cold and calculating in the highest degree, Crauford pretends warmth, sympathy, and idealism; at the same time, he succeeds in gradually pinching off the writer's small income by turning editors and publishers against him. Crauford makes a veiled proposal to Glendower, but the answer is so rigid and clear-sighted in its ethical analysis that Crauford is rebuffed. Reduced to the final degree of poverty and tortured by the miseries of his wife and child in their garret, Glendower is bitter but uncompromising. Persuaded at last that Glendower's honor is impregnable, Crauford sets out to find some more manageable tool. Glendower recovers his estate and becomes Mordaunt once more, though too late for his personal happiness. Eventually he is the accidental victim of an assassin. Crauford is hanged.

The attempt to entangle an innocent man as a confederate is not part of the Fauntleroy record, but in many other respects Bulwer makes his Crauford a close and unmistakable representation of the actual swindler.[38] Crauford, like Fauntleroy, is brought up in a family of strict Noncomformists; he is "fond of the laborious acquisition of money" and equally fond of the "laborious pageantries of expense." He carries on "at his luxurious villa, the orgies of a passionless, yet brutal, sensuality." There is rather little about the swindle itself, which is magnified in extent and duration, but the account of events following upon its discovery is close to fact, the chief addition being the burning of some bankers' houses. Many of the actual circumstances are used. Crauford's picture is sold in the print-shops; he has "a likeness to the King of Prussia." Crauford is about to be granted a title; Fauntleroy had been maneuvering for one and had made a gift to the wife of a man in the College of Arms.[39] Crauford is shown as treating his wife badly. As with Fauntleroy, she visits him in prison; and the mistress sends him a pigeon pie. Crauford escapes from prison but is soon brought back; an escape had been prepared for Fauntleroy, though he apparently feared to make the attempt.[40]

In sum, Bulwer made very large use of a criminal case not yet four years in the past, in such a way that his novel had immediate topical appeal. (Its immediacy was heightened by the accident that another well-known forger, Joseph Hunton, was brought to trial on October 28, a few days after publication of *The Disowned,* and was executed on December 8.) In this book, however, Bulwer made no reference to the argument about capital punishment for forgery, a sufficiently lively question. Crauford remains the contemptible foil to Mordaunt's virtue; we are not asked to regret that he is hanged. Since Bulwer was soon to make an attack on the harshness of the criminal law, it is interesting to see that he did not choose to do so with the materials of a famous forgery case.

Instead, he saw the typical commercial swindler as an interesting study in commercial morality and a significant figure, along with others, in an intellectual analysis of modern society. "At the time this work was written," he said later, in the "Advertisement" of the 1852 edition of *The Disowned,* "I was deeply engaged in the study of metaphysics and ethics." In episode and discussion, the book presented the utilitarian ethic—Benthamism, with a Godwinian flavor—with illustrations of how it might be twisted by a selfish man, whether a banker or a scheming scion of an aristocratic family. Bulwer did better than most novelists of the period who depicted swindlers; he finds the banker Crauford related to powerful currents of new ideas as well as to mere trains of events. In opposing Crauford to Mordaunt, he set up a meaningful contrast of symbols. Crauford is the crude and unprincipled result of social changes, without tradition and without honor; Mordaunt, though idealized nearly out of recognition, represents the honor of an ancient code and the possibility of a new enlightenment. Crauford existed, and every reader would recognize him; Mordaunt was unconvincing, but he was to show (along with one or two others) what the young aristocrat of the new age might be. In the forties, the ideal was to become well known as Young England. Crauford is the corrupted spirit of money-getting; although he has no real interest in the ideas of the new age, such as the Benthamite ethic, he is clever enough to lay hold on them and twist them to his purpose. Mordaunt, a conservative, is nevertheless a student of past and present, whose command of new and old philosophy is to serve the public good. Still in his Radical period, Bulwer was predicting, as Disraeli was to do, the direction which enlightened Tories were to take in the next generation even though that direction was not yet visible to the Tory leadership in Parliament.

Bulwer's intentions in *Pelham* and *The Disowned* deserve substantial praise. Some of his contemporaries, like later readers, found it hard to overlook his extreme defects: unjustified condescension, dandyism, wordy rhetoric, pompous claims to intellectual attainments, and, most distressing of all, the implication that Bulwer, proud of name and family, shared the finest qualities of his unbelievable heroes. From the distance of the next century, however, one is able to feel that there is a considerable sincerity and a commendable, if boyish, ambition in the sort of pictures which the young Bulwer presents as his ideals in L'Estrange and Mordaunt. They meant something to him; one feels it a pity that these admirable aims had to be deflected by personal vagaries in the author. And those intellectual pretensions are more than forgivable—they are praiseworthy—when one thinks of the intellectual barrenness of fiction in the earlier part of the century. Bulwer was setting out on a project all his own: to deal with scenes and affairs of the time in novels that should not be without ideas. The people in his books were to have more than the personal relationships which are always the substance of the novel; they were to be persons in relation to class, to both written and unwritten social law, and to history. In fiction Bulwer was a pioneer.

Fauntleroy's other appearances in fiction can be examined very briefly. The second novelist to use him was Theodore Hook, whose

Maxwell was published in 1830. But it is perhaps an overstatement to say that Hook used Fauntleroy; he took none of the facts of the case and only a little of the legend. It appears that upon rare occasions hanged men have revived.[41] No attempt at resuscitation was made upon Fauntleroy; but the relatives, determined to avoid a public exhibition or a theft of the body, had it sealed in a leaden coffin after the hanging, so that it was not seen at the funeral. This unusual precaution allowed the growth of a rumor that Fauntleroy had prevented strangulation by placing a silver tube in his throat and that he was later seen in another country. It was this part of the affair that Hook employed, along with the current interest in the use of bodies by surgeons. This latter topic was much in the public mind because of Burke and Hare.[42]

Hook's *Maxwell* is named for its chief character, a successful physician and surgeon. Early in the story a well-known merchant, Hanningham, who has been convicted of fraud and of the murder of his business partner, suffers hanging; but he is brought to Maxwell's house, is revived, and escapes to the Azores. This event, not at first disclosed, constitutes the mystery which lies behind the greater part of the novel.

It must have been fairly easy to guess, however, for readers of 1830. Maxwell unwisely entrusts his financial speculations and his daughter's hand to Apperton, an able but vulgar young broker. When Apperton fails in business, Maxwell is so much implicated in his debts that he thinks it necessary to flee the country. In the end, however, he recovers part of his fortune, Hanningham is cleared of the charge of murder, and all is well.

Hook's easy naturalness of style is a pleasant asset to *Maxwell*. His tone is all satirical amusement and condescension. Unlike Bulwer, he keeps at a distance from his characters, never identifying himself with any of them. With his fraudulent stock-broker and his surgeon intent on building up large holdings, Hook gives a more realistic impression than Bulwer of the extent of the new fabric of wealth.*

Thomas Love Peacock could not fail to use the subject which

* The Fauntleroy case was notorious enough to furnish inspiration, nearly twenty-five years after, for one of the plots of G. W. M. Reynolds' *Mysteries of the Court of London*, described later in another connection.

the financial world had to offer. With the swindling banker he paired the speculative financier, an even better representative of the new age of commerce and fluid capital. There had never been so many of the type before—the man who formed companies, sold stocks, manipulated magnificent enterprises in figures, and watched the market closely, because his substance was on paper, changing from day to day. As he went about among his associates, he was envied as wealthy and important. But he was called a charlatan, or worse, by those who respected the traditional forms of wealth and disliked the morality, mores, and politics of the new rich.* Peacock, who considered paper money and the theories of political economy not much sounder than Fauntleroy's conversions, included the ways of bankers and financiers in the collection of current foibles he dealt with in *Crotchet Castle*, in 1831.

Susannah Touchandgo, the amiably vague heroine of the little book, is the virtuous daughter of Timothy Touchandgo, a defaulting banker. He appears in the story only by letter, having absconded to the United States. He is very well situated there, he writes to his daughter, though he cannot, as he might at home, buy a seat in the national legislature.

> I am happy to say, I am again become a respectable man. . . . The notes of Touchandgo and Company, soft cash, are now the exclusive currency of all this vicinity. . . . The people here know very well that I ran away from London, but the most of them have run away from some place or other; and they have a great respect for me, because they think I ran away with something worth taking, which few of them had the luck or the wit to do.[43]

Timothy Touchandgo may be all the swindlers, including Fauntleroy; the specific inspiration for him was probably Rowland Stephenson, whose frauds came to light less than three years before the publication of Peacock's book. Stephenson was at one time a member of parliament, and he was, like Fauntleroy, head of a banking firm. In the last days of 1828, he disappeared with a large

---

* The new bankers of the paper-money system had already been roughly treated in two novels by Thomas Skinner Surr, an employee of the Bank of England and a hard-money man: *The Magic of Wealth*, 1815, and *Russell, or the Reign of Fashion*, 1830.

sum of money, got passage to America, and there fought extradition successfully.[44]

Peacock's Crotchets, father and son, have no such definite originals. The elder, who owns the "castle" and who gets together the Peacockian house-party, has done well in business and has set up his son; the son has gone into the more modern and intangible realms of finance. The chief bubble which young Crotchet has helped to blow up bursts before the tale is done, and he is forced to make his way to America, where he joins Timothy Touchandgo.

In the brief descriptions of young Crochet, Peacock sums up this new type in life and fiction. One can imagine him, with a comparable set of worries, in Wall Street in 1929.

> "Why, he is very smooth, and spruse [sic] as far as his dress goes; but as to his face, he looks as if he had tumbled headlong into a volcano, and been thrown up again among the cinders. . . . They say he was good-looking, till his bubble-schemes, as they call them, stamped him with the physiognomy of a desperate gambler. . . . He is almost always dreaming and *distrait*. It is very likely that some great reverse is in store for him." [45]

Peacock catches there the look of all the Fauntleroys and Stephensons as they moved about in the restless gaieties of the eighteen-twenties. On any morning the officers might be waiting for them, and if there had been forgery, the noose waited too.

Other cases of the twenties had almost as much notoriety as Thurtell's, though fewer connections with polite literature. In 1827, a certain William Corder, by a promise of marriage, lured from her home Maria Marten, who had already had a child by him. Months later, her body was discovered under the earthen floor of a nearby barn; Corder was found guilty, and was hanged at Bury St. Edmunds. Between the finding of the body, in April 1828, and the execution on August 11, there was plenty of time for publicity. Souvenir hunters nearly stripped the Red Barn; the hangman sold the rope by the inch for a high price; and the dissection of the body attracted eager crowds.[46] Catnach's broadsheet of Corder's confession is said to have sold more than 1,100,000 copies; and a printed copy of a book on the case was bound in a portion of Corder's skin.[47]

This murder entered at once into the realm of folklore and drama. There is record of at least three melodramas of 1828, and the story became a standard theatre item; it has been made into a motion picture and has been revived on the stage within this century.[48] There is probably no way of knowing how long it lasted in the puppet shows, at the fairs, and in the shoddy penny theatres. It was still a popular—and characteristic—feature of such shows in 1841.[49]

There was at least one fictional account of the case, *The Red Barn, a Tale Founded on Fact*, probably by Robert Huish.[50] Besides the novel of some 150,000 words, the volume contains appended materials which include accounts of Corder's trial and execution. A single incidental matter in the story is interesting enough to attract one's attention: the account of a large and well-organized crew of boy thieves and pickpockets.[51] The gang which appears briefly here precedes Fagin's, in *Oliver Twist*, by nine years. But the author was without talent; and he had the bad judgment to build his tale upon the murderer instead of on one of the boys.

One other case of the eighteen-twenties passed into enduring legend, though it had little connection with contemporary literature. Lecturers on anatomy had always had difficulty in getting cadavers; they paid good prices for subjects and showed no indelicate curiosity about the provenance of those which were offered them, for exhumation was illegal. In Scotland, where the problem was harder than in England, there was an import trade. During 1828, two Irishmen in Edinburgh, William Burke and William Hare, found an easy way to make a living; they murdered lonely and friendless persons, suffocating them after making them drunk, and sold the bodies to Dr. Robert Knox, one of the medical lecturers competing with the University professor of anatomy. Between February 12 and November 1, they did away with sixteen people, but they grew careless and were reported. Hare was given immunity for turning king's evidence, but Burke was hanged in January 1829. Public interest was naturally very great, and there is a large body of information about the case, both contemporary and later—to say nothing of ballads, prints, and miscellaneous allusions.[52] In 1844, R. S. Surtees could joke about it in a novel with assurance that the reader would understand—Mr. Jorrocks was better acquainted with William Burke than with Edmund.* The murders by Burke and Hare, followed by the somewhat less notorious ones by Bishop and Williams in London, brought about in 1832 the passage of the Anatomy Act, which regulated the conditions under which cadavers might be supplied to anatomists, and which ended the dissection of the bodies of murderers.[53]

Such mercenary villains as Burke were not the material for imaginative literature, even though his name became a verb of the English language. There was one paltry anonymous fiction, of the usual sort, a "tale founded on fact," illustrated by the young Robert Seymour.[54] Wholesale murder seems to have repelled even the makers of melodrama; one hears of only a single play on the subject.[55] With the grave-robbers, the case is otherwise; they have a long history in literature and humor, and living men still tell tales of them.

These notorious cases of the twenties did of course go to swell the collections of criminal biography. Borrow's work has been mentioned, but the chief collection of the period was made by two attorneys, Andrew Knapp and William Baldwin. Their work first appeared in four volumes in 1809 and 1810, but became best known in its final enlarged form, *The New Newgate Calendar*, the six volumes of which came out from 1826 to 1828. The original *Newgate Calendar* of 1773 had been revised and extended in 1814 and in 1818, and the name was used again for a new collection in 1841, by "Camden Pelham"; but all through the eighteen-thirties, "Newgate Calendar" usually meant the work of Knapp and Baldwin.** The twenties saw the completion also of

---

* In Chapter XII of *Hillingdon Hall*, the Duke of Donkeyton says to Mr. Jorrocks:

"And so you are a great fox-hunter? Glad of that—fine amusement fox-hunting —monstrous fine amusement. I remember Burke saying he would willingly bring in a bill to make poaching felony, another to encourage the breed of foxes—that he would make, in short, any sacrifice to the humour and prejudices of the country gentlemen in their most extraordinary form, provided he could only prevail upon them to live at home. Fine speech of Burke's; monstrous fine speech."

"He was 'ung for all that," observed Mr. Jorrocks to himself, with a knowing shake of the head. . . . *H.H.* (New York [1931]), p. 106.

** An obscure Calendar of the thirties was no rival to the well-known collections, but it had its own significant character. Martin's *Annals of Crime, or New Newgate Calendar, and General Record of Tragic Events* was a penny weekly, published

a serious work of legal history, the *State Trials*. This was begun in 1809 by William Cobbett, who prepared eleven volumes, and was continued by F. B. Howell and T. J. Howell. The thirty-third volume appeared in 1826 and an index two years later. This fifth edition remained a standard work for many decades.

The most enthusiastic observer of the crimes of the twenties was neither a compiler of Newgate Calendars nor a novelist. He was Thomas DeQuincey; his tribute to the galaxy of contemporary crimes, "On Murder Considered as One of the Fine Arts," is an illustrative document. As now printed, it consists of three parts, two papers and a postscript, but the first paper appeared alone, in *Blackwood's Magazine* for February 1827. In form this was a lecture before the Society of Connoisseurs in Murder, preceded by a letter purporting to be from a scandalized discoverer of the Society; and the paper was followed by an editor's note explaining that the lecture was all in jest, like the *Praise of Folly* or the *Modest Proposal*. No doubt it was wise to bolster up the reader with illustrious examples.

The mock-heroic and grisly humor of the lecture, now dulled by the passage of time, repelled some readers even in 1827. This is no reformer's document—it is a tribute to the seventeenth, eighteenth, and nineteenth centuries as the Augustan age of murder. The lecturer comments disparagingly upon the Thurtell case but for lack of space cannot allow himself even to begin the discussion of John Williams, who killed the people of two families in 1811:

> With respect to the Williams murders, the sublimest and most entire in their excellence that ever were committed, I shall not allow myself to speak incidentally. Nothing less than an entire

---

by William Mark Clark at 19 Warwick Lane. It began March 2, 1836, and continued for some two years. It combined accounts of crime, usually old but sometimes new, with descriptions of current social injustice. One series of articles was headed, "Slavery in England! The Factory System." Obviously designed for workingmen and the poor, the periodical was to attract them with notorious murders and such things as "Forms of Military and Naval Torture," which were assumed to have a natural interest for them; and at the same time it informed them about the evils of the corn laws and urged the need for Oastler's factory reforms. The tone of the little weekly was vigorous but not inflammatory.

lecture, or even an entire course of lectures, would suffice to expound their merits.[56]

The second paper, likewise in *Blackwood's*, was not published until November 1839, twelve years after the first. In the same vein of ponderous whimsy, it touched upon some modern crimes and reached back to ancient history for parallels. Besides Burke and Hare, it ranged to include the Thugs, a newly popular topic because of Meadows-Taylor's *Confessions of a Thug*, published in the same year. The third part never came out in the magazine; it appeared as a "postscript" to the others in the Collective Edition of DeQuincey's works in 1854. Though it contains an account of the Mackeans, the greater part is a minute narrative of the murders of John Williams, for which—since the author would not "speak incidentally"—the first readers had waited twenty-seven years.

In his fiction, DeQuincey made use of the murder theme in certain tales, notably "The Avenger," carrying over the manner of Gothic romance into his later years when it was out of fashion; but he did not make use of contemporary crime.

The fiction of the twenties has been drawn upon, so far, to illustrate the notoriety of criminal cases and the readiness of certain authors to turn them to immediate use. There were other books, not all arising from famous cases, in which the affairs of criminals appeared significantly, and here it is curious to observe the parallels in a few instances in France. In the two countries recently at war, between which were the barriers of temperament and circumstance, similar trends of events produced certain literary equivalents, though few books crossed the Channel and reciprocal influences were at a minimum. In both countries, the organized pursuit of criminals made possible the first narratives of detection. In both countries, the codification of law had been a problem—already solved in France and being haltingly approached in England. In both countries, during the twenties, reformers were causing public discussion of capital punishment. In both, a few writers began to use the situation of the condemned man as a theme for literary works. In giving it artistic form, France came first.

As for the detective stories, they were not usually Newgate novels since they did not make criminals their central characters;

moreover, they did not exist in sufficient numbers in the twenties and thirties either to be recognized as a new literary form or to figure in the controversy about the fiction of criminal life. Their development as a type is another subject, but the earliest examples, which appear during the twenties, show how fiction took up the materials of crime. The detective story could not, of course, be written until there were detectives, that is, until there was at least a little of specialization in the craft of hunting out a criminal for punishment. Without such action by police authority, one might have the story of a chase, as in *Caleb Williams*, but that is not the same thing. French procedures were formalized in 1812, by the establishment of a bureau of detection, the Sûreté, for which there was no equivalent in England.

The earliest book, in England, to rely for its substance upon the police officer as detective—that is, the first English detective novel—came out in 1827. It was written by Thomas Gaspey; its title was *Richmond, or Scenes in the Life of a Bow Street Officer, Drawn Up from His Private Memoranda*.[57] (Incidentally, it has suffered undue neglect at the hands of historians of detective fiction.) The author was a reporter and newspaperman; at the time he wrote *Richmond*, apparently his sixth novel, he was thirty-nine years old and was sub-editor of a weekly paper, the *Courier*.

Richmond does not get away from the tradition of the picaresque chronicle, and the hero becomes an officer only with the beginning of the second volume; but from that point on, the story consists of a series of episodes of detection, all fairly realistic and credible. (The title's statement about an actual source may possibly be true.) The two longest episodes involve investigations of kidnapping and counterfeiting, which Richmond brings to a successful conclusion. The story is the thing—the author indicates no wish to improve the criminal law—and the story, taken part by part, goes very well indeed. It does not romanticize low life nor gloat over scenes in underworld haunts of London.

A decade earlier, Bow Street men had been in bad odor; certain of them had arranged a crime to obtain the reward for catching the criminals.[58] Usually, however, the runners were regarded as glamorous figures, and Gaspey was one of their supporters. His Richmond is not mercenary in demanding his fees for

private service, and is pleased when a man he has caught is transported instead of hanged: "I would much rather never touch a
guinea, than have the reflection of its being the price of life."

Richmond preceded by a little the classic of roguery and
detective literature, the Memoirs of Vidocq, published in Paris in
1828–29 and translated into English almost immediately.[59] Eugène
François Vidocq (1775–1857), having wandered across Europe
in and out of the French armies, was convicted of a crime of which
he said he was innocent, and after a couple of escapes was caught
and held. He won freedom by becoming a paid spy; he was not
the first of these, but apparently the most faithful and the most
successful. For some three years he worked secretly; after the
formation of the Brigade de Sûreté in 1812, he was openly in the
public employ as its chief agent. Beginning with a few men, he
directed the work of twenty-eight or thirty in the last years of
his office.[60] With a reputation already legendary, he resigned in
1827, and then, by an unhappy turn, lost his savings in operating
a factory where he employed ex-convicts. Some years later, he had
a short term as head of the political police of Louis-Philippe; he
spent his last days in poverty in Brussels.

Vidocq's authorship of the memoirs was in doubt from the
first—the names of E. Morice and L. F. Heritier are now attached
to it along with Vidocq's—for he complained in his preface about
the interference of an editor. Apparently materials beyond his own
were foisted upon the unsuspecting and unwilling Vidocq.[61] The
authorship of the first English translation is uncertain; it has been
attributed to William Maginn, a plausible but unsatisfactory
candidate.[62]

The earlier parts of the memoirs form a picaresque tale of high
spirits, wanderings, and adventurous scrapes. A footloose young
man might have had some, if not so many, such experiences on
a continent that was with difficulty being taught the curse of pass-
ports. The descriptions of prisons and prisoners are convincing,
the escapes are remarkable but not impossible, and the accounts
of Vidocq's success as a police agent (which fill most of the two
last volumes) are likewise the stuff of legend but not impossible.
As for credibility, the main trouble is that there is too much of
everything, and Vidocq's pride in himself makes one prepare to

discount him. The writers took their material where they found it. The English translator identified a little theft from Colquhoun's *Police of the Metropolis*,[63] and Vidocq's tale of being seduced by a milliner follows a pattern of folk-drollery older than Boccaccio.

Vidocq enjoyed being a detective. As we see him in the memoirs, he loves drama, he loves surprises, he loves activity. He knows the underworld perfectly, and is happiest if he has an opportunity to re-enter it in disguise. If not assigned to find a particular criminal, he goes out to drag up what he can—and never fails to create adventure. Short tales make up the bulk of his matter, but there are one or two which occupy several chapters and achieve continuity. In one such, the story of Raoul and Court, he mentions the careful methods of gathering evidence which he employed.[64] Usually, though, he seems to rely on his knowledge of the underworld and on his information-gatherers. He professes himself opposed, however, to filling the Sûreté with former criminals, and expresses contempt for the nature and methods of the political police.[65] His final volume, though filled like the others with bits of narrative, contains a classification of thieves according to their operations, so that honest men may be on their guard.

In this odd and cheerfully sex-spiced mixture, Vidocq expresses some humanitarian convictions with apparent seriousness. He pities the nonprofessionals, who are reduced to thieving by sheer want, and he would like to see punishments graduated according to the individual nature and circumstances of the guilty one. He feels pity for the released criminal, always rejected by society; if such a man is to live honestly, he must have not merely virtue but heroism. Thieves stay together as a class because, after imprisonment, they can turn to no one else; a six-month sentence becomes a life-long punishment. He sees the whole system of penalties as worse than a failure; in spite of "correctional punishments" the worst criminals are those who have been punished. "I have seen thousands, but have never known one who, during his capitivity, had formed determinations or found inducements to reform and lead a better life." [66] Any impulse toward reform comes from something other than the period of imprisonment, which, with its ill treatment, leaves only "irritation, spite, rage; a vague resentment, deep and without repentence." But Vidocq does not discovered just in time.[68] A better story is the anonymous "Le Revenant," printed three years later, which purports to be the statement of one who has remained alive after hanging.[69] Since the writer does not emphasize the startling nature of the escape, the cheating of the rope serves mainly as a device to allow the criminal to tell his own story. Having committed a series of small forgeries over a period of months, he felt relief when he was caught. Now penitent, he is about to take his wife with him to one of the colonies. The story aroused Charles Lamb's enthusiasm: "There is in Blackwood this month an article MOST AFFECTING indeed called Le Revenant, and would do more towards abolishing Capital Punishments than 400,000 Romillies or Montagues."[70] It is not hard to see why Lamb wrote thus. In spite of being over-literary at the beginning and contrived at the end, the story has convincing qualities. The Revenant's easy step into forgery, his feelings during confinement, his minute recollection of the last days and the last visit of his betrothed—all these things are done in detail and are the work of a writer of great sensitiveness. With some exceptions, the style has a suitable simplicity. Most novels of the twenties do not, unfortunately, command so much of domestic realism.

The man about to be hanged may next be seen in a novel— the work, like *Richmond*, of Thomas Gaspey. His *History of George Godfrey* (1828), already briefly cited, has an amusing mixture of themes and subjects, among which Newgate scenes occupy perhaps half a volume. The whole book is an adjustment of the picaresque method, with its episodic plotting, to the uses of contemporary topical satire. But Gaspey is a conservative, not a legal reformer, and does not arrange the situation of his hero for the sake of attacking the criminal law. The prison episode achieves a kind of tension, though the context is that of comedy. After a series of scenes showing the tricks of auctioneers, the rascality of bubble-scheme riggers, and the hypocrisy of enthusiasts for Greek freedom, the author leads George Godfrey into Newgate. The charge is robbery, whereas George's only connection with the crime lies in his having tried to catch the robber.

The Newgate scenes, lively and realistic, satirize the people who surround the prisoner. Godfrey casually engages one of the lawyers favored by the underworld, and finds, as he has expected, that it does no good; he is pronounced guilty and condemned to death. Besides his mother and step-father, he is visited by politicians, journalists, and phrenologists. The prison ordinary does not intrude unnecessarily, but Dr. Fudge, a volunteer spiritual counselor, gives George "a most vivid description of the New Jerusalem, to which he assured me I might expect to proceed, straight from the Old Bailey." There were others, he says, and "upon the whole, I had a pretty respectable levy." Godfrey's social standing is improved; the other prisoners

> now thought me somebody. The attentions I received from many, whom they called nobs, seemed to move their envy. They looked as if they wondered at my getting on so, regarded condemnation as a great accession of dignity, and thought it a fine thing to be hanged.[71]

The Newgate scenes are not all comedy. Godfrey is reunited with a friend and benefactor, receives a visit from the girl he loves, and is genuinely affected by a last meeting with his mother. On the morning of the execution he goes through the preparations with two others. They take communion, they follow the sheriffs to a room where a blacksmith removes their irons and the watching reporters scribble, their hands are tied, they hear the beginning of the burial service. It is all particularized, even to the involuntary mechanical movement which Godfrey, in a moment of leisure, observes in his right leg. At the last moment, however, his reprieve comes. He is transported and experiences further adventures which lead to a happy conclusion.

Gaspey is not adept at giving the minutiae of feeling, but the externals of the story persuade us easily. He has first-hand observation at his command and sets out to make the most of it. He is interested enough to have chosen to use *this* material—but it is a spectator's interest, not more. If his knowledge of Newgate had belonged to a writer who passionately cared, such scenes as these would have taken fire.

The year 1829 brought a second book which received much attention in France. Unlike the memoirs of Vidocq, it was not translated immediately, but it was reviewed in English periodicals and thus had English readers. Victor Hugo's story, *Le Dernier jour d'un condamné,* undertook to make an argument against capital punishment by treating sympathetically a man convicted according to the law, and it succeeded better than most books in uniting a non-literary purpose with the sincerity of a work of art. It was published early in the year, without Hugo's name, though the authorship soon became an open secret.

The story takes the form of a journal kept by a man condemned to death for murder. Beginning well in advance of the time of execution, it includes recollections of the trial, but it is chiefly taken up with the prisoner's thoughts during his last three days. He sees convicts put in irons for the galleys, finds his own plea for clemency refused, is moved from one prison to another, and receives the formal attendance of the chaplain. He writes the last words of his journal in a few moments of respite before going to the guillotine.

The narrative, with its supremacy of feeling, its concern for one of the world's outcasts, shows the characteristic union of Romanticism and humanitarian sympathy. Direct and single as a lyric poem, it has deliberate and obvious omissions: nothing of the prisoner's history, no details of his crime, no extenuation, no passion of remorse, no deep searching of the self. Hugo believes that capital punishment is inhumane, vicious, wrong; he therefore avoids whatever might draw attention to any other issue than his central one. Within the story, however, there is no argument—nothing but the momentary observations of the man who is to die. He is given notable advantages in his assault upon the reader's sympathies; besides being an articulate observer, he is a man of tender feeling, who loves his wife, his mother, his three-year-old child. Obviously, such a man cannot really be an enemy of society. For the sake of its thesis, the story needs a hero who cannot obtain compassion on such easy terms.

Le Dernier jour was immediately popular in France, to the extent of three printings in a fortnight, and soon became known in England, where most of the periodicals avoided taking it as serious propaganda. Except in the *Westminster,* reviewers either ignored the author's opinion of capital punishment or waved it aside with good humor.[72] The *Blackwood* treatment was peculiarly gentle, in comparison with its way of dealing with English proponents of reform. Perhaps this tenderness was accorded to a poet, a French poet—but also to one whose political opinions, up to that time, were known to be conservative and Royalist.

It is true that the earlier reviewers had not seen the preface which Hugo wrote in March 1832. Disappointed that capital punishment had not been abolished after the July revolution, and observing that his book had not always been taken as argument, he reissued it under his own name, with a preface nearly a third as long as the story. The preface left no uncertainty. Is there a criminal who must be withdrawn from society? Imprison him, then, said Hugo: let there be no hangman, where the jailer is enough.[73] The whole utterance was, and is, eloquent with psychological insights, with sarcasm, and with passionate sincerity. Along the way, he turned practical England to his purpose, aware of the doctrines of her economists and also of the tarred bodies of murderers dangling from her gibbets. An economical country, he said, where hanged men were preserved as long as possible. (*"O terre d'économie! goudronner les pendus!"*) At the end, he described crime as illness—a conception that was still a novelty a generation later— and asked that it be dealt with according to Christian principle.

Whether taken as fiction or persuasion, *Le Dernier jour* aroused more comment in England than any other of Hugo's books before *Notre Dame de Paris*.[74] In 1840, when major battles had been won but when argument was still lively, there were two translations, one by G. W. M. Reynolds and the other by Sir Peter Hesketh Fleetwood, a member of parliament.

To recapitulate, the fiction of the twenties, though dominated by Scott's historical novels, shows numerous lesser writers making use of the contemporary scene. The fashionable novelists reflected the glitter, but now and then included a glimpse of the underworld which the sporting fringe of the upper classes did not mind mixing with. The most important of the new novelists of the twenties, Bulwer, drew upon the copious materials of contemporary crime, though not for the main elements of his books. The several sober middle-class realists had almost nothing to say of demi-monde or underworld, but the essayists and miscellaneous writers did not neglect it. "Founded on Fact" had for many years past been considered a lure to the novel-reader. Now, in the twenties, novels based on contemporary crimes took their place among the literature for unsophisticated readers, to rival the long-popular Newgate Calendars and reports of trials. A journalist-become-novelist produced prison scenes and the first English detective novel. A few novelists uttered passing criticism of some feature of criminal justice, as did Hook in "Merton" and Lister in *Arlington*, but no English novelist of the twenties used fiction to attack the severity of the criminal law. The English writers who wanted to use the sensational materials of crime took one of two paths: they made the criminal character a real villain; or they put in the toils of the law a man who was not a malefactor. Only Hugo took an admitted criminal and used his case for an argument against the law.

IV

THE FIRST NEWGATE NOVELS, 1830–34

CRIME, SATIRE, AND PERSONAL CONTROVERSY IN *Paul Clifford*

Since the criminal literature of the eighteen-twenties met no opposition, the Newgate fiction which critics were to enlarge into a school properly begins with the book which called forth the first attack. It was *Paul Clifford*, published in April 1830, the fifth work of fiction by Edward Lytton Bulwer. It was to be an influence upon the decade then beginning, a stimulus to Newgate productions by Ainsworth, Dickens, and Thackeray; indeed, it is one of the books which now mark the time as the threshold of a new literary period. Its author, who had already written *Pelham* and *The Disowned* and two other novels, was publishing so frequently both because he needed money and because his inspiration was copious. He came from two notable families: the Bulwers had held lands in Norfolk since the Conquest, and the Lyttons, only a little less old, included men of intellectual distinction. Proud of his lineage, he nevertheless wished to make his own mark in the world; he was at the beginning of an important career in letters and government. He could expect to inherit property, but he had married in 1827 against the wishes of his widowed mother, and at this time was working feverishly in order to spend too freely. His strong sense of family tradition had not made him a Tory; at the end of the same month in which *Paul Clifford* was published, he was elected to parliament as a Radical. He voted for the Reform Bill which did away with the borough that elected him, and returned to the reformed parliament from another constituency. He had great talent and extreme sensitiveness.

As a novel of purpose, *Paul Clifford* was a new departure for its author; and it has been called the first example of a new type, the "social novel," [1] which is to be distinguished from the older novels

65

of doctrine. In the work of Godwin, Bage, and Holcroft general questions about society had been argued at stratospheric heights; the social novel was to examine the life of a particular social group and thereby exhibit an evil remediable by law or by aroused public sentiment. The specific evil in Bulwer's view as he wrote *Paul Clifford* was society's treatment of the criminal. His attack was clear, though it was accompanied by the trappings of musical comedy, diluted with politics, and hampered by the intrusion of his own idiosyncrasies. It was the first English novel to make such a direct attack in twenty years of repeated parliamentary agitation for reform of the criminal law; and it came when Peel's revisions, then being concluded, had disappointed public opinion.

In the preface to the 1840 edition of *Paul Clifford*, Bulwer wrote that he had had a double object: "First, to draw attention to two errors in our penal institutions, viz., a vicious Prison-discipline and a sanguinary Criminal Code"; and second, more lightly, "to show that there is nothing essentially different between vulgar and fashionable vice—and that the slang of the one circle is but an easy paraphrase of the cant of the other."

He amplified his statement of the first object in another preface in 1848, which might be a summary of many twentieth-century novels:

> A child who is cradled in ignominy; whose schoolmaster is the felon;—whose academy is the House of Correction;—who breathes an atmosphere in which virtue is poisoned, to which religion does not pierce—becomes less a responsible and reasoning human being than a wild beast which we suffer to range in the wilderness—till it prowls near our homes, and we kill it in self-defence.
>
> In this respect, the Novel of "Paul Clifford" is a loud cry to society to mend the circumstance—to redeem the victim.[2]

The story which made the "loud cry" was as follows: Paul Clifford, whose mother dies during his infancy and about whose father some mystery is suggested, is brought up by the mistress of a disreputable public house in London, in the eighteenth century. Observing that he has a dangerous liking for reading about the highwayman, Dick Turpin, Mother Lobkins provides him with some education, but her efforts to keep him out of bad company are unsuccessful. In an episode Dickens was later to parallel in *Oliver Twist*, Paul is taken up for a pocket-picking he has not committed; his older companion escapes, but Paul, aged sixteen, is sent to the House of Correction. Instructed in crime, he escapes after three months and is introduced by a friend to a band of highwaymen. He becomes in time their leader, known as Captain Lovett, and spends seven years with them before he is caught.

Going about in society under the name of Captain Clifford in Bath, where his gang suppose him to be setting out to acquire a fortune by a cold-blooded marriage, Paul falls in love with Lucy Brandon, whom he has previously seen on the occasion of a minor hold-up. Lucy is the daughter of Joseph Brandon, a dull, well-meaning country squire, and an heiress in her own right; her father's brother is William Brandon, a lawyer ambitious to rise, and the man whose prosecution had first sent Paul to prison. Lucy has a better-placed suitor, the middle-aged, cynical Lord Mauleverer, who is favored by her uncle; Mauleverer assists the uncle, William Brandon, to a judgeship. Sincerely in love, Paul intends to quit the road. He helps carry out a long-planned robbery of Mauleverer and is later captured when he effects the escape of members of his company taken in the affair. Captain Lovett, now seen as Captain Clifford, is to be tried before Justice William Brandon.

Meanwhile, Brandon's life has been recapitulated. Ambitious, able, calculating, he wishes to found a family and restore the ancient fame of the Brandon house. The reader discovers that an act of cold villainy first secured to him the obligation of Lord Mauleverer: he connived at Mauleverer's seduction of his wife but kept the infant son, who was his own. (Thackeray, with his Lord Steyne many years later, is not more opposed than is Bulwer to the licentious, unprincipled aristocrat.) When Mauleverer discarded Mrs. Brandon, she became a prostitute and an intimate of thieves; she took the child from her husband's house, and Brandon heard no more of him. Brandon's inquiries have just resulted in success at the time of Clifford's trial; he is about to pronounce the sentence when a message is brought to him that Paul Clifford—as veteran novel-readers must have guessed—is his son.

He has no alternative but to pronounce the sentence of death, though it is commuted, by his efforts and Mauleverer's, to transportation for life. The final pages tell of Clifford and the faithful Lucy in America, where they have lived happily for twenty years after his escape from the Australian penal colony. Clifford has become a leading citizen, and the author points his moral: " 'Circumstances make guilt,' he was wont to say; 'let us endeavor to *correct the circumstances*, before we rail against the guilt!' " [3] Bulwer closes the tale with a quotation from John Wilkes: "The very worst use to which you can put a man is to hang him!"

For the general nature of Clifford's career as a highwayman, Bulwer made a study of the Newgate Calendar—his wife read it through in order to help him [4]—but Clifford's life does not correspond exactly with that of any one Newgate character. Dick Turpin had a cave; Clifford has a better one. Other borrowings from fact, if any, are too slight to be recognized.[5] Nor did Bulwer take his tone from the Newgate Calendars, always severe, factual, and full of ancient stereotypes. Instead, he clothed his highwayman with the daring and the happy zest of legend, with delicacy of feeling and a sense of honor. Paul is the boys' own outlaw.

Other sources, except the *Beggar's Opera*, are even less important. Brandon's sentence of death upon his son has some similarity to the judge's sentence upon the girl he seduced, in *Nature and Art*. Bulwer probably knew also Hogarth's scene in which the industrious apprentice, become a judge, sentences the idle apprentice to Newgate, but he may have written his own trial scene without thinking of either Hogarth or Mrs. Inchbald. Various trivia, of no importance to the plot, show his acquaintance with Fielding, Smollett, Sterne, and the picaresque writers.

The story of Paul, in its main outlines, is satisfactory for the author's purpose. Paul is potentially good, but his childhood innocence is corrupted by evil circumstances; in maturity he still keeps honor among thieves; and in his later life, when he has made a start in a new country, he is an exemplary citizen. But the impact of the fable is weak: Bulwer's slums and his house of correction are unrealistic. Actually measuring a cell did not help him.[6] There is no life in his cardboard settings, and the flash language with which he seasons the conversations is obviously the work of an outsider attemping a trick of flavor. The prison in which Paul is supposed to be educated in crime is passed by in the utmost haste; it provides chiefly the setting for an escape scene, of the sort which was to be a set piece in other Newgate novels. Moreover, the story of Paul is far from having the author's single-minded attention. Entangled with politics and burlesque, to say nothing of romance, it seems to lose sight of its serious object; and one is almost startled, when Paul makes his defense in court, to observe that the author has intended the events of his hero's life to enforce an impressive conclusion.

Paul's eloquent speech (until the year 1836, as mentioned above, the accused in a felony trial had to make his own defense) expresses what Bulwer seriously wanted to say. The prisoner, dignified and unrepentant, despises the law which condemns him:

> Your laws are but of two classes; the one makes criminals, the other punishes them. I have suffered by the one—I am about to perish by the other. . . . Seven years ago I was sent to the house of correction for an offence which I did not commit; I went thither, a boy who had never infringed a single law—I came forth, in a few weeks, a man who was prepared to break all laws! . . . your legislation made me what I am! and it now *destroys me, as it has destroyed thousands, for being what it made me!* . . . Let those whom the law protects consider it a protector: when did it ever protect *me?* When did it ever protect the poor man? The government of a state, the institutions of law, profess to provide for all those who 'obey.' Mark! a man hungers—do you feed him? He is naked—do you clothe him? If not, you break your covenant, you drive him back to the first law of nature, and you hang him, not because he is guilty, but because you have *left* him naked and starving![7]

The story of Paul's life has failed to provide realistic backing for this eloquence, but contemporary readers seem not to have felt the inadequacy.

Bulwer's message is conveyed by a variety of means other than speeches in the mouth of the hero. In one place is a footnote referring to a judicial injustice, in another a citation of the author's conversation with a prison governor; and there are appendices as well. The author as interpreter may be seen when Bulwer comments that Paul was

> conducted in state to his retreat, in company with two other offenders, one a middle-aged man, though a very old "file," who was

sentenced for getting money under false pretences, and the other a little boy, who had been found guilty of sleeping under a colonnade: it being the especial beauty of the English law to make no fine-drawn and nonsensical shades of difference between vice and misfortune, and its peculiar method of protecting the honest to make as many rogues as possible in as short a space of time.[8]

All the early part of Paul's life is thus developed with persistent irony and with much of the lighthearted humor which characterized *Pelham*.

Along the way, Bulwer's wit glances at politicians and clerics. His cynical Lord Mauleverer has it that "our Coriolanus of Tory integrity is a corporal kept by a prostitute; and the Brutus of Whig liberty is a lacquey turned out of place for stealing the spoons; but we must not tell this to the world." [9] Dr. Slopperton, a sluggish and selfish village clergyman, thus explains the prevalence of highway robbery:

> "It all comes of educating the poor," said the doctor. "The moment they pretend to judge the conduct of their betters, there's an end of all order! They see nothing sacred in the laws, though we hang the dogs ever so fast; and the very peers of the land, spiritual and temporal, cease to be venerable in their eyes." [10]

The law as an instrument of class control remains the central theme, to which we constantly return. Paul says:

> "I come into the world friendless and poor—I find a body of laws hostile to the friendless and the poor!" To those laws hostile to me, then, I acknowledge hostility in my turn. Between us are the conditions of war. . . .[11]

This point of view does not go unreproved; on another occasion, Paul attempts to soothe his spirit by "cheating himself into the belief that, if he was a highwayman, it was altogether the fault of the highways." [12] It is Paul's own attitude, however, that Bulwer wishes to propound, in order to shock people into thought. It is expressed on all sides, sometimes in Bulwer's character as author, sometimes by Paul, from whom we expect it, and sometimes even by the cynical Augustus Tomlinson. The law, says Tomlinson, is an apothecary who

. . . stands behind the counter, and dispenses to each man the dose he should take. To the poor, it gives bad drugs gratuitously; to the rich, pills to stimulate the appetite; to the latter, premiums for luxury; to the former, only speedy refuges from life. Alas! either your apothecary is but an ignorant quack, or his science itself is but in its cradle. . . . He relieves you, it is true—but of your money, not your malady; and the only branch of his profession in which he is an adept, is that which enables him to *bleed* you!— O Mankind! . . . You have not a notion how you ought to be governed!—you cannot frame a tolerable law for the life and soul of you! . . . You invent all sorts of vices, under pretence of making laws for preserving virtue; and the anomalous artificialities of conduct yourselves produce, you may say you are born with;—you make a machine by the perversest art you can think of, and you call it, with a sigh, "Human Nature." With a host of good dispositions struggling at your breasts, you insist upon libelling the Almighty, and declaring that He meant you to be wicked. Nay, you even call the man mischievous and seditious who begs and implores you to be one jot better than you are.[13]

Like other thematic passages, this harangue represents the blending of intellectual influences which went into *Paul Clifford*. The mischief-producing doses of the apothecary are an inversion of the right treatment recommended by Jeremy Bentham, by which a therapeutic adjustment of penalties should correct the evildoer and work for the health of society. The influence of Bentham may be seen, of course, in the general purpose of the book—the mitigation of the criminal law—as well as in the political satire.

The latter part of Tomlinson's apostrophe is Rousseauist and Godwinian in its attitude to human nature; the man "who begs and implores you to be one jot better than you are" is an allusion, surely, to the author of *Political Justice*. From that work perhaps comes Paul Clifford's conception of the poor as a class at war with the other classes of society. Godwin had it thus:

The superiority of the rich, being thus unmercifully exercised, must inevitably expose them to reprisals; and the poor man will be induced to regard the state of society as a state of war, an unjust combination, not for protecting every man in his rights and securing to him the means of existence, but for engrossing all its advantages to a few favored individuals and reserving for the portion of the rest want, dependence and misery.[14]

It may have proceeded to Bulwer by way of Raymond, the misguided but noble head of the band of robbers, who told Caleb Williams, "We, who are thieves without a license, are at open war with another set of men who are thieves according to law." [15] It is this conception which forms the link between the two objects of Bulwer's attack—the evil of the criminal laws and the general evils of the two old political parties. If this came solely from Godwin, Godwin's influence is at the center of the book.

At the same time, certain of the opinions that may be located in Godwin's work—for example, that poverty was the chief source of crime, or that the prison system was vicious—were beliefs held by many thoughtful men, inherited from the period of the Enlightenment and the Revolution. Moreover, Bulwer is at variance with Godwin on important matters. He is theistic rather than atheistic, and he does not hold Godwin's doctrines of necessity and anarchism. In the section of *Political Justice* which dealt with crimes and punishments, Godwin made certain practical concessions to the evil state of the world; although declining, by the doctrines of utility and necessity, to allow the conception of punishment as retribution, he admitted the usefulness of imprisonment or some similar method for the prevention of future criminal acts by an individual likely to commit them. In spite of this concession, his main argument led to a state of affairs in which law would disappear. Truth-seeking men would discover that reliable evidence about an individual's future acts was rarely to be had, and eventually some justly limited acts of coercion, reasoned to fit the individual cases, would take the place of the punishments once imposed by the law of the state. Though Bulwer admires Godwin's moral fervor and agrees with many of his convictions, he shows no sign of being ready to follow to these Utopian conclusions.

As for any personal connection between the two men, it is not certain that they met before the publication of *Paul Clifford*. As far back as 1824, Bulwer wished to know Godwin, but their conversation in May 1830 seems to mark one of their earliest meetings, if not in fact their first.[16] Godwin admired and respected Bulwer but warned him against Bentham's moral heresy in "the great question of self-love and benevolence." A career of virtue would be hindered, he said, by a creed which held that there was "no such thing as virtue."

But *Paul Clifford* was not all Newgate novel. It had political satire including both Whigs and Tories and personal satire including among its objects a literary man whom Bulwer would have scourged out of the London world of letters. Bulwer's novel was remembered for all these things.

The aspect of *Paul Clifford* which interested most readers in 1830 was the portrayal of public figures as members of the band of highwaymen. Though the model of the *Beggar's Opera* must very early have suggested itself, Bulwer gave credit for the idea to an unnamed friend, whom he complimented in the course of a long Dedicatory Epistle.[17] The book, indeed, began with this idea for a political satire, proposed by William Jerdan, editor of the *Literary Gazette*, but Bulwer enlarged the plan: "This idea, had the work been shorter, would have pervaded the whole . . . I have made use of his idea rather as an adjunct to my story, than as the principal groundwork of the story itself." [18] *Paul Clifford* was therefore a dual conception even in its beginnings. That Bulwer should have kept the satirical element is evidence of his humor, his daring, and his unresolved artistic perceptions. The device gave an outlet to his genuine high spirits, and it was a commercial asset, which his publisher exploited successfully in advance notices of the book.[19] It remained, however, a burlesque diversion, out of keeping with the realistic parts of the tale.

Paul Clifford is introduced to the gang of highwaymen by Augustus Tomlinson, a polished rogue, master of the niceties of political language, who represents the spirit of Whiggism. Their resort is "a flash public-house in the country," kept by Gentleman George. "He has a great deal of wit," says Tomlinson, "is a very good whist-player; has a capital cellar, and is so fond of seeing his friends drunk that he bought some time ago a large pewter measure in which six men can stand upright." [20] The portrait of the king proceeds in this slightly scandalous but good-humored tone, with references to his desire for money and his fondness for building. Buckingham Palace was still under construction; contemporaries complained of both its cost and its architecture.*

Besides George IV, the other well-known persons in the gang are the Duke of Wellington, Fighting Attie; Lord Eldon, Old Bags; Lord Ellenborough, Long Ned; Sir James Scarlett, Scarlet Jem; the Duke of Devonshire, Bachelor Bill; Lord Henry de Ros, Harry Finish; William Huskisson, "the sallow gentleman"; Lord Alvanley, Allfair; and Sir Francis Burdett, Mobbing Francis.[21] The list has its method. It omits Sir Robert Peel, whose modern intelligence would represent the best tradition of Tory government; it includes instead the opposite, the old-Toryism of Lords Eldon and Ellenborough and the Duke of Wellington. Certain others, such as Lord Alvanley, are the irresponsible men of leisure. Huskisson is present, presumably, as a Whiggish Tory, smeared with mercantile politics. Scarlett, nominally still a Whig, was considered to have practically completed his change of party, having held cabinet office under more than one Tory prime minister. Burdett, a Whig or a Radical, had indicated some Tory leanings, in particular by pledging support, like the vastly different Scarlett, when Canning formed his government in 1827; and he eventually joined the Tories (as did Bulwer himself later). But as a vigorous Reformer, he is out of place. Hidebound Old Tories, Canningite Tories, and men who accept none of the duties of their rank make up Bulwer's gang.

The tone of all the sketches is that of burlesque rather than satire. Fighting Attie is "a devil on the road . . . lots of gumption, and devil a bit of blarney." [22] The second edition adds praise for Wellington's decisiveness in action, and only approaches satire in a

---

* George IV died in June 1830, less than two months after the publication of *Clifford*. In the second edition (which appeared on August 27), Bulwer inserted a valedictory character of him in the last chapter of the novel: "Thieving with thee took a substantial shape, and the robberies of the public passed into a metempsychosis of mortar, and became public-houses. . . . And thy parasites, and thy comrades, and thine ancient pals, and thy portly blowens, they made a murmur, and they packed up their goods. . . ." The deceased king is criticized for his libertinism, but is otherwise leniently treated.

The insertion concerning George IV and another on the Duke of Wellington were at a later time removed from the text of the final chapter but retained as notes at the end of the book.

remark upon his simple elements, "few thoughts not confusing each other." [23] When *Clifford* appeared in April 1830, the Duke was first lord of the treasury as well as prime minister, so that Bulwer could joke about the manner in which he took people's money.

Sir James Scarlett is called "a dangerous fellow for a *press*," [24] in allusion to suits which Scarlett, as solicitor-general, instituted against a London paper for alleged libels on the Duke of Wellington.

Lord Eldon's caricature, though as little serious as the others, embodies more of the public complaints which had been current. Still living, Lord Eldon had not been in office for three years, but he had been Lord Chancellor from 1801 to 1827, except for the short interval of the Grenville ministry. Among the most important of the Tories, he had always been one of the strongest influences for conservatism. The name Old Bags was commonly known; it is said to have been applied to him by the Prince of Wales near the beginning of the Regency. The delays of the Court of Chancery, as well as the abuses of costs and fees that flourished within it, were an ancient and bitter joke.[25] Though the Lord Chancellor's personal honesty was not impugned, he countenanced the traditional and now astonishing exactions of judges, clerks, and barristers; and he had a habitual unwillingness to come to a decision. When his cases were heard by another, during a week's illness in 1811, Romilly, who knew the Chancery Court well, wrote in his diary that if the Lord Chancellor would stay ill for two terms, all the court's arrears of business would be cleared up.[26]

So vast a reputation made a ready reception for the appearance of Lord Eldon as Bagshot the highwayman. Bagshot robs a country gentleman and strips him naked; when the victim asks to keep his flannel drawers, Old Bags replies, " 'Tis not my way . . . I be's slow about my work, but I does it thoroughly." Or again, when the highwaymen turn in their spoils to the general store:

> Old Bags, in especial, preserved his well earned reputation, by emptying six pockets, which had been filled with every possible description of petty valuables. Peasant and prince appeared alike to have come under his hands; and, perhaps, the good old man had done in one town more towards effecting an equality of goods

among different ranks than all the Reformers, from Cornwall to
Carlisle. . . . "May new cases [said Clifford] never teach us to
forget Old Bags!" [27]

The especial prominence of the characterization of Lord Eldon makes one look for some distinct or influential source. It is reasonable to suppose that Bulwer's period of Radical reading had led
him to Bentham's *Indications Respecting Lord Eldon*, a pamphlet
published in 1825. This was Bentham's most sarcastic piece of topical writing; his friends had been alarmed for his safety at the time
of its appearance. Amid this mass of detailed "indications" Bentham describes Lord Eldon as the supreme head of Judge and Company, a joint-stock association of persons banded together to extort
money from the public. Bulwer's conception of the gang of highwaymen is not dissimilar to Judge and Company (this phrase Bentham had used for many years); Bulwer has simply expanded his
predatory group beyond the judicial and legal establishment to take
in the whole of the governing party. His laughing caricature may
owe something of its impetus to Bentham's bitter attack, where
judges figure as generals:

> *General Jefferies* had his one "campaign": *General Eldon* as many
> as his campaign lasted years.—The deaths of Jefferies's *killed-off*
> were speedy: of Eldon's, lingering as his own resolves. The deaths
> of Lord Jefferies's victims were public—the sufferers supported and
> comforted in their affliction by the sympathy of surrounding thou-
> sands: Lord Eldon's expired, unseen, in the gloom of that solitude,
> which wealth on its departure leaves behind it. Jefferies, whatso-
> ever he may have gained in the shape of royal favour—source of
> future contingent wealth—does not present himself to us clothed
> in the spoils of any of his slain. No man, no woman, no child, did
> Eldon ever kill, whose death had not, in the course of it, in some
> way or other, put money in his pocket. In the language, visage, and
> deportment of Jefferies, the suffering of his victims produced a
> savage exultation: in Eldon's never any interruption did they pro-
> duce to the most amiable good-humour, throwing its grace over
> the most accomplished indifference. Jefferies was a tiger: Eldon, in
> the midst of all his tears, like Niobe, a stone.[28]

But that is not the tone of *Paul Clifford*—Bulwer did his satirical portraits with a hearty camaraderie intended chiefly to

amuse. He may have feared that the solicitor-general would again prove himself a dangerous fellow for a press. At any rate, the expectation of the preface was fulfilled, for the Duke of Devonshire "left his name on the author as Bachelor Bill." [29] The *Beggar's Opera* element, however, gives the novel a hodge-podge aspect and its author the look of a playboy among the reformers.

On the other hand, the whole device is not out of keeping with Bulwer's Radical analysis of English politics, and indeed is intended to be a vehicle of it.[30] That Tomlinson, standing for all the Whigs —though certain elements of his portrait must have made readers think of Henry Brougham—should be part of the Tory gang was hardly an exaggerated representation of the years 1827 to 1830; at that time, Whigs themselves were not very sure what the party stood for. Tory ministries were maintained with Whig support, and the Whigs had not yet adopted parliamentary reform as the issue of their party. If the individual portraits are not drawn with acid and the exploits of the gang are told with boyish high spirits, Bulwer nevertheless had a thoughtful, even revolutionary, idea to popularize. In previous books he had professed to find new values in *noblesse oblige*, but in *Paul Clifford* he showed the ruling groups at war with the rest of society. Casual readers might take it as a pure jest, if they chose. Actually, Bulwer showed consistency and prescience in comparing the aristocracy to a class of outlaws no longer feared. *Clifford* is a youthful and confident book; in the dangerous Reform contest of the next three years, there was all too little room for such good-humored satire.

In *Paul Clifford*, we must add up in Bulwer's favor a humanitarian intention expressed with some eloquence and some absurdity; a meaningful and pleasant political fable; and best of all an ingenious, persistent, successful effort to give to the novel intellectual liveliness. The large reputation which came to the author with his early books was well deserved.

The first fiction, then, which attacked the criminal law was politically irreverent, and the Radical coloring of the original Newgate novel was not soon to be forgotten. Compounding his hazards, Bulwer did more—he injected into the mixture of *Paul Clifford* the expression of some personal dislikes, which, like the political allegory, aroused continuing antagonism against him and the Newgate novel too. His animosities included two men, two magazines, and Scotch-men.

The first of the unworthy trivialities came in the Dedicatory Epistle, a preface hastily written just in time for publication. *Fraser's Magazine* had judged Bulwer's work unfavorably in its recent third number, in an article on fashionable novels.[31] In his preface, then, Bulwer alluded to the new magazine and referred to the critics of *Pelham* as "the Great Unwashed." He commented on the arrogance and jealousy of the Scotch, and invited all opponents to do battle:

> For any occasional retaliation on critics, enemies, or Scotch-men—(With me, for the most part, they have been found three appellations for the same thing,) for many very hard words, and very smart hits against myself—I offer no excuse:—my retaliation is in the spirit of English warfare—blows at one moment, and good humour the next.[32]

In the novel itself, Bulwer carried on his personal warfare through the comic figure of Peter MacGrawler, a Scot. He is the pot-house scribe whom Mrs. Lobkins engages as Paul's tutor, and he is the "editor of an obscure periodical, entitled 'The Asinaeum,' which was written to prove that whatever is popular is necessarily bad." When Paul goes out into the world, he writes for Mac-Grawler until he finds himself defrauded. By that time he has learned the three branches of criticism—"to tickle, to slash, and to plaster"—better than his employer. MacGrawler goes down in the world, from editorship to picking pockets; assisted by Paul, now leader of the highwaymen, he becomes cook in their cave; and it is he who repays this favor by betraying Paul to the Bow Street runners.

The attack on the young *Athenaeum* was good-humored; it may be called justified, for Bulwer had been harshly treated there.[33] By the time *Paul Clifford* came up for review, the magazine was in the hands of C. W. Dilke; its treatment of Bulwer, then and later, was severe but impersonal. The *Asinaeum* gibes, therefore, had no consequences of great importance.

With MacGrawler, the case is otherwise. The graceless attack on the Scots in general probably prevented the *Edinburgh Review* from giving Bulwer's novels the consideration they would otherwise have had.[34] But MacGrawler, despite Rosina Bulwer's key to the figures in the novel, was not merely a type.[35] He was a caricature of an individual, intended to be recognized, and the effect of the recognition continued for years.

MacGrawler does not resemble any editor of the *Athenaeum*, nor is he a portrait of any Scottish editor. He is, instead, a caricature of an Irishman, William Maginn, the editor of *Fraser's Magazine*. By changing the nationality and attaching MacGrawler to the wrong magazine, Bulwer avoided a public identification of Maginn, which might perhaps have been answered by a libel suit or a challenge to a duel, and he made an open retaliation difficult because embarrassing. MacGrawler as a Scot came close enough, and had the advantage of being a glancing blow at John G. Lockhart and at *Blackwood's Magazine*, which had called Bulwer a charlatan.[36] Even with nationality and magazine disguised, MacGrawler resembles Maginn in so many ways that contemporary literary men in London can have had no doubt about the intention. MacGrawler, in the novel, acts as tutor; Maginn, before coming to London, had been a schoolmaster. MacGrawler, to qualify for his place, recites the opening sentences of a Latin grammar and parades an insignificant learning; Maginn had a well-deserved reputation as a Latinist. MacGrawler writes best when he has drunk well; Maginn was known for conviviality and heavy drinking. MacGrawler borrows money from Paul and is always in low circumstances; Maginn, though he had a satisfactory income, was always short of money and constantly in debt to his friends. MacGrawler likes the low company at Mrs. Lobkins' house, the Mug, where pickpockets and fences meet; Maginn was known and welcomed in low dives in London and Paris.[37] On being taken into the band of highwaymen, MacGrawler is a failure and is demoted to the place of cook; Maginn had assisted on several Tory papers, and MacGrawler's demotion may parallel the failure of Maginn's political hopes or his separation from one of the papers when he was considered irresponsible.[38] The list of correspondences could be extended. Taken all together, they constitute a derisive insult to Maginn which his acquaintances must have recognized at once. Reviewers of the time did not mention it, but R. H. Horne, in his essay on Bulwer in 1844, spoke of MacGrawler as a satire upon a known person.[39]

Maginn recognized Bulwer's intention to caricature him. The

notice of *Paul Clifford* in *Fraser's* says of Paul's being tutored by MacGrawler, a Scotchman: "The author has done this to take his revenge of *Blackwood's Magazine and of ourselves,* because we have honestly expressed our several opinions—that Mr. Lytton Bulwer is no novelist." [40] Whether or not Maginn wrote the whole of the article, the italicized words spoke officially for the editor; he accepted the challenge.

Critical disapproval, on literary grounds, was a good enough reason for public consumption, but something more specific and more personal is required to account for the creation of Mac-Grawler. Moreover, there was not time enough—the caricature could not have been inserted in the book after the first appearance of *Fraser's.* It is not possible to say what provocation moved Bulwer to an extended insult so gay and so contemptuous. Michael Sadleir speculated on the origins of the hostility, and Miriam Thrall, historian of *Fraser's,* countered his suggestions, though neither writer identified MacGrawler as Maginn. [41] Whatever the beginning of the matter, Bulwer must be held responsible for bringing a restricted quarrel—though probably not a merely personal one—into the more public domain of fiction.

To see Maginn in MacGrawler illuminates, as nothing else can, the bitter series of attacks on Bulwer which appeared in *Fraser's* for a decade. These ranged from derogatory allusions to full-scale "critical" reviews; their frequency makes Bulwer the author most often mentioned in the magazine. Although Maginn left the editorship in 1836, the policy toward Bulwer continued. The "Preface to our Second Decade" recalled achievements and controversies:

> Bulwer did not admire the appreciation of his character, which was given in the letterpress accompanying his portrait, and talked of personality. Alas! poor baronet! He has had a specimen of more irritating personality since that time, and he ought to have recollected that with us he began the ungentle amusement. . . . [42]

That Bulwer "began" the exchange of personalities is an utterly incomprehensible statement if MacGrawler is not seen as Maginn.

This quarrel was significant in the reception of the Newgate novels that were to come. Bulwer was to be the chief user of Newgate materials, and nothing Bulwer did could be approved in *Fraser's*, though Maginn could allow praise, as we shall see, of other Newgate novels. In the latter half of the thirties, Thackeray's early work shows him taking over the Maginn practice of making Bulwer a constant object of raillery. On the principle of an eye for an eye, we may say that Bulwer deserved all he got from Maginn. But when we see Thackeray renewing the attack, then seven years old, we begin to say Unfair—MacGrawler has been paid for.

Paul Clifford was immediately popular, but the reviewers were, of course, not unanimous in their opinions. Despite the attack on the *Athenaeum*, that magazine showed notable restraint, even warning the reader that perhaps its judgment was not, in view of the circumstances, to be trusted. It found Bulwer deficient in humor, and it deprecated the caricature of actual persons, which involved "grossness and personality," but it made no objection to the material of the serious plot—that is, the Newgate material.[43]

In *Fraser's*, the appearance of *Paul Clifford* was the occasion for an article on all of Bulwer's novels; in it for the first time Bulwer was tagged as a Newgate Calendar novelist. *Pelham* had merit, but also many faults: " 'Fore Heaven, we would rather read the Newgate Calendar than the last volume and a half of this novel of fashionable life!" As for *Clifford*, "Its moral is reprehensible to even the extremest degree"; its hero, who deserved hanging fifty times over, is "made happy in the end, as though he had been the most virtuous of mankind." [44] It was wrong, *Fraser's* held, to put the blame upon society rather than on the criminal. The article did not neglect other grounds for criticism, but warped morality was the chief of them. In one form or another, this argument—that Bulwer treated criminals sympathetically—was to be used against him repeatedly for more than fifteen years to come.

Such a paper as the *Examiner*, on the other hand, made no objections. *Paul Clifford*, it said, "abounds in pointed applications to politics and morals, and the satire is ever in the right direction." The review, presumably by Albany Fonblanque, was amusing in itself; it dealt with Bulwer's parallel of highway robbery and politics rather than with his sermon on the criminal law. The *Spectator*, which had not liked *Pelham*, had a good-humored and discriminating review of *Paul Clifford*: "this exceedingly clever work . . . is a satire upon the hollowness and hypocrisy of the world, and on the inequality and frequently the injustice of the laws; it may be said to be an Utilitarian satire upon London morals and English legislation." It objected to the hostile treatment of the Scotch and to MacGrawler ("this ebullition of spite is a blemish"), but agreed that "the state of criticism at the present day is undoubtedly a disgrace to literature." [45]

Blackwood's Magazine did not review Clifford, but Bulwer was discussed briefly in one of the "Noctes Ambrosianae" in 1831. Christopher North complained of Bulwer's "horrid puppyism," but gave him substantial praise. He approved specifically the morality of Bulwer's works.[46] A review in a less important periodical was exceptional in that it took notice of Bulwer's serious theme, society's treatment of the criminal. The Monthly Review quoted from the trial scene and praised the book, though it objected to the use of slang in a work "destined to meet the eyes of females." [47]

As for the quarterlies, the Westminster Review, which had had an article on Pelham and The Disowned, did not deal with Bulwer's novels during the eighteen-thirties. The Edinburgh, two years after Paul Clifford, dealt with the several novels judicially; the story of Clifford, it said, "lingers too long in the haunts of vice, and deals too much with its jargon." [48] The Quarterly took no direct notice of Bulwer's novels in these years. The only reference to Paul Clifford, in a review of a book by Morier, was a criticism of Bulwer's political caricatures.[49]

Altogether, then, the reviews paid more attention to the political satire of Clifford than to anything else in it. The only periodical which objected to the morality of the Newgate story was Fraser's, whose editor was personally attacked.

Eugene Aram: PSYCHOLOGY OF THE GENTEEL CRIMINAL

Bulwer's next novel, published in January 1832, was to become a storm-center of the Newgate controversy. Unlike Paul Clifford, Eugene Aram contained no message of social reform, and its hero was an actual murderer, whose crime was a matter of record, no matter how it might be explained. Eugene Aram had been a strange and extraordinary man, inexplicable despite being well known to history. Bulwer tried to bring him to life as the central figure in a romance and attempted a psychological character study of an unusual criminal mind.

He was led to the subject by his own interest in the abnormal, by his keen sense of the direction of popular interest, and by special circumstances which put the idea in his way. He must have read about Aram when he went through the Newgate Calendars in preparation for *Paul Clifford;* Aram's case, which had never been forgotten since his execution in 1759, appeared in these and in pamphlets.[50]

In any such source Bulwer would have found the story of the self-taught scholar and village schoolmaster who, with a confederate, arranged a murder in such a fashion that the victim seemed to have disappeared in order to defraud creditors; who then buried the body in a cave, and continued his occupation as a gentleman usher in other places; and who was tried and executed fourteen years later, when the finding of a skeleton not that of his victim had brought suspicion upon him. The most curious feature of the case has always been the commission of a sordid crime by a man who labored passionately as a scholar. The old accounts probably exaggerate the extent and depth of Aram's scholarship, but he is said to have learned, besides Latin and Greek, French, Hebrew, Chaldee, Arabic, and Celtic; and he undertook a comparative lexicon. His best achievement was to discern the relation between Celtic and the European languages. For being the first to see it, he is still spoken of with respect.[51] Richard Garnett wrote in the *Dictionary of National Biography* that Aram, under favorable circumstances, might have advanced the progress of comparative philology by fifty years. In the company to be found in the Newgate Calendars, he remains impressive and unique.

Attractive enough in itself, the story of Aram had a slight link with Bulwer's family history, explained in the preface to the 1840 edition of the novel. Bulwer's grandfather had employed Aram at one time as tutor to his children; and Bulwer, hearing of the connection in 1829 or 1830, collected some local traditions of the man. Former pupils of Aram, always impressed by his gentleness and benevolence, still expressed belief in his innocence, and contributed to the generally favorable character which Bulwer was to give him in the novel.[52]

There was a third circumstance which must at least have given the novelist confidence that a book about Aram would be popular. Thomas Hood had written a serious poem, "The Dream of Eugene Aram," which appeared in his annual, *The Gem*, for 1829. This short fiction in verse shows Aram as usher at a school and takes for its climax the moment of his arrest. Troubled in mind, he tells a boy a dream about a horrible crime; when an officer comes to take him in charge, the crime is discovered to be his own.[53] The poem was immediately popular; it was reprinted and republished and came to be known everywhere. A novelist who had already noticed Aram's story could not have failed to be impressed. Michael Sadleir, Bulwer's admirably sympathetic biographer, speaks of Bulwer's "skill in pre-judging popular taste" and his opportunism in the choice of subjects.[54]

Thus Hood and Bulwer together caused a renewal of interest in Eugene Aram; after the novel there was a spate of minor publications,[55] and the controversy over Aram's guilt and motives, started afresh by Bulwer, continued for many years. However, the case had a considerable literature before Hood, and Bulwer required other printed sources than the short entries in the Calendars. A modern investigator thus sums up the history of the bibliography:

> From 1759 until the publication of Hood's poem in 1829 there was a constant stream of reports of the trial. Many magazines printed accounts of it, and a multitude of pamphlets appeared. Of these pamphlets most became early out of print, but one, sold by Bristow in London, it is said, as agent for Ann Ward, of York, established itself as the standard version, and continued to be reprinted, sometimes with, sometimes without, Aram's literary remains, by a succession of Yorkshire publishers. . . . Hood's poem and Bulwer's novel appearing within a short period of one another, a remarkable revival of interest was manifested, and Aram enjoyed for a season a factitious fame, exceeding that of 1759 itself.[56]

Bulwer must have had some of these pamphlets, and he had read what Smollett said of Aram in his continuation of Hume's history of England.

It was, therefore, a well-known story which Bulwer chose for his novel, and the record was available to any curious reader who might want to scrutinize his literary treatment of a real criminal. He had exercised on the facts, he said in his preface, "the common and fair license of writers of fiction," but he insisted that his changes were chiefly in the minor parts of the story.

Bulwer's Aram is not a schoolmaster but a morose and gloomy scholar, "one of those earnest and high-wrought enthusiasts . . . not uncommon in the last century, who were devoted to knowledge yet disdainful of its fame; who lived for nothing else than to learn." Unlike modern schoolmen, says Bulwer, Aram does not incline to the consoling hope of human perfectibility; he is a model of tenderness to individuals, but he cares nothing for society. We find him a plaintive fatalist and a pre-Darwinian evolutionist. When he goes to the highest chamber of his house for his astronomical studies, he looks out on the stars and soliloquizes thus:

> The colours of our existence were doomed before our birth—our sorrows and our crimes;—millions of ages back, when this hoary earth was peopled by other kinds, yea! ere its atoms had formed one layer of its present soil, the Eternal and the all-seeing Ruler of the universe, Destiny or God, had here fixed the moment of our birth and the limits of our career. What then is crime? What life? —Submission! [57]

After two years' aloof residence in Grassdale, the moody stargazer yields to the friendly advances of a country gentleman of the neighborhood, Rowland Lester, and becomes acquainted with Lester's nephew, Walter, and two daughters, Ellinor and Madeline. The latter is secretly adored by her cousin Walter; heedless of him, the high-minded and romantic girl becomes infatuated with the middle-aged Aram, whose severe nobility arouses her quite remarkable capacity for hero worship. Aram resists, but gives way, and Madeline's father is pleased with the prospect of the marriage. (Madeline is happily unaware that she is in love with Manfred and Faust and with worse than these.) Aram, who is apparently a reader of Wordsworth as well as other authors, keeps her mournfully happy with his prose poems:

> If, my beautiful love, you have selected one whom the world might deem a strange choice for youth and loveliness like yours; you have,

at least, selected one who can have no idol but yourself . . . how few are the lovers whom solitude does not fatigue! they rush into retirement, with souls unprepared for its stern joys and its unvarying tranquillity: they weary of each other. . . . I do not enter the temples of Nature as the stranger, but the priest: nothing can ever tire me of the lone and august altars, on which I sacrificed my youth: and now, what Nature, what Wisdom once were to me—no, no, more, immeasurably more than these—you are! Oh, Madeline! methinks there is nothing under Heaven like the feeling which puts us apart from all that agitates, and fevers, and degrades the herd of men. . . .[58]

While Madeline, entranced by such eloquence, prepares for the wedding, the disappointed Walter Lester sets out on his travels to forget her. He searches for his father, long unheard of, and discovers evidence that the wastrel parent, under the name of Daniel Clarke, was murdered fourteen years previously by Eugene Aram. The legal machinery is set in motion, and the officers arrive with a warrant for Aram on—of course—the day of the intended marriage. Madeline steadfastly believes in Eugene's innocence; Walter, instrument of justice on behalf of a worthless father, is the bringer of sorrow to all the family. Aram is tried, speaking in Bulwer's pages part of the actual defense, and is convicted and hanged. Madeline dies heartbroken. After a long voluntary exile, Walter marries her sister Ellinor.

The facts of the case, which may be seen in Eric R. Watson's study of it, Bulwer rearranged with a romancer's facility. He removed those inconvenient persons, the wife and seven children, whom Aram deserted some few months after the crime. He changed the victim from a young married man to a practised and cold-hearted seducer. He omitted any account of the very considerable suspicion against Aram at the time of the crime. In Aram's later life, he added the Lester family, providing Aram with friends and a fiancée and the murdered man with a son to trace him. From the trial he removed all the witnesses who gave important, though circumstantial, evidence, and he thus made the conviction depend solely upon one witness, the companion Houseman, who turned king's evidence. In general, Bulwer tidied Aram up for romantic presentation, making him attractive in everything except the central fact of being a murderer. This he retained; he kept Aram morally guilty.

Despite all the matter which Bulwer thought it necessary to replace or discard, there were in the story many elements attractive to him; the substance and the legend contained the seeds of a Bulwer novel, the possibilities for popular development. First, Aram was a criminal, and the more usable for being genteel. This criminal, moreover, could be given stature. He was capable of serious treatment, Bulwer conceived, as a tragic hero in the classical tradition; but he was Romantic, he could be made a Byronic hero, and the murder could be Gothicized. Quite above these was another possibility: to analyze the ethical confusion which might lead a man to crime and to show the corruption which would follow—an intention not unlike Dostoevsky's in *Crime and Punishment*. How Bulwer supposed that all these elements could be reconciled is inexplicable. He tried, nevertheless, and added the inevitable love-story for the circulating libraries.

That Aram could, in all but rank, be dignified as a tragic hero according to Aristotle was no mean advantage to a writer like Bulwer, whose aims included intellectual distinction as well as popularity. Even if Aram's abilities had been exaggerated, they were substantial enough for the novelist's purpose. Bulwer is vague and unconvincing about the nature of Aram's genius, but his intention is clear: Aram is a man risen to intellectual if not worldly eminence who is ruined by a tragic flaw and a single crime against the moral order. Bulwer wrote in his original preface that he had tried to "impart to this Romance something of the nature of Tragedy"; and in a later preface, perhaps feeling that the classical quality had not been properly appreciated, he tried to make the point more emphatically.

The romanticizing of the hero was an equally deliberate effort. Bulwer presents Aram as a seeker of knowledge with the boundless curiosity of a Faust, a forerunner "of the intellectual spirit that broke forth when we were children, among our countrymen." [59] As for the Byronic, Aram's monologues, his scorn of popular interests, his nearly mystical search for the ultimate in knowledge, his loneliness and his secret guilt mark him as one of Manfred's descendants.[60] At one of the crucial chapters the identification is suggested by an epigraph from Byron's poem: "The spirits I have raised abandon me;/ The spells which I have studied baffle me."

For a character so conceived, Gothic accessories must have seemed the most appropriate ones. Up to this time, Bulwer had shown only the mildest taste for Gothic sensations; in *Eugene Aram* he supplied the deficiency and became what Mr. Sadleir calls him, inheritor of the mantle of Ann Radcliffe.[61] Aram, in his quiet country cottage, lives in un-Gothic surroundings; but Bulwer contrives, on one splendid night-time occasion, to bring him before an improbably romantic background. Aram joins his old confederate, Houseman, at the Devil's Crag, "consecrated by many a wild tradition," in a forest "that might have reminded a German wanderer of the darkest recesses of the Hartz." The two criminals meet in a firelit cave near a roaring cataract, and they come out to find a thunderstorm in progress:

> With every instant, the lightning broke from the river chasm of the blackness that seemed suspended as in a solid substance above, brightened the whole heaven into one livid and terrific flame, and showed to the two men the faces of each other, rendered deathlike and ghastly by the glare.[62]

The fortissimo passage does not end without a Gothic skeleton. Having escaped in the storm from four horsemen, robbers of Houseman's band, Aram comes to a gibbet, "with its ghastly tenant waving to and fro, as the winds rattled through the parched and arid bones; and the inexpressible grin of the skull fixed, as in mockery, upon his countenance."

The interesting thing about this gibbeted body (apart from the "arid" condition of the bones just after a storm) is that Bulwer did not have to invent it; he only transposed it to a fitting scene. One of the best-known pamphlets about Aram told of his discomposure at passing a gibbet after his arrest; the Gothic imagination was at work on the story before Bulwer took it over.[63] The matter had gone this way from the start; the criminals themselves, who lacked the advantage of a castle vault, had at least buried the victim's body in a cave, an acceptable substitute. When the materials of the tale invited Gothic treatment, how could such a novelist as Bulwer decline? He did what was indicated; and he added to the Gothic an element of the homely supernatural, imitated from Scott, to whom *Eugene Aram* was dedicated. In developing the Aram story, Bulwer thus united the romance of Gothicism with the realistic factual tradition of the Newgate Calendars.

The serious problem for the novel, one which attracted Bulwer, lay in the character of Aram: how could the scholar, apparently gentle and devoted, have committed a vicious crime? On the question of motive, the materials of history provided almost nothing. Aram was reported to have admitted his guilt orally, after conviction, and to have explained that he suspected Clarke of seducing his wife.[64] Bulwer discarded this excuse, to be free to set the psychological problem in his own terms. What he wished was to demonstrate, in Aram's reasoning, the practical fallacy in Utilitarian ethics. In *The Disowned*, the fraudulent Crauford had consciously tried to deceive another by means of Utilitarian arguments; Eugene Aram is shown deceiving himself. Disregarding any moral absolute, he balances one choice against another, considering the greatest good of the greatest number, and self-interest betrays him.

In the fictional confession, Aram describes this mental process at length. (It strikingly resembles, in outline, that of the later Raskolnikov.) Miserable under the restraints of poverty, he is approached by Houseman, a plausible outlaw whose language, when he speaks of his war against society, resembles that of Paul Clifford or of the antisocial heroes of the romantic tradition. A great discovery is within Aram's grasp, but he has not the means to complete his work. Would it not be better for mankind for him to "commit one bold wrong, and by that wrong purchase the power of good?" Aram half accepts Houseman's view that he owes nothing to society; yet he insists that he loves mankind, and rationalizes the proposed robbery and murder on the ground of social good. The problem is easier because the intended victim is an evil man, "aged with vice":

> Within myself I felt the will—the spirit that might bless mankind. I lacked the means to accomplish the will and wing the spirit. One deed supplied me with the means. Had the victim of that deed been a man moderately good . . . it might have been yet a ques-

tion whether mankind would not gain more by the deed than lose.
But here was one whose steps stumbled on no good act. . . .

Arousing himself for the deed, Aram mounts on wings of rhetoric:
is not his aim more glorious than that of the soldier who strikes
for patriotism? When the time comes, he has arrived at a high
pitch of exaltation:

> I had wrapped myself above fear into a high and preternatural
> madness of mind. *I looked on the deed I was about to commit as a
> great and solemn sacrifice to knowledge, whose Priest I was.* The
> very silence breathed to me of a stern and awful sanctity—the re-
> pose, not of the charnel-house, but the altar.[65]

Since these were his motives, Aram calls himself a man "be-
wildered by his reason rather than yielding to his vices." The outcome proves the fallacy of his reasoning and vindicates the moral
order. After the murder, he finds that his noble aims have vanished:

> I occupied my thoughts, I laid up new hoards within my mind
> . . . but where, with the passion for wisdom still alive within me
> —where was that once more ardent desire . . . the desire of ap-
> plying that wisdom to the service of mankind? Gone—dead—
> buried forever in my bosom. . . . When the deed was done, man-
> kind seemed suddenly to have grown my foes.[66]

He then finds himself reasoning away the validity of his former
ambition—where is the good for mankind in intellectual advance-
ment? He loves knowledge still, but as a private solace.

As for remorse, he feels it for the first time when he discovers that the murdered man belonged to the family of his betrothed; to have brought harm to them and to her is, he feels,
the real evil. The murder might still be justified if it had affected
only the intended victim:

> In the individual instance it was easy for me to deem that I had
> committed no crime. I had destroyed a man, noxious to the world;
> with the wealth by which *he* afflicted society *I* had been the means
> of blessing many; in the individual consequences mankind had
> really gained by my deed; the general consequences I had over-
> looked till now. . . . All my calculations were dashed to the
> ground at once; for what had been all the good I had proposed to

do—the good I had done—compared to the anguish I now inflicted on your house? Was your father my only victim? Madeline, have I not murdered her also? . . . How incalculable—how measureless—how viewless the consequences of one crime, even when we think we have weighed them all with scales that would have turned with a hair's weight! [67]

It is a distinctly limited ground of repentance; Aram is still weighing evils quantitatively. In the same spirit he explains his false plea of Not Guilty at the trial: he felt that he would give less pain to Madeline and her family if they could still believe in his innocence. He feels it creditable that the "struggle against truth was less for myself than for them . . . for them, a bold, a crafty, a dexterous villain I became!"

After disclosing his secret in such terms, Aram ends his confession with an appeal to the Great and Unseen Spirit and his life with the Stoic gesture of suicide.

Aram's ethical progression, as thus outlined, may contain an element of the author's reaction against Godwin as well as against Bentham. Other Godwinian youths before Bulwer had come to feel that pure reason and individual judgment might delude their follower into moral anarchy. Aram finally affirms conventional morality: one should not go beyond "the line allotted to the rest of men." But the lesson is chiefly for Benthamites. Bentham's doctrine was more capable of general misuse than Godwin's, and cheap appropriations of it were not hard to find. Aram's confession, entirely Utilitarian in principle, is intended to undercut misapplied Utilitarian ethics with a single objection. Aram, repenting, does not attribute unique importance to a man's life, nor deny the right of the private individual to kill, nor speak of the inevitable blindness of self-interest, nor consider the need of some harmony between ends and means. The sole argument is that one cannot foresee all the consequences of an act. Still expressing a calculating morality, Aram raises a practical caution against it when it is employed to condone a visible evil.

In this novel, despite its tangle of literary derivations, Bulwer laid hold of an important and original theme. He lacked the spiritual firmness to deal with it greatly, and subjected it to indignity and triviality. Overcome by his fatal inclination and talent for popularity, he subordinated his psychological theme to a commonplace romance, cheapening the whole with a plaster covering of sentiment according to current fashions. He evaded the true difficulty of analyzing Aram's motives, performing this essential task summarily in the secret autobiographical confession. He had not the capacity to execute the novel on the plane of his finest perceptions, and left us only a reminder that he might have been among the greatest of the English novelists.

Whatever Bulwer intended, and failed to do, he did not intend *Eugene Aram* as a protest against capital punishment nor even against a miscarriage of justice. He never wished to abolish the death penalty for murder; and in his novel of 1832 he did not deny, he did not question Aram's guilt. Aram, it is true, says "my hand struck—but not the *death*-blow," but this is of no legal consequence; as for the intention to murder, Bulwer inserted a footnote to emphasize that it had been present.[68] He described Aram as morally responsible, and did not suggest that he ought to escape hanging.[69]

Nevertheless, the tone of the book is not quite right. Although Aram never, not even at the end, seems morally heroic, it is possible to suppose at times that the author thinks him so. A writer less hasty and more subtle might have prevented this confusion, even while arousing some sympathy for the misguided criminal. Not the subject but Bulwer's failure to dissociate himself from his hero—basically a failure of imagination and of technique—became the source of contemporary objection, whenever it was sincere. First *Clifford*, then *Aram*. Bulwer had taken the side of the criminal again.

As soon as published, *Eugene Aram* was an immediate popular success; it "took Europe by storm and became one of the most abidingly popular of all Bulwer's works." [70] Two individuals whose notice of the book is recorded testify—even better than the literary reviews—to its general circulation. That literate courtesan, Harriette Wilson, who had drawn Bulwer into an occasional correspondence, mentioned *Aram* as the favorite of "the boarding school miss." [71] The other person, Pierce Egan, called upon Bulwer to present him with a curio; it was, he said, the caul of Thurtell, and Bulwer alone among literary men was worthy of possessing it.[72]

If readers were favorable, reviewers were divided, and the author's treatment of a criminal subject was put in question at once. The *Athenaeum* found genius manifest in the book but wished it had never been written. The *Edinburgh*, noticing Bulwer's novels for the first time, found Aram incredible as a murderer for money. These reviews were balanced, and some others were entirely favorable. The *Spectator* commented upon the idealized portrait of Aram, adding: "In this we see nothing to blame: we are merely informing our readers that Mr. Bulwer's tale is far more like *Manfred* than the *Newgate Calendar*,—a compliment, certainly; though not of the kind that will contribute, in these days, to the sale of the book." The *Monthly Review* called the new book the best of Bulwer's works and found in it a fine tone of Christian philosophy.[73] The chief attack upon it came, not surprisingly, from *Fraser's Magazine*. Novelizing the *Newgate Calendar*, said Maginn,[74] was a work suited to Bulwer's capacity, and he gleefully charged Bulwer with the taste for low life which Bulwer had attributed to him as MacGrawler:

> When the author of *Pelham* affects to describe refined feelings and distinguished society, he forthwith labors and becomes overstrained; but among thieves and blackguards—in the tap, the ken, the hedge-row pot-house—in the purlieus of the Minories and Whitechapel, he writes with an easy felicity of phrase that betokens an intimate acquaintance with the scenes described. . . . If the Bill is carried, and a representative given to the Tower Hamlets, let Mr. Bulwer canvass them: he will be popular and appreciated there.[75]

The last sentence reminds us that Bulwer, besides caricaturing Maginn in *Paul Clifford*, was of the reform party in the House of Commons.

Maginn objected to Bulwer's departures from fact, to the disparities in Aram's character, and to the literary imitations evident in the novel. His last charge was this: "Finally, we dislike altogether this awakening sympathy with interesting criminals, and wasting sensibilities on the scaffold and the gaol. It is a modern, a depraved, a corrupting taste." [76] Extraordinary crimes, such as those of Burke and Hare, induced imitation, he added; a book like this might have the same effect.

The evil of arousing a wrong sympathy with a criminal had sometimes been alleged against the newspapers.[77] Here it was charged against a novel for probably the first time. Maginn's objections, the essence of all the criticism of Newgate fiction, were to be repeated by others—some of whom, unlike Maginn, believed what they said—against Bulwer, Ainsworth, Dickens, and lesser persons. *Eugene Aram* greatly extended its author's popularity, but it allowed a hostile critic to complain that Bulwer had shown his intellectual hero, though a thief, a liar, and a murderer, to be among the noblest of mankind.

The reader using any copy of *Aram* printed in the last hundred years may be puzzled by the strength of the attack upon the book, for he finds Eugene not guilty of murder. The change was made late; in 1840, when there was a new edition of his works, Bulwer wrote a preface for *Aram* in which he defended both the choice of subject and the treatment. In that year, the controversy over Newgate literature was lively, but he had not recently been at the center of it; with a little condescension, he set his work apart:

> The guilt of Eugene Aram is not that of a vulgar ruffian; it leads to views and considerations vitally and wholly distinct from those with which profligate knavery and brutal cruelty revolt and displease us in the literature of Newgate and the Hulks.[78]

But in the eighteen-forties, as will appear, there was a resurgence of attacks upon Bulwer. When these had quieted, and when he was preparing *Aram* for re-issue in 1849, he made the significant changes which have been followed ever since. In the new preface for this edition, he announced that he had changed his mind about Eugene's guilt: having restudied all the evidence, he had concluded that Eugene Aram was an accomplice in the robbery but no more.[79] In the text of the novel, Bulwer changed the substance of the criminal's confession, made his attitudes more palatable both before and after the crime, and altered some passages which had been interpreted as showing the author's admiration for the criminal. Aram looked, after all this, a different man indeed. One has to remember that from 1832 to 1849, over the whole period of attack and defense of Newgate novels, Eugene Aram was guilty of premeditated murder.

As material for the theatre, *Eugene Aram* was far more popular than *Paul Clifford*, which was dramatized in 1832 and made a melodrama in 1835.[80] There were four stage versions of *Aram* in 1832, the year of publication; one of these was played in Edinburgh. The most successful of them was also the earliest; it was that of W. T. Moncrieff, which opened at the Surrey on February 8, 1832, not much more than a month after publication of the novel.[81] A competing theatre had its version on stage five days later. Moncrieff's play was included in standard collections of the nineteenth century—Dick's Standard Plays, Cumberland's Minor Theatre, Lacy's Acting Editions—and in French's Acting Editions. Eric Watson, historian of the trial, records other instances of the later dramatic use of Hood's poem and Bulwer's novel.

The chief attack of the year upon *Eugene Aram* was not a review but a fictional parody, "Elizabeth Brownrigge: a Tale," which appeared in two issues of *Fraser's Magazine*.[82] This story was once attributed to Thackeray, but it is more reasonable to accept the suggestion of Miss Miriam Thrall that the authors were William Maginn and his friend J. G. Lockhart.[83] The title came from the chief character, a woman who figures in the Newgate Calendars as a monster of cruelty. She ill-treated the girls apprenticed to her from a foundling hospital, and one of them died. Elizabeth Brownrigg was hanged September 14, 1767. Before Maginn's time, she had already served as material for parody: in the first number of the *Anti-Jacobin*, in 1797, was an "Inscription" for the door of her cell in Newgate, which read in part:

> Dost thou ask her crime?
> She whipp'd two female 'prentices to death
> And hid them in the coal-hole. For her mind
> Shap'd strictest plans of discipline. Sage schemes!
> Such as Lycurgus taught, when at the shrine
> Of the Orthyan goddess he bade flog
> The little Spartans; such as erst chastised
> Our Milton when at college. For this act
> Did Brownrigg swing. Harsh laws! But time shall come
> When France shall reign, and laws be all repeal'd! [84]

The tale about her in *Fraser's* is prefaced by a long dedicatory letter addressed to the author of *Eugene Aram*; the purported author, eager for success, finds that he can achieve it by studying and imitating the works of Bulwer. "Elizabeth Brownrigge" is the result. The sarcasm is elaborate and sometimes witty, but it descends sometimes into sober diatribe. The letter parallels the preface to *Aram:* the author remarks that he has "taken a few slight liberties with the story."

> As you have omitted any mention of the wife of your Eugene, I have not thought it necessary to recall the reader's attention to the husband and sixteen children of my Elizabeth. As you have given your hero more learning and virtue than he possessed . . . I have presumed to raise the station of my heroine. . . . I have represented her in my tale as a young gentle-woman of independent fortune, a paragon of beauty, a severe and learned moral philosopher, and the Lady Bountiful of the village of Islington.[85]

The attack is exuberant, and it makes undeniable hits. What extends it to its considerable length—its more than twenty-five thousand words seem at first to be bad editorial judgment—is that the writers make a literary game of parallels, imitating *Aram* closely at a hundred points. Some of the parallels have little satirical effect, but these contribute to the whole appearance of sedulous imitation and must have provided amusement for anyone who had just read the novel. Bulwer had prefixed a quotation, in Greek, from *Oedipus the King;* the parody uses a still apter one from *Medea,* beginning with the same "Alas, alas." Bulwer revealed that he had first begun a verse tragedy about Aram; "Brownrigge," we are told, was begun as a burletta. The damaging likeness to the novel runs through the whole of the parody: it mocks Bulwer's mannered descriptions, his rhetoric of emotion, his genteel purple passion. The young lover of Elizabeth, "who stood six feet two without his shoes, united, in the compact and slender structure of his person, the vigour of the Hercules with the elegance of the Apollo." Elizabeth has been made beautiful, too; but of course the essence of the satire (following the line of the *Anti-Jacobin* verses) lies in the conversion of the sadistic murderess into a fine-souled being who weeps at the stripes she inflicts and who explains her actions in the kind of exalted language Bulwer had put in the mouth of Aram. Some parts of the attack fall short of consistency—Elizabeth's

Benthamism, surely, leaves Bulwer unscathed—but the burlesque is frequently diverting. Like Aram, Elizabeth is high-minded even in prison:

> She completed a large stock of baby-linen for the poor; she perused and commented upon the principal new publications of the day; and she composed an elaborate parallel between the characters of Socrates and Lady Jane Grey, after the manner of Plutarch.[86]

Though "Elizabeth Brownrigge" had its origin in personal hostility, it kept on proper literary ground in exposing and exaggerating the weaknesses of Bulwer's book. It showed, to readers not aware of its authorship, only the degree of malice which makes satire possible. In this instance, personal animosity moved Maginn and Lockhart to express opinions about *Eugene Aram* which they might well have felt, though less strongly, if the book had been written by someone else.

But this entirely appropriate satire was only a visible surface over a turbulence. Despite the parody, the controversy with Bulwer was not really about the morality of the criminal theme, and the next exchange of verbal blows did not even mention it. In December 1832, the *Quarterly Review* carried a review of Morier's *Zohrab the Hostage*, commenting unfavorably on several of Bulwer's novels but saying nothing of *Eugene Aram* or Bulwer's attitude toward criminals. The tone was not improper. Bulwer, then editor of Colburn's *New Monthly Magazine,* replied in his January number with a "Letter to the Editor of the Quarterly Review." [87] This was an open attack on Lockhart as a writer; the tone was contemptuous and angry. There was, the letter said, "no man living who possesses the same power of incorporating the narrowest sentiments in the meanest language." Michael Sadleir explains the reasons for this burst of temper, and they had nothing to do with *Paul Clifford.*[88] The ostensible issue—the morality of Bulwer's novels—had been left behind as the quarrel progressed.

To sum up the matter, Bulwer's two novels were criticized chiefly by Maginn, with the collaboration of Lockhart, for reasons calculated to enlist the support of right-thinking people. Mr. Sadleir, sympathetic to Bulwer, calls it "Tory-cum-Grub Street" persecution. However one apportions blame in the confusion of political and personal quarreling, the critics' conviction that the novels had a dangerous tendency seems the least of their motives.

NEWGATE ROMANCE WITH LYRICS: *Rookwood*

After *Eugene Aram*, Bulwer moved to other interests. He was followed, as a Newgate novelist, by a popular romancer, William Harrison Ainsworth, whose *Rookwood* appeared in April 1834. Like *Eugene Aram* (from which it differed vastly in other respects) it combined the Gothic tradition with the lore of the Newgate Calendar.

Ainsworth began his career as a writer of Gothic tales for the magazines; some of them were published in book form in the early eighteen-twenties. He became one of the imitators of Scott with a historical novel, published in 1826. He occupied himself in various ways, including publishing, and began to write his next novel, *Rookwood*, in 1831, which upon publication three years later made him extremely popular. He was then twenty-nine. He followed it with another successful historical novel, *Crichton*, in 1837, and with another Newgate novel, *Jack Sheppard*. Thereafter he produced a long series of historical novels; those published in the early eighteen-forties increased his reputation and have continued to be read to the present time, but the works of his later years had, in comparison, few readers.

Rookwood is a story by Mrs. Radcliffe transplanted. Ainsworth's own expression of the obvious debt occurs in the preface he wrote for the novel in 1849:

> Wishing to describe, somewhat minutely, the trim gardens, the picturesque domains, the rook-haunted groves, the gloomy chambers, and gloomier galleries, of an ancient Hall with which I was acquainted, I resolved to attempt a story in the bygone style of Mrs. Radcliffe (which had always inexpressible charms for me), substituting an old English squire, an old English manorial residence, and an old English highwayman, for the Italian marchese, the castle, and the brigand of the great mistress of Romance.[89]

"Substituting" is the accurate word for Ainsworth's process. There is probably no single item of originality in all the profusion of

Gothic elements. The ancient hall, the family curse, the gruesome burial vaults, the secret marriage, and all the rest had long been in the common domain. The central conflict of the tale is that between two half-brothers for the family inheritance, a plot used a few years earlier by Scott, in St. Ronan's Well.[90] From the same novel Ainsworth acquired Miss Mowbray, even using her name, and Rookwood was suggested by Ravenswood, of The Bride of Lammermoor. Ainsworth followed the fashion of taking poetic keynotes for his chapters; these he drew from a variety of sources, including Schiller and John Gay, but especially from John Webster, of whose works there was a new edition in 1830.

The English robber whom Ainsworth chose to entangle incongruously in his Gothic tale was Dick Turpin, executed in 1739. The actual Turpin of record is not a very engaging character. Besides highway robbery, his affairs included stealing sheep and breaking into farmers' houses, sometimes with the aid of confederates; and he took a turn at smuggling. There was, however, enough singularity in his career to set a legend going and make him one of the several highwaymen best known to English boys even before Ainsworth took him up. Under an assumed name Turpin was able to hunt with country sportsmen without being detected; for a time he lived in a cave or brush-covered retreat and made his forays from it; and there is an attractive story, possibly true, of his association with another highwayman, Tom King. He confronted King upon a road at night; King recognized him, invoked the fraternity of their occupation, and was thereafter his friend and companion. Turpin later killed King by accident, in attempting to shoot a constable who had set upon them. When he was brought to trial in 1739, the indictments were for horse-stealing, not highway robbery, but the imprisoned horse-thief had been identified as Turpin. He was a model of easy behavior up to the time of his execution.[91]

Possibly Ainsworth reread some of the Newgate Calendars, but he may not have needed to. He had prepared himself long before:

> Turpin was the hero of my boyhood. I had always a strange passion for highwaymen, and have listened by the hour to their exploits, as narrated by my father, and especially to those of "Dauntless Dick," that "chief minion of the moon." One of Tur-

1. George Cruikshank, The Death of Black Bess. Chapter xii, Book IV, *Rookwood*, 1834.

pin's adventures in particular, the ride to Hough Green, which took a deep hold of my fancy I have recorded in song. When a boy, I have often lingered by the side of the deep old road where this robbery was committed, to cast wistful glances into its mysterious windings; and when night deepened the shadows of the trees, have urged my horse on his journey, from a vague apprehension of a visit from the ghostly highwayman. . . . No wonder, in after-years, in selecting a highwayman for a character in a tale, I should choose my old favorite, Dick Turpin.[92]

Although Turpin appears in a considerable part of *Rookwood*, he has no inherent connection with the plot. By stealing a marriage certificate he introduces a minor complication, but this seems a triviality—merely one of the weary quantity of arranged motions that the puppets must go through. But in spite of his being forced within the pages of the book, Turpin's presence does all that anything could do to lighten them. Unreal as he is, he is far more lively than any of the other figures of the tale. Ainsworth shows him masquerading under the name of Palmer, making himself comfortable in Rookwood Hall and laying a wager against the capture of Turpin with a mean-spirited lawyer who aspires to be a thief-catcher. Turpin is ready to make money where and how he can, but his heart is in the right place, and he does not hesitate even to endanger himself for the sake of friendship. He has no scruples against violence when it is necessary, but he prides himself on his gallantry and honor.

Turpin takes possession of a large section of the book when he sets out to escape pursuit and rides his fine mare, Black Bess, from London to York; Black Bess dies after keeping ahead of the pursuers, who have had fresh horses at intervals. The account of the ride impressed contemporary readers more than the stale Gothic omens, and they were right. The style is less turgid in this passage than elsewhere; Ainsworth, always fluent, was proud of the speed with which he wrote it.

The real Turpin, after shooting Tom King, rode to a town in Lincolnshire, a journey of no great difficulty. In his fondness, Ainsworth attributed to his hero the extraordinary feat of the ride to York, which seems to have been performed by two other highwaymen if by any at all. (S. M. Ellis, Ainsworth's biographer, compares

the real with the fictional Turpin.) One of the traditional stories
had a pleasing feature which Ainsworth did not use: a highwayman
established his alibi after such a ride by inquiring the time from the
Lord Mayor, on the Bowling Green at York. Whether there had
been several rides, or only one which duplicated itself in the manner of legend, Ainsworth himself became a legend-maker. Inn-
keepers along the highway from London to York adopted Turpin's
exploit as Ainsworth told it; the new legend became as well established as the old.[93]

Ainsworth makes his highwayman a merry fellow, with a high
regard for his profession. No undercurrent of seriousness, such as
ran through *Paul Clifford*, comes near it. Speaking as Palmer, Turpin argues warmly that

> It is as necessary for a man to be a gentleman before he can turn
> highwayman, as it is for a doctor to have his diploma, or an attorney
> his certificate. . . . England, sir, has reason to be proud of her
> highwaymen. They are peculiar to her clime, and are as much be-
> fore the brigand of Italy, the contrabandist of Spain, or the cut-
> purse of France—as her sailors are before all the rest of the world.[94]

Turpin thereupon sings a ballad in praise of some eight or ten re-
nowned criminals; and an Irishman in the group replies patriot-
ically with his ballad about the Rapparees. Elsewhere the author
memorializes Turpin as the last of the Romans:

> Several successors he had, it is true, but no name worthy to be re-
> corded after his own. With him expired the chivalrous spirit which
> animated successively the bosoms of so many knights of the road;
> with him died away that passionate love of enterprise, that high
> spirit of devotion to the fair sex. . . .[95]

Why has the race declined, Ainsworth inquires, when the times
seem to furnish so much excellent material for the profession? He
regrets that "we are now degenerated from the grand tobyman to
the cracksman and the sneak, about whom there are no redeeming
features."

Ainsworth was well aware of the delight with which he had
written about Turpin; in the Envoy he recalled the tales his father
had told him:

We shall, perhaps, be accused of dilating too much upon the character of the highwayman, and we plead guilty to the charge. But we found it impossible to avoid running a little to extremes. Our earliest associations are connected with sunny scenes in Cheshire, said to have been haunted by Turpin; and with one very dear to us—from whose lips, now, alas! silent, we have listened to many stories of his exploits—he was a sort of hero. We have had a singular delight in recounting his feats and hairbreadth escapes. . . . Perhaps we may have placed him in too favorable a point of view— and yet we know not. . . . Such as we conceive him to have been, we have drawn him.[96]

Ainsworth, who sang at the first of the Fraserian dinners, was indulging another personal taste when he filled *Rookwood* with songs. He may also have had an eye upon the theatre, in which he had been dabbling.[97] The first edition of the novel contained twenty-three; the fourth edition saw the total raised to about thirty, for the songs had been popular. Half of them, including those most favored at the time, were highwayman ballads and flash songs, with a quality of lively movement. The others were mechanical Gothic pieces (about corpses, yew trees, carrion crows), with gypsy love songs and even a couple of hymns tossed in for good measure. A few of the ballads were written for familiar tunes; others were set to music after the publication of the book.[98]

One of Turpin's songs, "The Scampsman," begins as follows:

> There is not a king, should you search the world round,
> So blithe as the king of the road to be found;
> His pistol's his sceptre, his saddle's his throne,
> Whence he levies supplies, or enforces a loan.[99]

"Jerry Juniper's Chant"[100] may furnish an example of Ainsworth's flash songs. The first stanza runs thus:

> In a box of the stone jug I was born,
> Of a hempen widow the kid forlorn,
>   *Fake away,*
> And my father, as I've heard say,
>   *Fake away,*

Was a merchant of capers gay,
Who cut his last fling with great applause,
*Nix my doll pals, fake away.**

Bulwer had gone slumming for his thieves' talk and liked to recall his acquaintance with gypsies; it is not clear whether Ainsworth did the same. The romanticized scenes in *Rookwood* may represent only book knowledge. This was Ainsworth's explanation, when Edmund Yates suggested that he must have interviewed thieves and gypsies in order to gain such a knowledge of flash:

> Not at all. Never had anything to do with the scoundrels in my life. I got my slang in a much easier way. I picked up the Memoirs of James Hardy Vaux—a returned transport. The book was full of adventures, and had at the end a kind of slang dictionary. Out of this I got all my "patter." Having read it thoroughly and mastered it, I could use it with perfect facility.[101]

Such a highly respectable answer may be open to doubt, but the quality of the conversation in *Rookwood* does not prove it untrue.

Besides using gypsies as a part of the furniture of unconventionality in his tale, Ainsworth followed Bulwer and Hook in introducing persons of contemporary notoriety. The first, Jerry Juniper, who sings the flash songs, seems to have been a true jolly beggar who was known at all the race tracks. The second, John Tom, who also sings a ballad of his adventures, called himself Sir William Courtenay, Knight of Malta; he had come to Canterbury in 1832

---

* Ainsworth supplied brief notes to interpret the slang to his readers. "Nix my doll," according to his notes, means no more than *nix* alone: "nothing," or "nothing's the matter," perhaps. If "my doll" is taken, somewhat awkwardly, as a term of direct address, like "pals," it would mean *doxy* or mistress. This may well have been intended. Although *cly-faking* was an old word for pocket-picking, Ainsworth's *fake* as an imperative verb was not idiomatic. (See J. S. Farmer, *Slang and Its Analogues*, London, 1890, II, 368.) The lines translate thus:

In a cell of the prison I was born,
Child forlorn of a widow whose husband had been hanged,
          Go on stealing,
And my father, as I've heard,
          Go on stealing,
Was a dancing-master,
Who cut his last fling with great applause,
          (as he hung from the gallows)
          Never mind, pals, keep on stealing.

and had proposed himself as a candidate for parliament. He was a crazed impostor and fanatic, but his deception succeeded for a considerable time. Both Juniper and John Tom were alive at the time of publication of *Rookwood*, though the Knight of Malta was confined in an asylum, from which he emerged to die in 1838 at the head of a messianic "insurrection." [102]

In the preface of 1849, Ainsworth wrote that his aim in *Rookwood* had been

> To see how far the infusion of a warmer and more genial current into the veins of old Romance would succeed in reviving her fluttering and feeble pulses. The attempt has succeeded beyond my most sanguine expectations.[103]

The warmer and more genial current *was* a great success. *Rookwood* sprang into immediate popularity; there were five editions in three years.[104] A French translation was appropriately entitled *Les Gentile-hommes du grand chemin*. A set of six drawings illustrating Turpin's ride to York was a popular item, often seen in roadside inns.[105] The popularity of *Rookwood* is responsible for the appearance of a song about Turpin in Chapter XLIII of *Pickwick Papers*. (It is odd to find Ainsworth's Gothic verses imitated there: "The Ivy Green," of Chapter VI, is very like "Mandrake" and "Churchyard Yew," in *Rookwood*.)

Ainsworth became a celebrity and a dandy. He received letters of praise from various notables; he was bidden to the soirees of Lady Blessington and the gatherings at Holland House. There is no reason to suppose that he disliked the advertising custom which placed his pictures in the omnibuses. An Edinburgh lawyer sought out more information about Turpin in the Advocates' Library; Ainsworth used it in additional notes to the fifth edition. His hero, moreover, was to be endlessly used and imitated by the writers of cheap literature. As soon as the penny serials began to appear, perhaps in 1840, there were serials about Turpin. E. S. Turner, recording the names of some of them in *Boys Will Be Boys*, says that *Rookwood* "directly inspired the scores of highwaymen 'penny dreadfuls' which fascinated the next two generations." [106] Turpin was extremely popular all through the forties, fifties, and sixties, and could be revived much later; a new serial about him had reached two hundred numbers in 1908.[107] It was Ainsworth who set Turpin going on so long a career as a hero.

It seems likely that the fame of *Rookwood* was spread by the London theatres. Ainsworth's biographer says it was produced at the Adelphi and elsewhere.[108] One would certainly expect this, though the only regular play listed in Nicoll's *Early Nineteenth Century Drama* is a later version, produced in 1840.[109] Certainly the best-known dramatic result of the book was an equestrian spectacle produced by Ducrow at Astley's Amphitheatre; with what delight must the producer have discovered the book which made possible *Turpin's Ride to York and the Death of Black Bess*.[110] But Turpin's story had been exploited by an earlier manager at Astley's; an entertainment called *Richard Turpin, the Highwayman* had been given there in 1819. It was devised by William Barrymore, who romanticized various criminals and outlaws for the stage.[111]

Fraser's had jested that Bulwer was setting out to novelize the entire *Newgate Calendar*. Apparently Ainsworth, impressed by all this popularity of Turpin, actually entertained the idea of doing so, for he wrote

> Turpin . . . is only a part of a plan, as this work is part of a more extensive edifice, which in time, I may be able to construct. . . . The portrait of the robber is not, I am free to admit, complete in all its details, but, though I have not yet found canvass [sic] enough for it, the tablet exists fully wrought in my imagination.[112]

Turpin was the robber on the road, DuVal was to be the robber at the theatres and public places, Sheppard to be the robber in Newgate. The plan for a novel about DuVal went as far as an agreement between Ainsworth and his publisher, signed in June 1836.[113] The book was not written, and the most gentlemanly of all highwaymen made only a minor showing in *Talbot Harland*, more than thirty years later.

The periodicals which reviewed *Rookwood* judged it, naturally, as a romance. John Forster, in the *Examiner*, found the Gothic horrors "mouldy" and the highwaymen's slang "loathsome."

> Turpin, whom the writer is pleased with loving familiarity to call Dick, is the hero of the tale. Doubtless we shall soon see Thurtell

presented in sublime guise, and the drive to Gad's Hill described with all pomp and circumstance. There are people who may like this sort of thing, but we are not of the number. . . . The author has, we suspect, been misled by the example and success of "Paul Clifford," but in "Paul Clifford" the thieves and their dialect serve for illustration, while in "Rookwood" the highwayman and his slang are presented as if in themselves they had some claim to admiration.[114]

The review concluded, on the other hand, by saying that another opinion was possible: the book had admirers among people of good judgment.

The objection to Turpin was not typical of the reviews; most did not complain. The *Athenaeum* reported ironically: "In breadth of delineation, and depth of coloring, it is most complete; its villains are most villainously villanous [sic], and its terrors are most terribly terrible." [115] The reviewer considered that the book strained the horrible to the point of making it ludicrous, but he was able to praise the portrait of Turpin's horse and the account of Turpin's ride.

Because Ainsworth had been since 1830 a member of the group writing for *Fraser's Magazine*,[116] he received his most favorable attention there. It began with the notice of a book published shortly before *Rookwood*: the reviewer of Charles Whitehead's *Lives and Exploits of English Highwaymen*, casting a nostalgic glance at various celebrated figures, inquired in the mood of Villon, "Nay, what is most and more than all, where is Turpin? All, all hung upon that fatal Tyburn tree. . . ." [117] In view of the imminent publication—by a Fraserian—of a novel in which Turpin appeared, this portion of the article reads like a subtle puff for *Rookwood*, in spite of the fact that the latter part, in a quite different tone, calls for a serious nonfictional study of such criminals without "poetic adornment and speculative reverie." [118]

When Ainsworth's novel appeared, *Fraser's*, punning on the name of a famous Latin dictionary, entitled its review "High Ways and Low Ways; or Ainsworth's Dictionary, with Notes by Turpin." [119] *Rookwood* here became the occasion of a comparison between Ainsworth and Bulwer, much to the latter's disadvantage. *Rookwood* was first issued with no preface and a modest dedication;

Bulwer's prefaces and dedications were "bloated with vanity, mean-ness, an ostentatious exaltation of self, and a despicable deprecia-tion of others." Ainsworth's work was "natural, free, and joyous," whereas Bulwer's was "forced, constrained, and cold." Ainsworth's flash songs (some of which were quoted) were the most original feature of his book; the songs in *Paul Clifford* were not to be com-pared with them, for Bulwer had no sense of humor. As for the story, the *Fraser* writer praised it with a handful of clichés and sum-marized it at length. In the next issue, that of July 1834, Ainsworth took his place in the Gallery of Literary Characters,[120] a monthly feature in which a drawing by Maclise was accompanied by a page of letterpress by the editor; the chitchat about Ainsworth was lauda-tory. In 1836, Maginn noticed the third edition of *Rookwood* and approved the author's inclusion of more ballads.[121]

Ainsworth had also the fortune to be mentioned, in a review of current novels in the *Quarterly Review*, as a young writer of promise, with "a fresh and stirring fancy."

> But he must lop his luxuriancy, and chastise his taste. The odious *slang* with which he has interspersed his third volume is as false as base; and his energetic and animating picture of Turpin's ride to York needed not the setting off of such vulgar and affected orna-ments.[122]

Flash language, which had pleased *Fraser's*, offended the *Quarterly*; but the objection was on the grounds of taste, not moral tendency.

The *Edinburgh* did not deal with *Rookwood* for three years, until it had come to a fourth edition and *Crichton* had appeared. An article on "Recent English Romances" then gave Ainsworth qualified praise as a writer of "considerable powers and resources." He had attempted a bold experiment and had ventured, success-fully, to "revive the almost exploded interest in the supernatural." Other recent attempts had failed, but Ainsworth's narrative pace carried the reader on to the end without allowing time for sober ob-jection. The reviewer admired Ainsworth's ability but not Gothic romance as a type. "Is this a romance," he inquired, "or a melo-drama compounded of the *Castle Spectre* and the *Newgate Calen-dar?*" [123]

To sum up the reception of *Rookwood*, the periodicals dealt with it according to the standards of the decade. Although some criticized it for including a low element, *Fraser's* was not among them, and no one expressed fear that the novel would lead young men into a life of crime.

In the five-year span from *Paul Clifford* to *Rookwood*, there were a few other crime novels. The climactic year of the forgery debate, 1830, saw the publication of a short novel, *Carwell, or Crime and Sorrow*, by Mrs. Frances Sheridan. It phrased no arguments against the forgery or other laws; it merely told a pathetic story. A young man, entangled in bad company, is convicted of forgery, sentenced to death, and transported; his wife, thinking to join him and help him make a new life, passes a forged note, but her death sentence is not commuted. In spite of the lesson of the tale, neither *Fraser's* nor anyone else objected that *Carwell* aroused sympathy for a criminal.[124]

Horace Smith's *Gale Middleton, a Story of the Present Day* (1833), a novel unfairly neglected even in its own time, breathed the optimistic spirit of the first year of the reformed parliament. The main characters are middle-class people, but a crime is central in the action, much of which is admirably natural and realistic. There is an attack upon the criminal law, summed up in language like that of *Paul Clifford*:

> We punish the crimes, and in some cases even the misfortunes of the poor, with severity; but we offer them not a single incentive to virtue and good conduct; our criminal system creates a hell for them, but does not offer to their hopes anything that approximates toward a heaven.[125]

Charles Whitehead, remembered for his early connection with Dickens and already mentioned as author of a book about highwaymen, published in 1834 a novel whose title page reads, *The Autobiography of a Notorious Legal Functionary*; it is also called *Autobiography of Jack Ketch*. It might be expected to tell of the actual seventeenth-century hangman, but the story has no connection with the Ketch of history. Apparently it is intended to be an account of a life suitable for any aspirant to the position. The early chapters contain an incredible amount of punning and word-play about jails, courts, and hanging, and the illustrations aim at a gruesome humor; but many episodes of the story are grimly realistic, and the life described is drably unattractive. If four editions mean anything, this strange production had some popularity, though it is hard to see why.[126]

Notwithstanding the popularity of Bulwer's and Ainsworth's books, the early and middle thirties were not filled with counterparts of Aram and Turpin. There was crime in other novels; T. H. Lister's *Arlington* (1832), for example, has a plot which hangs on a murder. But Lister, with his upper-class characters, was a silver-fork novelist, and *Arlington* is not a Newgate novel. Crime in the novels of the early and middle thirties—outside those selected for special attention here—was not more common or more noticeable than in the novels of the twenties or in the novels of Scott. After a short interval, *Clifford*, *Aram*, and *Rookwood* were to be followed by another little cluster of Newgate novels, but those, published in the standard three volumes and at the standard price of one and one-half guineas, could always be counted on the fingers.

V

THE NEWGATE NOVEL AND THE MORAL
ARGUMENT, 1837–40

THE "REAL" WORLD OF *Oliver Twist*

Although Dickens' interest in crime and criminals was lifelong, it
was the early novel, *Oliver Twist*, which for a time placed him
among the Newgate novelists. Its "low" material was disliked by a
few readers even to the beginning of the twentieth century.
(George Saintsbury, who had a favorite joke about "grime" novels,
wrote deprecatingly of it in 1917, in the *Cambridge History of English Literature*.) *Oliver Twist* was attached to the contemporary
scene in a fashion not equalled in the other Newgate novels. It reflected the prevalence of juvenile crime; the recent development of
the trade in stolen goods, which seemed in the twenties almost to
be keeping pace with legitimate commerce; and the general attention to crime and punishment.

The story originally appeared in the new *Bentley's Miscellany*,
of which Dickens was undertaking the editorship and for which he
was to furnish original fiction. The first issue of the magazine came
out in January 1837; the first of twenty installments of the novel
appeared in the February number. On three occasions it was omitted: June 1837 (after the death of Mrs. Dickens' sister, Mary Hogarth), October 1837, and September 1838. During the early
months of *Oliver Twist*, when Dickens was also finishing the *Pickwick Papers*, he was less than a week ahead of the printer with each.
In the spring of 1838, though he then had *Nicholas Nickleby* under
way also, he was apparently getting far ahead of monthly deadlines;
he finished the writing of *Oliver Twist* early in September 1838.[1]
The completed book was published two months later; the serial ran
on in *Bentley's* through April 1839.

Both the serial and the book were extremely popular.[2] A second edition came out in 1840 and a third in 1841, to say nothing of various extra printings. There were no further editions until 1846, when *Oliver* was published as a ten-part serial, and in one-volume and three-volume forms. There were minor changes between the magazine version and later editions—chapter numbering is not the same, for example—but the revisions of text are inconsiderable.[3] George Cruikshank's twenty-four plates for the story in *Bentley's* were redrawn in a larger size for the book.

Besides observing the streets of London, Dickens must have read what came to hand about youthful criminals, and he probably sought out more.[4] The newspapers of any year of the period show the kind of notice given to young thieves: when they were brought before a magistrate there was little opportunity for discrimination between the novice and the professional criminal. Judges had certain discretionary powers, but the jury, deciding between guilty and not guilty, knew that the penalty of imprisonment or transportation or indeed death was as applicable to the boy of ten or twelve as to the man of thirty. The attitude of the judge did of course make a great difference in the handling of an individual case.* Real innocence might receive pity, but the system and the minds which carried it on were not constituted to deal with boys who were still at the beginning of a criminal career.

The newspapers had made Dickens' readers equally well prepared to accept Fagin. Isaac or Ikey Solomon, whose name (with *s* added) Thackeray was to take as a burlesque pseudonym for *Catherine*, had become known as the most successful and elusive of London fences, and his activities had been extensively reported. Dickens' receiver is not shown to have so large a business as Solomon's nor does his character parallel Solomon's in detail, but the notoriety of the actual person was such that every adult reader must have thought of him. The case had been closed, so far as the Eng-

---

* Dickens might have read in a Newgate Calendar about Patrick McDonald, a destitute boy of fourteen, whom the jury reluctantly found guilty of stealing a jacket but to whom each of them first gave a shilling. His unaffected tears drew similar gifts from the sheriff and all in the courtroom. The judge undertook to obtain for him a situation and a pardon. Crook, V, 87–88.

In the same year, 1810 (or 1811), a shop-boy, Samuel Oliver, whose name may not be without significance, came up at the Old Bailey for defrauding his master. Samuel Oliver was sent for seven years to Botany Bay. Crook, V, 89–90.

lish courts were concerned, when Solomon was transported to Australia in 1831, but references to him were frequent for years thereafter. Born in 1785, he was first a peddler, a passer of bad coins, and a pickpocket.[5] He learned to deal in stolen goods and made enormous profits. For many years the police knew of his operations, but the requirements of the law for identifying stolen goods were so stringent that a conviction was hard to obtain. No great ingenuity seems to have been matched against Solomon's, but the accounts do not suggest that he paid for immunity. In making the traffic of a fence into a well-organized business, Solomon was extremely careful to see that identifying marks on all objects were removed before the goods came to rest in his house. It was a precaution which no one had applied so consistently before. (Dickens' Fagin sets Oliver Twist at removing the marks from handkerchiefs.) One writer has it that as Solomon advanced in his career he dealt only in big lots; he advised the thieves who supplied him not to take continual risks on small jobs but to live better by carrying off one or two well-planned large operations in a year.[6]

He was a successful dealer in stolen notes of the Bank of England; he had agents outside London who sent the notes (as well as other goods) to the Continent, whence they returned to the bank through legitimate channels of trade. (Fagin remarks of a stolen note that it will have to be sent out of the country.) Property in Solomon's house at the time of his arrest was supposed to be worth £20,000. He was tried at last on July 9, 1830, and transported the next May. In the course of his career, he had become legendary—a modern businessman who made Jonathan Wild seem a crude amateur.

Oliver Twist reflects also the parliamentary attention given to revision of the criminal law, an attention nearly constant between 1833 and 1837. For observing the social and political legislation of a great period of change, Dickens had experience unparalleled by that of other novelists, for he began a four-year period of parliamentary reporting in the reform year, 1832. He was twenty years old when he first entered the reporters' gallery of the House of Commons.[7] After or concurrently with work on another paper, he was employed by the Mirror of Parliament, a journal which emulated the completeness of Hansard; he was with the Mirror for two sessions. By August 1834, he had achieved a coveted position with the *Morning Chronicle*, which he resigned two years later, at the close of the session in August 1836.[8] His work for the *Chronicle* kept him chiefly in the Commons, but on numerous occasions he was sent to cover important parliamentary elections in the towns. Such absences were of short duration, a few days at a time. He must surely have been aware of every important measure which the House of Commons dealt with between March 1832 and August 1836.[9]

Although Dickens was no longer a reporter in this conclusive year, 1837, there is every reason to suppose that he followed the course of the pending legislation. Bills proposed by the Royal Commission were introduced in the Commons in March and passed without difficulty; they were delayed in the Lords, where the second reading did not occur until July 4, after which they had to return to the Commons in their amended form. The completed acts, which received the royal assent at the close of the session on July 17, were certainly among the principal achievements of that parliament.

The dates are interesting. It cannot have been by accident that Dickens inserted an argument against capital punishment into *Oliver Twist* while the long-awaited measures were at the obstacle of the House of Lords. Fagin, the vicious exploiter of other men's theft, looks over his treasures and mutters to himself:

> What a fine thing capital punishment is! Dead men never repent; dead men never bring awkward stories to light. Ah, it's a fine thing for the trade! Five of 'em strung up in a row, and none left to play booty, or turn white-livered! [10]

Nothing could have been more topical and current at the beginning of July 1837, when this came to the readers of *Bentley's Miscellany*.

If certain features of *Oliver Twist* came to it directly from the contemporary scene, others came by way of Dickens' earlier work. What signs of Dickens' interest in criminals and their milieu preceded *Oliver Twist*? The two sets of *Sketches by Boz*, which contain thematic indications for so many of the novels, show the subjects of his observation, the aspect of London which his criminal novel was to use, and a few very specific anticipations of the characters in it.

Among the frankly fictional items, there is some indication of

Dickens' special interest in "The Black Veil," in which a physician is engaged in advance to try to resuscitate a hanged man, and "The Drunkard's Death," the chronicle of an evil wretch responsible for the deaths of his daughter and his son. The reporting pieces begin to show us the parts of London we might expect. As a boy of nine or ten, Dickens had been fascinated by walking through Seven Dials, and this locality served for one of the street scenes.[11] The sketches "Gin-Shops" and "The Pawnbroker's Shop" contain further observation of poor neighborhoods.

Others draw much closer to the scenes and characters of *Oliver Twist*. "Criminal Courts," published in the *Morning Chronicle*, October 23, 1834, describes a visit to the Old Bailey, newsworthy because the recent act of parliament had reorganized it as the Central Criminal Court. From a scene in the New Court there, he recorded some words from an ingenious young offender like Jack Dawkins.[12] "The Prisoners' Van" tells of two young girls being taken away from the Bow Street police office; one is a novice, the other still in the first steps of a life of vice and crime. "A Visit to Newgate" gives an account of what was apparently Dickens' first experience of the interior of the prison.[13] Dickens noticed that the women in Newgate had needlework to do, whereas the men had no employment. The relics of famous criminals—Sheppard, Turpin, and the recent Bishop and Williams—were for him incidental; he had come to record the human reality of the present.

The sketch most closely connected with *Oliver Twist* is "The Hospital Patient." In the police-office Dickens heard a young man charged with having beaten a woman, and he accompanied the magistrates when they found it necessary to confront the accused with the victim in the hospital where she was confined. She was a girl of twenty-two or twenty-three, badly beaten, who cried and covered her bruised face when she at length recognized the hand-cuffed man before her. She was sworn, that her testimony might be taken. The man looked anxious, but said nothing.

> "Oh, no, gentlemen," said the girl, raising herself once more, and folding her hands together; "no, gentlemen, for God's sake! I did it myself—it was nobody's fault—it was an accident. He didn't hurt me; he wouldn't for all the world. Jack, dear Jack, you know you wouldn't!"

Her sight was fast failing her, and her hand groped over the bedclothes in search of his. Brute as the man was, he was not prepared for this. He turned his face from the bed, and sobbed. The girl's color changed, and her breathing grew more difficult. She was evidently dying.

"We respect the feelings which prompt you to this," said the gentleman who had spoken first, "but let me warn you, not to persist in what you know to be untrue, until it is too late. It cannot save him."

"Jack," murmured the girl, laying her hand upon his arm, "they shall not persuade me to swear your life away. He didn't do it, gentlemen. He never hurt me." She grasped his arm tightly, and added, in a broken whisper, "I hope God Almighty will forgive me all the wrong I have done, and the life I have led. God bless you, Jack. Some kind gentleman take my love to my poor old father. Five years ago, he said he wished I had died a child. Oh, I wish I had! I wish I had!"

The nurse bent over the girl for a few seconds, and then drew the sheet over her face. It covered a corpse.[14]

Bill Sikes and Nancy are here, and Nancy's unshakable devotion, her repentance, and her murder. Dickens states that the incident happened "a twelvemonth ago," thus placing it approximately in the summer of 1835.[15] Whether fact or fiction, this may be called the tangible beginning of *Oliver Twist*. The tale is turned too neatly to be unadulterated fact, but Dickens may well have seen the essence of it. His later preface to *Oliver Twist* is vehement in its assertion that Nancy's devotion to Sikes "IS TRUE." In the novel itself, the scene seems to be alluded to in Nancy's words to Rose Maylie: persons like herself have "no friend in sickness or death but the hospital nurse." [16]

The subjects of the sketches were Dickens' own—it was not assignments from editors which took him to police court and prison. The localities he sought out were not unnatural for an enterprising reporter, who wanted salable feature materials, but the subjects do betray an individual and special interest.

This concern with the prison may also be seen in *Pickwick Papers*. Full of laughter though it was, it was written by the author of the sketches, the same author who was to begin *Oliver Twist* before *Pickwick* was ended. The prison there was the Fleet. It had not the same kind of associations as Newgate, nor had the Marshalsea, where Dickens' father was; but all were prisons. Any prison might extend itself broadly to an imaginative boy, as a symbol of authority and law; he might transfer easily and without volition his experience of rebellious fear to his images of other persons confined by the law and find himself readily provided with a fund of sympathy for outcasts. The prison went with Dickens all his life. Edmund Wilson, in "Dickens: the Two Scrooges," pointed out the thematic relation of parts of *Pickwick* to Dickens' obsession with crime; and Lionel Trilling, in a more recent discussion of *Little Dorrit*, remarked that "The prison obsession was due not only to the Marshalsea but also to Dickens' consciousness of the force and scope of his will." [17] All this, however, is the study of modern critics. To Dickens' contemporaries, the debtors' prison, which was no new thing in literature, was pathetic or sometimes funny, but not completely outside the range of ordinary life. *Pickwick Papers* did not prepare them for *Oliver Twist.*

The underworld part of the second novel, drawing upon the social scene and upon Dickens' earlier work, was also touched by certain literary influences. E. A. Baker sees one of them as Marryat.[18] *Snarleyyow, or the Dog Fiend* (1837) had appeared serially in the *Metropolitan Magazine.* Baker calls Smallbones, in that novel, the prototype of Dickens' friendless boys, and has it that Dickens copied Nancy Corbett, the prostitute who has become an honest wife. There seems no reason to doubt that she contributed something, but in view of the scene in "The Hospital Patient" one hesitates to say that it was much more than her first name. Incidentally, Mr. Bumble's method of naming foundlings may owe something to the similar comic naming in *Japhet in Search of a Father*, the Marryat novel which preceded *Snarleyyow.*

Victor Hugo's *Le Dernier jour d'un condamné*, had been mentioned by a reviewer of *Sketches by Boz.*[19] The circumstance may well have sent Dickens to Hugo, if he did not already know the little book. Elizabeth Barrett, reading *Le Dernier jour* later, was convinced that Hugo, whom she thought more powerful than the author of *Oliver Twist*, had had a strong influence upon him: "In his serious powerful Jew-trial scenes, he has followed Hugo closely, and never scarcely looked away from 'Les Trois Jours d'un Con-

damné." [20] She may well be right, although there are few specific
likenesses between the two books. One of them must be responsible for the way she remembered Hugo's title: the greater part of
Le Dernier jour deals with the last three days of the man's life, and
Dickens' chapter, "Fagin's Last Night Alive," containing the trial
scene, also covers Fagin's last three days. Hugo's work offered an
example persuasive in two respects: it had a criminal in a contemporary setting, and it employed psychological realism with an unprecedented acuteness of detail. Dickens, like Hugo, presents moments of sharp attention alternating with uncontrolled trivial
reverie.[21]

Other contemporary influences involved close personal relationships. It would be surprising if Dickens, ambitious as he was,
had not paid attention to the most popular books of the early thirties; and his association with their authors, Ainsworth and Bulwer,
forms part of the background of Newgate novel controversy. The
relations of the three, or four when we include Forster, may be followed in Dickens' letters and in the several biographies. At some
time in 1834, Dickens met Ainsworth; he was one of Ainsworth's
numerous guests in 1834 and 1835. Ainsworth then was a literary
lion, Dickens still a reporter. Through Ainsworth he met in 1836
John Forster, literary editor of the *Examiner*, who was to be his life-
long friend and his biographer; probably through Ainsworth he met
Bulwer.[22] After he met Forster, the relation between the two grew
faster than the friendship of either with Ainsworth; but both were,
for the next two years and more, increasingly associated with Ainsworth. They rode together, dined together, and called themselves
the Trio. Ainsworth and Dickens talked of collaborating on a
book.[23] During January and February 1839, Dickens was effecting
his separation from his publisher, Bentley. He was not sorry to have
Ainsworth replace him as editor of *Bentley's Miscellany*, though
Ainsworth may have been hoping for that outcome.[24] A breach
came, however, when Dickens was led to suspect that Ainsworth
had misrepresented Forster's part in the negotiations.[25] After Dickens' letter of protest, March 26, 1839, the familiar letters and the
trio dinners ceased. Forster's attitude will be spoken of in connection with *Jack Sheppard*. The friendship of Dickens and Ainsworth,
despite some later exchanges of dinners, was not on its old footing,

and by 1845 even their meetings were rare accidents. A small residue of the association with Ainsworth remains in the name of Sikes, in *Oliver Twist*; a James Sykes figures in the historical accounts of Jack Sheppard. Perhaps there is another in Fagin's giving Oliver a *Newgate Calendar* to read.

Bulwer's literary influence must have been more substantial; he had shown a boy in miserable surroundings turned into a thief by bad companions. *Paul Clifford*, later mentioned in the preface to the third edition of *Oliver Twist*, was certainly one of the books Dickens set out to surpass with his realistic story of a workhouse boy. But neither Paul nor any other boy in a book (such as Humphry Clinker) can have been as important for the making of Oliver as the boy Charles Dickens. Bulwer's books were a stimulus of importance, but in some respects Dickens saw in them what to avoid. Though the two authors shared the same view of the criminal law and also an interest in criminals, one cannot say that either learned from the other a manner of handling such themes. Between the men themselves, there was no intimacy but a kind of reciprocal appreciation. Already having met, perhaps in 1835, they were on terms of mutual respect from the time when Dickens emerged as a writer.[26] John Forster, friend of Bulwer and close friend of Dickens, knew both of them better than they knew each other.

The plot of *Oliver Twist* is improbable, yet the book has force. Born in a workhouse, of a mother who dies almost immediately, Oliver is farmed out up to the age of nine. After an unhappy experience as an apprentice, he runs away to London, where he is brought by a chance meeting to the house of Fagin, thereafter one of the chief actors in Oliver's affairs.[27] Though Oliver is at first ignorant of it, Fagin's business gradually becomes apparent to the reader. Fagin manages a gang of boy pickpockets, deals in stolen goods, directs the affairs of the thieves who sell to him, and turns them in for a reward when it becomes profitable to do so; he uses in various ways—for petty thievery, recruiting, and spying—the services of several prostitutes, of whom the chief is Nancy. (She is an early progenitor of the sympathetically treated fallen women who figure more largely in fiction in the latter part of the century.) Oliver finds two groups of protectors, ultimately drawn together. Saved by Mr. Brownlow when he is taken before a magistrate,[28] Oliver is recaptured by Nancy, who then takes a liking to him. Next used as an unwilling assistant to Sikes and Toby Crackit

2. GEORGE CRUIKSHANK, The Burglary. Chapter xxii, *Oliver Twist*, *Bentley's Miscellany*, January 1838.

in a robbery, Oliver receives a bullet wound, but is taken in by Mrs. Maylie and thereafter cared for. Through Nancy's assistance, Oliver's new protectors discover that the boy is being pursued by his villainous half-brother, a fairly Gothic creation called Monks, who seems to have wandered off the stage and into a novel; he is employing Fagin in order to wreak his spite on Oliver. With Nancy's information Mr. Brownlow is able to destroy Monks' schemes, solve the mystery of Oliver's parentage, and procure for the boy the remainder of his inheritance. Fagin falsely leads his burglar, Sikes, to believe that his faithful mistress has betrayed him to the law; Sikes kills Nancy with a "club," and accidentally hangs himself in full view of a crowd which is hunting him for the murder. Fagin is hanged and his gang broken up.

Oliver Twist has great vitality and a large measure of realism in its Newgate furnishings. There is force in the workhouse scenes; there is psychological conviction in the crisis of the murderer and the condemned man. "Fagin's Last Night Alive" employs essentially the method that was to be rediscovered later and named internal monologue or stream of consciousness. To enjoy the story, however, one must set no limit on coincidence, and be ready to accept a birth-mystery for the hero, with another added for good measure. This staple of fiction, unknown parentage—the use of which weakens the logic of the humanitarian sermon—was quite in harmony with Dickens' predilections; as a child he had noticed a handsome little chimney sweep and had been sure the boy was the lost heir of some illustrious man. The sweep "believed he'd been born in the Vurkis, but he'd never know'd his father." [29] Oliver, unfortunately, has no substance as a character.

Dickens makes an effort to have his several classes of characters speak appropriately, though Oliver has the improbable language and deportment of a little gentleman. There is a limited amount of underworld slang, introduced so carefully that the genteel reader need never be at a loss for the meaning. One gets the impression that Dickens had indeed heard the thieves' language in idiomatic context—but that his acquaintance with it was not extended or familiar. If it had been, he would not have been able, even in censoring them, to let his low characters relapse into the stately literary rhythms they sometimes use. George Gissing, quoting Sikes's exclamation, "Wolves tear your throats!" pointed out that the influence of contemporary melodrama reached beyond Dickens' plot to his very language. [30] The words of Toby Crackit, telling Fagin about the unsuccessful robbery, illustrate the author's divergencies. "The crack failed," Toby says in words of one syllable; but a little later, with an original nautical phrase, he says that Bill Sikes "scudded like the wind."

Both language and action are cleansed for presentation to the family circle. In the preface to the third edition Nancy is called a prostitute; she is never so named in the story, and her occupation is most delicately suggested, chiefly through her protestations of guilt. Dickens wishes to show repulsive truth, but—

> No less consulting my own taste, than the manners of the age, I endeavoured, while I painted it in all its fallen and degraded aspects, to banish from the lips of the lowest character I introduced, any expression that could by possibility offend; and rather to lead to the unavoidable inference that its existence was of the most debased and vicious kind, than to prove it elaborately by words and deeds. In the case of the girl, in particular, I kept this intention constantly in view.[31]

Much of Dickens' writing is affected by this practice of leading to "unavoidable inference"; he is thoroughly conscious of the method, but its application seems almost automatic. Humphry House comments that the atmosphere Oliver was plunged into in London would have been "drenched in sex." [32] Dickens could, it is true, have made Nancy more realistic if he had been willing to do so, but he would have had to heap disgust upon her, and he was sensitive to popular taste. His reticence, though, does not seem merely calculated. The whole conception of Nancy is sympathetic: one feels it to have been quite as important that Charles Dickens should be fond of her as that readers should not protest. For this, she had, while remaining a prostitute, to take on, in Mr. Brownlow's words, "the courage and almost the attributes of virtue."

Nancy's original, as we have seen, was the girl in the hospital. The development of the character, however, has another involvement, Nancy's association with Rose Maylie. Rose is the first of the several girl characters in the novels drawn, one feels sure, from Mary Hogarth, the young sister-in-law who lived with Dickens and his wife.[33] Seventeen years old, Mary died of a sudden illness in May 1837, when Dickens had been married a little more than a year. His diary and his letters at the time show a sorrow patterned by convention but as deep and as devastating as any tragedy of young love and death in romantic literature. The heightened quality of his feeling for her is hard to explain. He wrote in *Bentley's* (to account for the omission of the installment of *Oliver Twist* which he had been unable to work on) that the editor was mourning "the death of a very dear young relative . . . whose society has been for a long time the chief solace of his labours." Almost five years later he wrote to Forster, at the time of another death in the Hogarth family:

> The desire to be buried next her is as strong upon me now, as it was five years ago; and I *know* (for I don't think there ever was love like that I bear her) that it will never diminish. . . . I cannot bear the thought of being excluded from her dust. . . . I shall drive over there, please God, on Thursday morning, before they get there; and look at her coffin.[34]

The fictional Rose Maylie is, to take the words of Dickens' epitaph for Mary Hogarth, "young, beautiful, and good." Near to the first anniversary of Mary's death, in the June 1838 installment of *Oliver Twist*, he gave Rose a severe illness, though he stopped short of making it a fatal one.

Nancy, who was to be so much criticized, is the counterpart, among the low characters, of Rose Maylie. Rose is "not past seventeen"; neither is Nancy, although her original, the hospital patient, was five or six years older. Both girls are kind to the boy hero, with whose unhappy life Dickens had reason to feel a close identification. A penitent sinner, Nancy arouses pity for her ruined youth when she is brought face to face with the girl of sheltered virtue. If Rose and other innocent young in girls in Dickens are astral bodies emanating from Mary Hogarth, surely Nancy may be regarded as another, whose creation likewise afforded him satisfaction. The sentiment he lavished upon her thus becomes understandable, as well as his later warmth in her defense.

Dickens wrote no death scene for Rose Maylie—he allowed her to recover. In effect, Nancy dies in her place. When the time comes for the murder of Nancy, the event is given special fury and pathos. A degree of identification of the two girls' characters has been achieved. Nancy's good impulses have made her appealing, and she has become pure in heart through her contact with Oliver and Rose; her final supplication to Sikes is that he go away with her so that they may "far apart lead better lives, and forget how we have lived, except in prayers, and never see each other more." Unmoved, Sikes brutally kills her. In a sense, then, Dickens wrote the death scene after all. In emotional terms, he created and defended Nancy as the unadmitted sexual aspect of Mary Hogarth—and then expiated his sin with Nancy's death.

Oliver Twist was the more Newgate novel because of the author's fascination with crimes of violence, although his treatment of them brought him considerable praise and almost no specific blame. When Dickens was to do a murder he set himself to wring the most from it.[35] In the famous scene of the killing of Nancy he unfortunately tries for a stagey pathos before she dies, and so falsifies his conception, but the occasion has impressive moments. A little after her death, the morning sun lights the room; Sikes, in a daze, makes pointless efforts to remove, not the body, but the blood and the weapon, in a kind of unreasoned ritual:

> He struck a light, kindled a fire, and thrust the club into it. There was hair upon the end, which blazed and shrunk into a light cinder, and, caught by air, whirled up the chimney. Even that frightened him, sturdy as he was; but he held the weapon till it broke, and then piled it on the coals to burn away, and smoulder into ashes. He washed himself, and rubbed his clothes; there were spots that would not be removed, but he cut the pieces out, and burnt them. How those stains were dispersed about the room! The very feet of the dog were bloody.[36]

In following the behavior of Sikes after the murder, Dickens maintains urgency and tension to a high degree; and in the few minutes which Sikes spends with the boys of the gang in their last hiding-place, he makes both boys and man conscious of the murderer's isolation from mankind. Such parts of the story are impressive.

The murder is by no means a necessity of the plot. Indeed, it is forced. Nancy has been portrayed as deeply attached and Sikes as violent by nature, but there has been nothing to show that his feeling for her could be attended by murderous passion at a supposed betrayal. Evil-tempered as he is, he might be expected to clout her on the head and then to leave London till the trouble should blow over. Or, since he has had a hanging look from the beginning, he might have gone to the gallows; but Dickens found himself writing his way toward a murder, and Sikes must do it.

Whatever the Newgate novel owes, then, to social circumstances or literary fashion, it owes something more to the arrival, in the eighteen-thirties, of a writer who had a deep personal interest in crime. Edmund Wilson, in "Dickens: the Two Scrooges," points out the rebellion which compelled Dickens to an identification with murderers. He finds its origin in the psychic trauma of Dickens' childhood despair:

> He identified himself readily with the thief and even more readily with the murderer. The man of powerful will who finds himself opposed to society must, if he cannot upset it or if his impulse to do so is blocked, feel a compulsion to commit what society regards as one of the capital crimes against itself. With the antisocial heroes of Dostoevsky, this crime is usually murder or rape; with Dickens it is usually murder. . . . In Dickens' novels, this theme recurs with a probing of the psychology of the murderer, which becomes ever more convincing and intimate.[37]

The obsession with murderers can also be traced, outside the novels, in the interests which Dickens frequently displayed to the end of his life. The death of Nancy was the most exciting of the dramatic readings in his last platform appearances; no one can fail to be impressed by his determination, against all advice, to include it and by his extraordinary satisfaction in the performance. "In deciding to add the murder of Nancy to his repertory," says Edgar Johnson, "he was sentencing himself to death." [38] He would not give up, and the murder scene was in the renewed series of readings that began six months before he died.

Oliver Twist was certain to be popular on the stage. After his experience with *Pickwick*, Dickens would have liked to control the dramatization of his new novel by being his own adapter. For some reason, however, a proposal he made to Frederick Yates, actor-manager of the Adelphi, was not carried through, and other adapters were at work before the serial had run its course.[39] The first dramatic piece, by J. S. Coyne, opened at the St. James on March 27, 1838.[40] As with the earlier Newgate novels, fears were multiplied as soon as there was a stage version, and objection to this "burletta" was expressed immediately by the *Literary Gazette:* "unfit for any stage except that of a Penny Theatre." [41] There were probably two other theatre pieces during the spring. When the book was published, Dickens tried once more; through Forster he offered to dramatize the book for William Macready. Obviously Macready did not want to install a Newgate drama at the Covent Garden; his verdict was that it was "utterly impracticable for any dramatic purpose." [42]

The managers of lesser theatres had no such inhibitions—they found *Oliver Twist* quite practicable. A drama by George Almar opened at the Surrey in November 1838; the manager, Davidge, billed it fairly constantly, for it had reached its seventy-fourth performance by the middle of February. Forster preserves for us his friend's opinion of it: in the first scene Dickens lay down on the floor of his box and stayed there till the curtain fell.[43]

Other dramatizations included Thomas Greenwood's at Sadler's Wells in December 1838, and Edward Sterling's at the Adelphi in February 1839. It seems likely that there were more than those noted here, but the chroniclers give differing statements about both number and authorship.[44]

Oliver Twist was reviewed in general quite favorably.[45] It was not immediately described as another Newgate novel; that accusation came chiefly from Thackeray a little later. While it was still young in *Bentley's,* the *Westminster Review* spoke of it as fine but almost too painful; the *Quarterly's* first review of Dickens' work, though favorable, objected that he was writing too much and too fast. *Oliver Twist* was said to show improvement.[46]

The *Edinburgh Review* dealt with all his works when the magazine serial was two-thirds done, shortly before the book itself appeared; it gave the most confident praise which had come from the important periodicals. It compared him to Smollett, Fielding, and Washington Irving, but chiefly to Hogarth. (Hogarth was frequently used as a standard of comparison for the Newgate writers.) Admiring particularly the arraignment of evils, the tendency to "make us practically benevolent," the review found no evil in the book. On the contrary, Dickens

never endeavours to mislead our sympathies—to pervert plain no-
tions of right and wrong—to make vice interesting in our eyes.
. . . His vicious characters are just what experience shows the
average to be. . . . We find no monsters of unmitigated and unredeemable villany; no creatures blending with their crimes the
most incongruous and romantic virtues.[47]

Though Bulwer was not named, no doubt a contrast with him was
intended in those phrases.

The *Monthly Review*, crediting the author of *Oliver Twist*
with a moral aim, objected only to too much "muscular agony";
the *Athenaeum* raised no objection; and of course the *Examiner*
praised. The *Spectator* had a few compliments but a larger bulk of
dispassionate objections.[48]

In June 1839, the *Quarterly* built on *Oliver Twist* a substantial
article, the writing of which Lockhart assigned to Richard Ford. It
is an excellent article, still thoroughly interesting, with verve and an
allusive style not usually to be found in the solid reviews. It sets out
to place Dickens in the literary currents of the time, holding that
the search for excitement in contemporary novels is a reaction
against the dominion of the fashionable school and against the increasing seriousness of everyday life. The March of Intellect sobers
everything, and highwaymen became the delight of fiction when
they had disappeared. Dickens is the voice of a new class in a new
age:

> Life in London, as revealed in the pages of Boz, opens a new world
> to thousands bred and born in the same city, whose palaces over-
> shadow their cellars—for the one half of mankind lives without
> knowing how the other half dies; in fact, the regions about Saffron
> Hill are less known in our great world than the Oxford Tracts: the
> inhabitants still less. . . .[49]

With the slight condescension which flavors the article throughout,
he says that the upper classes enjoy Boz; the *centre gauche* fear to
demean themselves with his low book. Dickens' gentle and genteel
people are "unendurable" and his young ladies "awful," but he is
not vulgar when he deals with vulgar subjects: "He is natural, and
that can never be ridiculous." Is this entirely a compliment?

The reviewer (or perhaps reviewers—for the humorist of the first pages becomes a serious-minded critic after a time, and one does not know how much of Lockhart's work to find in Ford's article) puts himself to some trouble to praise Dickens' fidelity and his delicacy and yet to complain of the material of his book.* *Oliver Twist* brings to light evil that should not be made known: "Our youth should not even suspect the possibility of such hidden depths of guilt." The author must "shun Mr. Sikes and his gin-bottle."

The first distinct review of Dickens' work in *Fraser's* came a year and a half after the publication of *Oliver Twist*.[50] The verdict is generally favorable, but the tone is cool. Cruikshank is praised to the point of detraction from Dickens, though chiefly for his work in the *Sketches*. And the *Fraser* reviewer holds that Fagin's hanging is hardly legal: because Fagin was not present at the murder of Nancy he could not be called an accessory before the fact. (This same point, in a wittier form, is attributed to G. S. Venables, who was a practising lawyer: "Dickens hanged Fagin for being the villain of a novel".) [51] The whole review gathers up a variety of objections—but immorality and a Newgate tendency are not among them.

The next mention of *Oliver Twist* appeared in *Fraser's* in August 1840, not in a review but in the essay, "Going to See a Man Hanged." Thackeray went to see the execution of Benjamin Courvoisier, on July 6, and reported his observations, ending with a fervent prayer that these public spectacles should cease. He watched the crowd attentively, not accustomed to seeing such people as he mingled with that day. Amid much else, he noticed girls of sixteen or seventeen, and one who might have been a study for Nancy:

> The girl was a young thief's mistress evidently; if attacked, ready to reply without a particle of modesty; could give as good ribaldry as she got; made no secret (and there were several inquiries) as to her profession and means of livelihood. But with all this there was

* "Fagin, Sikes and the dog especially, are always in their proper and natural places, always speaking, barking, and acting exactly as they ought to have done. . . ." *Quarterly Review*, LIV (June 1839), 90. The presence of the dog in this sentence recalls "Elizabeth Brownrigge" and its burlesque of the cat in *Eugene Aram* which acted like a dog. This passage in the article, praising Dickens' avoidance of "false sentimentality," must have been written by Lockhart, perhaps as a message to Bulwer.

something good about the girl; a sort of devil-may-care candor and simplicity that one could not fail to see. Her answers to some of the coarse questions put to her, were very ready and good-humoured. . . . Her friend could not be more than fifteen. They were not in rags, but had greasy cotton shawls, and old, faded, rag-shop bonnets. I was curious to look at them, having, in late fashionable novels, read many accounts of such personages. Bah! what figments these novelists tell us! Boz, who knows life well, knows that his Miss Nancy is the most unreal fantastical personage possible; no more like a thief's mistress than one of Gessner's shepherdesses resembles a real country wench. He dare not tell the truth concerning such young ladies. They have, no doubt, virtues like other human creatures; nay, their position engenders virtues that are not called into exercise among other women. But on these an honest painter of human nature has no right to dwell; not being able to paint the whole portrait, he has no right to present one or two favorable points as characterizing the whole: and therefore, in fact, had better leave the picture alone altogether.[52]

The moral objection is here stated in critical terms, more persuasively than Thackeray usually took the trouble to state it. He presses Dickens closely on the point, but, as in the *Pendennis* preface later, he thinks it unnecessary to defend the first assumption—that the "whole portrait" cannot be painted.

One can imagine Dickens' objections, on several grounds, to being classified as a writer of the Newgate school, though he did not express them publicly for more than two years. His attitude is to be seen in a letter to R. H. Horne, written near the end of 1839, when Thackeray's *Catherine* and Ainsworth's *Sheppard* were still running their courses:

I am by some jolter-headed enemies most unjustly and untruly charged with having written a book after Mr. Ainsworth's fashion. Unto these jolter-heads and their intensely concentrated humbug I shall take an early opportunity of temperately replying. If this opportunity had presented itself and I had made this vindication, I could have no objection to set my hand to what I know to be true concerning the late lamented John Sheppard, but I feel a great repugnance to do so now, lest it should seem an ungenerous and unmanly way of disavowing any sympathy with that school, and a means of shielding myself.[53]

Dickens' delicacy does him credit, especially since this was during the time of his definite estrangement from Ainsworth. There would have been a certain embarrassment, too, in joining with Thackeray against Ainsworth, when Thackeray had already tarred Dickens and Bulwer with the same brush.

The temperate reply which Dickens planned was written in April 1841, as a preface to the third edition of *Oliver Twist*, and most of it has been retained in later ones. Dickens withdrew nothing and defended himself with vigor.

> It is, it seems, a very coarse and shocking circumstance, that some of the characters in these pages are chosen from the most criminal and degraded of London's population; that Sikes is a thief, and Fagin a receiver of stolen goods; that the boys are pickpockets, and the girl is a prostitute.
>
> I confess I have yet to learn that a lesson of the purest good may not be drawn from the vilest evil.[54]

He is answering, with the conviction of an evangelist, the satire of Thackeray, the chidings of reviewers, and most recently, the jesting of Bon Gaultier, in *Tait's Magazine*. He dissociates himself from the merely entertaining Newgate writers—even little Oliver represents "the principle of Good"—and asserts his reforming aim. He has read of scores of gallant seductive thieves, "great at a song" (*Rookwood* was full of songs): "But I had never met (except in Hogarth) with the miserable reality. It appeared to me that to draw a knot of such associates in crime as really do exist . . . would be a service to society." Dickens points out that his book offers no enticement "for the most jolter-headed of juveniles." Since he specifically exempts from censure *The Beggar's Opera* and *Paul Clifford*, this preface includes a pointed refusal to sanction Ainsworth publicly. It must have been interpreted so by Dickens' former friend, who in 1836 had praised Dickens in the preface to a new edition of *Rookwood*. The two prefaces, five years apart, compose an irony of time and change. The forceful effort which Dickens makes to separate himself from Ainsworth and assert his own purposes shows how strongly he felt the criticism. Thackeray's article, in particular, roused him to a vehement reply. The preface closes with a defiant word against hypocritical refinement ("It is wonderful how Virtue turns from dirty stockings") and an eloquent defense of the truth of Nancy:

> It is useless to discuss whether the conduct and character of the girl seems natural or unnatural, probable or improbable, right or wrong. It is true. Every man who has watched these melancholy shades of life knows it to be so. Suggested to my mind long ago—long before I dealt in fiction—by what I often saw and read of, in actual life around me, I have, for years, tracked it through many profligate and noisome ways, and found it still the same. From the first introduction of that poor wretch, to her laying her bloody head upon the robber's breast, there is not one word exaggerated or over-wrought. It is emphatically God's truth. . . . It involves the best and worst shades of our common nature . . . it is a contradiction, an anomaly, an apparent impossibility, but it is a truth.[55]

This last paragraph must surely have been written for Thackeray.

In 1844, R. H. Horne published his *New Spirit of the Age*, which contains echoes of the controversy. Although the author assumes a wide public appreciation of Dickens, he defends Dickens as a moralist, and the first book he undertakes to praise is not *Pickwick* but *Oliver Twist*. Though it is "the work which is most open to animadversion," it has a beneficial moral tendency. Of Dickens' defence in the 1841 preface, he says, "It is unanswerable, but ought not to have been needed." [56]

JACK SHEPPARD AND HIS PUBLIC

The book from which Dickens dissociated himself as well as he could, Ainsworth's *Jack Sheppard*, had appeared under conditions that linked it with *Oliver Twist* for one set of readers. It began in *Bentley's Miscellany* in January 1839; for four months, therefore, the two serials came out together in that magazine, both illustrated by George Cruikshank. Ainsworth, after his historical novel, *Crichton*, had gone back to pick up the second of his trio of robbers; his new story, like Dickens' concluding one, pictured boys associated with criminals. The connections were superficial, but the timing accentuated them. As in *Rookwood*, Ainsworth produced a standard romance—though not this time a Gothic one—in which a figure from criminal history might be involved. His instincts as an entertainer were very keen, his sense of the public taste good, and his craftsmanship improved to the point of excellence. *Jack Sheppard*, as a result, became a sensational success, more popular than *Oliver Twist*, and the high point of the Newgate novel as entertainment. It also became, though only five years had elapsed since *Rookwood*, a high point of controversy.

The Jack Sheppard of history was a petty thief known for his several ingenious escapes from prison. His exploits have frequently been described in print, but most authoritatively by Horace Bleackley's *Jack Sheppard*, in the Notable British Trials series.[57] Sheppard was born in 1702 and was hanged at Tyburn on November 16, 1724, at the age of twenty-one. Apprenticed to a carpenter at fifteen, apparently he committed no crimes until he was twenty; he was hanged about a year and half after his first petty theft. Within that period he escaped from prison four times. He got himself out of a small lock-up, St. Giles's Round-House; he got himself and Edgeworth Bess out of the New Prison, Clerkenwell; and he escaped twice from Newgate. His robberies were never remarkable, but the escapes made him famous. Sometimes he stole alone, sometimes with his older brother Tom, sometimes with Joseph Blake, called Blueskin. After escaping from the Clerkenwell prison, he stole from a man who had befriended him, a Mr. Kneebone, because knowing the premises made it easy. Kneebone, angry, employed Jonathan Wild, and one of Wild's men located the suspect; it was for this burglary that Sheppard was sentenced to death, though some half-dozen of his acts up to that time were also capital felonies as the laws then stood.

At the end of August 1724, he escaped from the Condemned Hold of Newgate in daylight, while Bess and another woman talked with him at the visitors' hatch; he was so small and thin that the filing and removal of a single bar enabled him to squeeze through. In eleven days he was caught and restored to Newgate, where he was a great attraction for visitors. On October 15, he achieved the famous second escape, this time from another part of the prison. Left unwatched during the late afternoon and evening, he slipped his small hands out of the heavy irons, removed an iron bar fixed in

3. GEORGE CRUIKSHANK, Jack Sheppard in Company with Edgeworth Bess Escaping from Clerkenwell Prison. Chapter iv, Epoch the Third, *Jack Sheppard, Bentley's Miscellany,* July 1839.

a chimney, and worked his way to freedom through an impressive series of locked doors and masonry walls. During his periods at large, he hid; but only once and briefly did he leave the neighborhood of London.[58] Two weeks after his last escape, he saw his mother, who begged him to leave the country. Instead, he went on a round of drinking in various taverns with one Moll Frisky. He was recognized, reported, and recaptured after being out sixteen days; he did not escape again. Friends had hoped to rescue him on the way to Tyburn, or to resuscitate him after the hanging, but these plans came to nothing.

Sheppard was a huge sensation in his own time; he had many visitors in prison, the newspapers were full of him, and pamphlets were numerous. Two of these have been the chief sources for other writers; though both have been attributed to Daniel Defoe, one was probably the work of another writer.[59] His youth and his daring escapes commanded sympathy, which was the warmer because he was tracked down by the hated Jonathan Wild. His story was first used on the stage—though incompetently—less than two weeks after the execution, and more than once thereafter; perhaps it contributed something to the *Beggar's Opera*.[60] Sir James Thornhill painted Sheppard's picture during the final imprisonment. William Hogarth may also have seen Sheppard then. In his pictures of the industrious and the idle apprentices, done much later, in 1747, Jack Idle has a bodily resemblance to Sheppard and follows the same downward course, though he goes further than Sheppard when he commits a murder.[61] When the major Newgate Calendars were compiled, Jack Sheppard naturally had a place in them.

Ainsworth's romance of 1839 renewed and increased this reputation which had lasted more than a century. The influence of Hogarth, already commented on, worked very directly here; for Ainsworth from the beginning thought of his project as "a sort of Hogarthian novel," and set about obtaining information which would make his backgrounds historically accurate.[62] He has the two apprentices: Jack, who gives way to temptation, and Thames Darrell, a boy of about the same age, whose early virtue obviously will continue and will be rewarded. We have, then, two careers to follow, the fictional one of Darrell and the real one of Sheppard, woven into the plot more intricately than Turpin's in *Rookwood*. Ains-

4. GEORGE CRUIKSHANK, Jack Escaping from the Condemned Hold in Newgate. Chapter x, Epoch the Third, *Jack Sheppard, Bentley's Miscellany*, September 1839.

worth keeps Sheppard as close to history as he can while carrying out his aim of involving him in the Darrell romance. Wood, the master carpenter, comes from history; so does Kneebone, though his character is altered; Jack Sheppard's older brother, Tom, becomes in the romance his father; Blueskin, Edgeworth Bess, the Ordinary, and the turnkeys of Newgate are all present under their own names. The infamous Jonathan Wild is of course present, perhaps not much more evil in the novel that he was in reality. In fact, he was employed and he willingly acted against a thief who had not joined his organization; in the novel he pursues vindictively both the elder Sheppard and the son Jack. Wild's helper, Quilt Arnold, comes from the contemporary accounts; Ainsworth supplies two others, Obadiah Lemon and Abraham Mendez. The latter, frequently referred to as "the Jew," is present perhaps because Dickens had successfully made use of the fearsome Fagin. Mendez, a minor character, has like Fagin the stage identification of a red beard.[63]

As for the escapes, Ainsworth takes minor liberties with the facts, the most notable of which is to have his hero get out of the jail of a village, Willesden, where the real Sheppard never was; but he keeps the three major escapes (one from Clerkenwell and two from Newgate) just as history records them, only filling in suitable details. Ainsworth, who was soon to plan whole novels about old buildings, is meticulous about the condition of Newgate and is interested in historic locations: "Skirting the noble gardens of Montague House (now, we need scarcely say, the British Museum), the party speedily reached Great Russell Street—a quarter described by Strype, in his edition of old Stow's famous Survey. . . ."[64] He cares about Old London Bridge, and he contrives to work into his story a fine set-piece showing the Thames during a great storm.

The Thames Darrell story is plotted with that ingenuity which was then so much enjoyed and which now seems so tiresome. Arranged in three sequences, dated 1703, 1715, and 1724, the action is so concentrated that the author must sometimes follow more than one set of persons through events of the same few hours. The invention is unflagging, the coincidences extraordinary. The complication need only be suggested, not followed. It involves a wealthy

Jacobite family, a secret marriage, and stolen children, ignorant of their name and birthright; a scheming heir seeking to confirm his title by destroying those in his way; essential papers hidden, stolen, retrieved; and the employment of Jonathan Wild, who, having all the knowledge in his possession, is ready to commit murder or marriage. It is a new role for Wild: as a turncoat political agent in the employ of Walpole, he seeks Jacobites as well as thieves. Everything is wrapped up when we reach the end. Thames Darrell, the industrious apprentice, is a French marquis, and he marries the carpenter's daughter.

Ainsworth's narrative technique has many virtues, perhaps because of his attention to the theatre. Except for the planned passages of description, such as a whole chapter at the appropriate point about Old Newgate, he carries the story swiftly. It always moves. His theatrical talent does not, however, extend to the writing of realistic dialogue: "I don't ask you to liberate me," says Thames Darrell, "but will you convey a message for me?" The stage clichés come naturally to Ainsworth. "Hell-hounds!" Jack says to Wild and his men, "Release me!" And Mrs. Sheppard has this line to speak: " 'Begone, wretch!' cried the mother, stung beyond endurance by his taunts, 'or I will drive you hence with my curses.' " [65]

The character of Sheppard all through the story is adroitly made acceptable and even admirable. Escapes are described in detail, robberies are not. There is no comment on Jack's willingness to rob a beneficent master; at one point Jack complains that the unkindness of the master's wife drove him toward bad company. He is unfailingly loyal to his fellow-apprentice, Thames Darrell, and heroically risks his life, in the contest with Wild, to promote Darrell's interests. Jack's noble impulses are explained by his origin: his mother, though herself unaware of it, is of high family. His devotion to her—after first repulsing her good influence—is his supreme virtue; the two captures which bring him to Newgate are possible only because of it. Ainsworth exploits this theme with unblushing sentiment and theatrical ingenuity. On the first occasion, Jack visits his mother in Bedlam, knowing that Wild can trace him there; Wild tears him from his mother's arms at the moment when she has come to her senses and joyfully recognized her son. On the second occasion, Jack attends his mother's funeral and betrays his identity by kneeling in tears at her grave; at this moment, Wild and Mendez seize him.

The novel contains no propaganda. Ainsworth holds the attitude of a nineteenth-century humanitarian—he causes Mrs. Sheppard to speak feelingly of "how much misery has to do with crime" —but his story is not aimed at reforming the law or the prisons. The evils he shows are all of the past:

> It is a cheering reflection, that in the present prison, with its clean, well-whitewashed, and well-ventilated wards, its airy courts, its infirmary, its improved regulations, and its humane and intelligent officers, many of the miseries of the old gaol are removed. For these beneficial changes society is mainly indebted to the unremitting exertions of the philanthropic HOWARD.[66]

He could indeed claim that, like Hogarth, he had shown a bad end for the idle apprentice; the criminal goes to the gallows. But he likes to think of his story as being in the tradition of the *Beggar's Opera* and of the Spanish chronicles of roguery.[67]

In avoiding the earnest tone of the reformer, *Jack Sheppard* forms an obvious contrast with *Oliver Twist*. The difference—the more noticeable because the two books show so many likenesses— is partly responsible for the censure to be incurred by Ainsworth. One pair of scenes will illustrate the point. Dickens had his gang of young boys being taught to pick pockets; Ainsworth has a flash-ken, where Jack and other boys are introduced to a life of depravity. But Ainsworth puts foremost the sexual element that Dickens carefully avoided: Jack is lured on to crime by the blandishments of Edgeworth Bess and Poll Maggot. The author, somewhat casually, calls their plan "odious," and goes on with his lively description. He does not realize how fast the times have changed.

As a serial in *Bentley's Miscellany*, *Jack Sheppard* ran for thirteen months, through February 1840. Bentley issued the book in three volumes in October 1839, shortly after Ainsworth had completed the manuscript. The sales were extraordinary—three thousand copies in a week. It was complimented by the appearance of imitations and plagiarisms before the year was out. In 1840, there was a second edition in one volume, and it was reissued as an independent serial in fifteen shilling numbers.[68]

The book was dramatized as soon as possible. In the autumn of 1839, there were eight versions in London—a number probably unequalled in the dramatization of novels. The first opened at the Pavilion on October 17. Four more opened on October 21: one by J. T. Haines at the Surrey, another at the Queen's, another at the City of London, and still another, by W. T. Moncrieff, at the Royal Victoria. Ainsworth endorsed the one at the Surrey (Cruikshank advising on the sets) and got twenty pounds for doing so; from the others he got nothing. All the managers were in haste to make use of a valuable theatrical sensation, and apparently the writers of these first versions were working without having seen the conclusion of the story in the published book. Ainsworth seems to have had a kindly regard for the blind Moncrieff, who had done a play about Sheppard many years before; he visited Moncrieff and promised to send him the conclusion of his story—this, if the reported dates are correct, only four days before the play actually opened.[69] On October 28, a version by Thomas Greenwood opened at the Sadler's Wells. Later there was still another at the Garrick, and in December a pantomime, *Harlequin Jack Sheppard*, at the Drury Lane. Sheppard plays were done also in Edinburgh and in provincial theatres; one of them preceded by a month the publication of the novel in book form.

But the most famous of all the dramas was that of J. B. Buckstone, which opened (like that at the Wells) on October 28; it ran steadily at the Adelphi until Christmas, and was often revived. Various memoirs recall the superlative delights of this performance, in which Mrs. Keeley played Jack. Cruikshank made a sketch of the scene in which Blueskin, Jack, Edgeworth Bess, and Poll Maggot sang "Nix My Dolly, Pals, Fake Away," the flash song from *Rookwood* which Buckstone had taken over for his Sheppard play. Of this song, Theodore Martin said:

> Nix my dolly . . . travelled everywhere. . . . It deafened us in the streets, where it was as popular with the organ-grinders and German bands as Sullivan's brightest melodies were in a later day. It clanged at mid-day from the steeple of St. Giles, the Edinburgh

Cathedral . . . my astonished ears have often heard it; it was
whistled by every dirty guttersnipe; and chanted in drawing-rooms
by fair lips, little knowing the meaning of the words they sang.[70]

Ainsworth and his theatrical collaborators had caught the
public fancy in an extraordinary way. Sheppard was not simply
a sensation in fiction, but an extra-literary popular phenomenon.
The theatres were chiefly responsible; not all the eight versions
continued, but apparently there was a choice of four on almost any
night. And who can tell how many Sheppard acts were seen with
amateur enthusiasm at the penny gaffs? The whole wave, seen in
perspective, was at least the equal of anything in popular entertainment in the present century. It had the magnitude of something
like *South Pacific* or *My Fair Lady,* different chiefly because there
were not so many mediums into which the story might be transferred. The original author and publisher had no control over
the transference, nor any possible way of making money on commercial use of the name. Ainsworth could not have profited from
the sale of exclusive trade-marked Jack Sheppard handcuffs for the
children. On December 1 and 2, Thackeray commented on the
Sheppard craze in a letter to his mother:

> I have not read this latter romance [*Jack Sheppard*] but one or
> two extracts are good: it is acted at *four* theatres, and they say
> that at the Cobourg [sic] people are waiting about the lobbies,
> selling Shepherd-bags—a bag containing a few pick-locks that is,
> a screw driver, and iron lever, one or two young gentlemen have
> already confessed how much they were indebted to Jack Sheppard
> who gave them ideas of pocket-picking and thieving w^h-. they
> never would have had but for the play. Such facts must greatly de-
> light an author who aims at popularity.[71]

Exactly why there was so much enthusiasm for Jack Sheppard
is a matter for wonder. Ainsworth's novel had, it is true, the elements to make a popular success: a spotless hero and an underdog
to sympathize with, both pitted against a fearful villain; a glimpse
of aristocracy, a suggestion of sex, hairbreadth adventures and
plenty of virtuous emotions. The theatre appealed even more
directly. Bess and Poll were *there,* and very pretty, too. Jack was
seen (as the curtain rose on Act III of Buckstone's play) prostrate

with grief upon his mother's grave. The whole house wept—and later watched with horrified delight when a crowd set fire to the house of Jonathan Wild. The theatre also added some songs and even a bit of dancing. But spectacle and sex and sentiment, as well as music, were standard in the theatre. Why did *this* combination arouse a unique response?

The reasons, surely, were psychological and social; they lay in the readiness of public feeling at the time. It was not that a plebeian hero was wanted. In certain persons, perhaps, a sense of injustice already present might flow into sympathetic identification with young Jack; but, despite some Chartist feeling in the populace, this was not the temper of the Sheppard enthusiasm, which was fundamentally gay. Frowning Newgate, the grim hangman, and the gallows represented old oppressions, maintained by the law of the rulers; and humanitarian feeling had made the middle class quite as uneasy about them as the class without property had ever been. If Jack himself was not quite everybody's darling, Sheppard-ism was not merely a working-class epidemic. Jack was not felt to be an enemy of society; he was a boy who scaled prison walls to be free and who set himself against the villain Wild, tolerated by the oppressors. The owners of Newgate had been forced to yield some of their power in 1832; the death-dealing laws had been swept away in the half-dozen years just preceding this novel and these plays; hangings had become few, the gallows less obtrusive; policemen walked the streets of a safer London. Prison reform was respectable. The crudest terrors of Newgate, well enough remembered, could be thought of as safely in the past. Freedom and opportunity were in the air. A vast public could, at such a moment, permit itself to idolize a young thief—could see him as a victim of the old system or as a rebel against it, or could merely be entertained by a daring scamp who loved his mother—without suffering a really inhibiting concern about the gravity of the issue. This general high-spirited extravagance would not have been possible twenty years earlier; its *raison d'être* would have been lacking twenty years later. Ainsworth provided his novel at the right time. The Sheppard mania which followed was an uncalculated, uncalculating paean to the end of the bad old days and the arrival of a time like morning.

But as Thackeray's private letter has already indicated, there

were some who could not share the lighthearted suspension of reason and morality. The first reviews were such as to disturb even an
elated author. The *Athenaeum,* which had developed a tradition
of impartial judgment, had a long article—hardly a review—on
Ainsworth's novel and public taste. The *Athenaeum's* disapproval
was complete, though impersonal. Authors of the present, said the
article, do not lead; they take their tone from their readers and
cater to the mediocrity of their customers. "*Jack Sheppard,* then, is
a bad book, and what is worse, it is one of a class of bad books,
got up for a bad public." The illustrations showed what unnatural
excitement was necessary to awaken sensation. Sheppard's life was
a "history of vulgar and disgusting atrocities." To enliven it, the
hero

> is involved in a melo-dramatic story of motiveless crime and im-
> possible folly, connected with personages of high degree; and an
> attempt is made to invest Sheppard with good qualities, which are
> incompatible with his character and position.[72]

The review pointed to Fielding and to John Gay as authors who
had found the right way of dealing with such subjects. It went on
to praise Dickens, but expressed uneasiness about his position
among the Newgate novelists. His works, although they seemed
to resemble those of Ainsworth and Mrs. Trollope (whose *Michael
Armstrong, the Factory Boy,* was then appearing as a serial), really
left the reader wiser and better; but the reviewer feared people
bought Dickens not for the "undercurrent of philosophy" but for
the "strong flavour."

The *Standard,* whose practice as a daily paper was to notice
plays but not books, mentioned the novel at the beginning of a
review of Buckstone's play at the Adelphi:

> Most persons have heard of Captain Ainsworth's *Life and
> Death of Jack Sheppard,* and many there are who have had suffi-
> cient pertinacity of purpose to wade through the almost endless
> rubbish, balderdash, twaddle, and vulgarity of which it consists.[73]

But the manager of a theatre was not to be blamed for making use
of something that pleased the public; the reviewer praised the play,
"a very effective dramatic piece," as better than the original work.

Despite the alarmists, it was fairly common to deal with drama according to easy standards not accorded to books.

Another blow came from the *Examiner*, this one probably more painful for Ainsworth. His association with Forster and Dickens had been close. He had introduced them to his Manchester friends, and Forster had been included in the party when Ainsworth and Dickens attended a public dinner in their honor in Manchester. It took place in January 1839, shortly after the first installment of *Jack Sheppard* had appeared.[74] Since that time, however, frictions had developed, and the trio was broken. It seems probable that despite some contact between Forster and Ainsworth after March 1839, Forster's disapproval of *Jack Sheppard* had not been communicated.

Forster's article appeared on November 3, 1839, shortly after the flood of advertising which marked the opening of all the dramatic versions. (These, by the way, did not receive notice in the theatre columns of the *Examiner*.) The review began with an expression of reluctance to deal with the book—the writer had been thought capable of better things—but the regret sounds perfunctory and impersonal. The *Examiner* could not keep silent because the book was "in every sense of the word so bad and has been recommended to circulation by such disreputable means." Of the book alone, nothing might have been said, but "we think the puffs even more dangerous." There was danger in the paragraphs in every town and country paper; there was danger "in the adaptations of the 'romance' that are alike rife in the low smoking rooms, the common barbers' shops, the cheap reading places, the private booksellers', and the minor theatres."[75] In the theatres, the worst passages of the book were served up attractively for the young —and Mr. Ainsworth was said to have superintended rehearsals at the Surrey.

> Mr. Ainsworth also travels about with assistance for the various adapters; honours Mr. Moncrieff with visits to supply material for his closing scenes, and has his visits duly chronicled; and writes to Mr. Davidge [manager of the Surrey] a public approval, which is advertised every morning in the *Times* and *Chronicle* and *Post*, of the very worst specimen of rank garbage thus stewed up.

The public morality and decency had not been so much endangered since the time of Tom and Jerry. The reviewer's objection was to the manner of treatment; he added the usual contrast with Fielding and Gay, and included LeSage as well. Finally, he objected to the slavish adulation of high birth and to the nice emotions, the sensitive affections, attributed to thieves and murderers.

All of this, consistent with what Forster had written of *Rookwood*, in 1834, may be no more and no less than the sober concern of a responsible critic supported by his editor-in-chief, both of them alarmed by the large-scale advertising of the publisher and the theatres. By connecting himself with the latter, Ainsworth, already culpable as author, had added to his guilt. Since there is a note of petulance in the thunder, however, one can excuse Ainsworth's biographer and defender, S. M. Ellis, for seeking another explanation. He has it that Forster could not bear to see his idol, Dickens, superseded: *Jack Sheppard* was selling even better than *Oliver Twist*.[76] This may be a partial explanation. Moreover, Forster's adverse judgment cannot have been softened by the fact that Ainsworth had dealt in friendly fashion with Moncrieff, whom he and Dickens despised. Moncrieff had dramatized both the *Pickwick Papers* and *Nicholas Nickleby*, and had responded impudently to the objections of Dickens and Forster; his reply to the Crummles chapters in *Nickleby* had appeared only five months before.[77] As Forster would see it, Ainsworth was fraternizing with the enemy. Ainsworth was grieved by the attack, but Ellis has it that he showed Forster no resentment and did not allow the matter to interfere with their friendship. There was even more: apparently as a result of the Sheppard furor, Forster somewhat later had to report that Ainsworth had been blackballed at the Trinity Club, of which Forster was a member.[78] Ainsworth was indeed good-natured.

Jack Sheppard had two outright defenders against a cohort of critics (William Jerdan in the *Literary Gazette*, and Albert Smith in the *Literary World*), and the *Spectator* at least found "nothing offensive to propriety, or with the slightest tendency to corrupt." [79] But Ainsworth had his legions of another sort: the customers who kept on reading the book and going to the play. A few more kind words came later. A reviewer in *Tait's* had a favorable, though incidental, word to say; and in 1842 (for the argument went on and on), a friend of Ainsworth, Laman Blanchard, wrote a strong defense of him in the *Mirror*. But the standard published opinion was like that of the *Monthly Chronicle*, which condemned *Jack Sheppard*, Newgate novels, fashionable novels, and the influence of the theatre, and finally—making the distinction Dickens so much desired—specifically exempted the author of *Oliver Twist* from its objections.[80] In the *Monthly Chronicle*, as in some other places, it becomes clear that Ainsworth was under fire not only for his treatment of the criminal but for his easy-going presentation of the prostitutes.

When Forster had fired his single shell, it exploded and was done. Thackeray mounted a whole offensive against the Newgate novelists, which included several attacks upon *Jack Sheppard* in 1840. These are omitted for the moment, since Thackeray's work will be noticed separately.

When the salvos of the reviews were long past, and when Ainsworth had withdrawn from candidacy for the Athenaeum club for fear of defeat, a new event revived the controversy in a way the unfortunate novelist could not have expected. On May 5, 1840, Lord William Russell, aged seventy-two, was murdered by his valet, B. F. Courvoisier. The murderer was reported to have stated, in one of several confessions, that the idea of the crime had come to him upon reading *Jack Sheppard*. The man was emotionally unstable, and it would have been easy enough for someone to suggest to him that blaming the novel would gain him sympathy. But the charge—if believed—seemed grave. No such consequence had been attributed to a Newgate novel before. After a three-day trial, Courvoisier was sentenced to death on June 21. On June 28, the *Examiner* recalled its previous judgment of the book and took up the new matter:

> In Courvoisier's second confession, which we are more disposed to believe than the first, he ascribes his crimes to the perusal of that detestable book, 'Jack Sheppard'; and certainly it is a publication calculated to familiarize the mind with cruelties and to serve as the

cut-throat's manual, or the midnight assassin's *vade-mecum,* in which character we now expect to see it advertised.[81]

With what was surely a feverish surmise, the writer thought it significant that Courvoisier's sentence, "I drew the knife across his throat," nearly duplicated a sentence in the book concerning Blueskin's murder of Mrs. Wood; and he closed by saying, "If ever there was a publication that deserved to be burnt by the common hangman it is *Jack Sheppard.*"

These remarks did not occur, however, in the literary columns of the paper. They were included in an editorial article (which began on the front page of the issue) criticising the conduct of one of Courvoisier's attorneys, the well-known criminal lawyer Charles Phillips. The article probably was written by Fonblanque, not Forster.

Ainsworth had to act in response to both the original report and the *Examiner* article, which obviously represented editorial judgment. He wrote similar letters to the *Times* and to the *Morning Chronicle,* the latter having reported Courvoisier as saying he wished he never had seen the book about Jack Sheppard. Ainsworth's reply ran as follows:

> I have taken means to ascertain the correctness of the report, and I find it utterly without foundation. The wretched man declared he had neither read the work in question nor made any such statement. A Collection of Trials of Noted Malefactors (probably "The Newgate Calendar") had indeed fallen in his way, but the account of Jack Sheppard contained in this series had not particularly attracted his attention. I am the more anxious to contradict this false and injurious statement because a writer in *The Examiner* of Sunday last, without inquiring into the truth of the matter, has made it the groundwork of a most violent and libellous attack upon my romance.[82]

Ainsworth's letter was published on July 7, the day after Courvoisier was executed before a crowd of thirty thousand. Two days later appeared a reply, from the sheriff of London and Middlesex, William Evans:

> I think it my duty to state distinctly that Courvoisier did assert to me that the idea of murdering his master was first suggested to him

by a perusal of the book called "Jack Sheppard," and that the said book was lent to him by a valet of the Duke of Bedford.[83]

On July 12, the *Examiner* printed Ainsworth's letter of denial from the *Morning Chronicle* and the sheriff's letter from the *Times*. In a short paragraph thereafter, it reaffirmed its judgment of *Jack Sheppard* as a book that would create a lust for cruelty, and added: ". . . we acquit the author of having intended or foreseen the encouragement of cruelty, but the admiration of the criminal is the studied purpose of the book." [84]

There the matter stood. A collection of criminal biography published the next year included Courvoisier; his written statements, as reproduced there, do not mention *Jack Sheppard* but do mention a book about thieves and murderers.[85] One cannot seriously blame Ainsworth's novel for a murder committed by a man of twenty-three. Nevertheless, the incident was a disturbing one. At the time, Ainsworth was already busy with *Guy Fawkes* and *The Tower of London*, performing the remarkable feat of keeping two serials going at the same time. He never wrote the contemplated book about the highwayman DuVal; he never again made an ordinary criminal the central figure in a novel.

As a result of the Courvoisier matter, the Lord Chamberlain refused to license the performance of any more dramatizations of *Jack Sheppard*. Apparently he did not revoke the licenses already issued—certainly not that of the Buckstone version—and managers later found they could evade the prohibition by giving a different title to a play about Sheppard.

In the first half of 1842, Ainsworth engaged in a new controversy, in which Jack Sheppard figured prominently but not significantly. Described in full by Ainsworth's biographer, it may be summarized briefly here.[86] Like Dickens before him, he quarrelled with Bentley; he left the editorship of the *Miscellany* in November 1841, taking with him Cruikshank, who was also at odds with the publisher. In the first number of his own venture, *Ainsworth's Magazine*, in February 1842, he printed an article in which Cruikshank described his relations with Bentley—and a new magazine war was on. Attack and counter-attack covered some four months. From the barricades of *Bentley's* Father Prout fired doggerel verse at Ainsworth, the final volley, in May, satirizing him in the figure of a barber's apprentice who "scribbled tales of NEW-GATE, which were used as curling-papers."

> The shop frequenters often wished he'd hold his peace or alter
> The staple of his tedious yarns, all ending in a halter.
> Soon, one by one, they dropped away—for life cannot afford us
> Sufficient time with maudlin tales of cut-throats to be bored thus;
> A listener by the button still he sometimes on the sly attacked,
> Till, finding that each new 'Romance,' like the reading of the Riot Act,
> Cleared out all decent customers, his master told him plainly
> That ''twere better for the nonce eschew a practice so ungainly,'
> That 'men of sense and learning loathed an overdose of folly,'
> Brief answer to his master made the varmint, 'Nix my dolly!' [87]

The verses included an insinuation that Ainsworth's book had influenced Courvoisier. By this time tempers had reached a strong boil.

Thus *Jack Sheppard* was denounced in the same periodical in which it had been appearing, with mounting popularity, two years before. The whole affair, though it developed bitterness, reads like schoolboy high jinks, a chapter out of Kipling's *Stalky and Company*. In moving to publicize the quarrel of Cruikshank, Ainsworth was being commercially shrewd: two great magazine successes, *Blackwood's* and *Fraser's*, had begun with personalities and continued with quarrels—and *Ainsworth's Magazine* by the same means got itself talked about. Then, as happened time after time, the Newgate novel became a topic of personal controversy, not a subject of thoughtful literary inquiry.

THACKERAY AS CRITIC AND SATIRIST: *Catherine*

In reaction against the popularity of *Jack Sheppard* and *Oliver Twist*, the most active and repeated opposition to the Newgate novel occurred in the years 1839 and 1840. It could not have come about without the presence of Thackeray. It was he who led the van, trying to arouse a not very articulate public sentiment against the prevailing enthusiasm. *Catherine*, his most sustained piece of propaganda, was both preceded and followed by other efforts against the Newgate writers.

The focal point is necessarily the attitude of *Fraser's Magazine*, Thackeray's chief outlet, toward the three novelists. Dickens' books were not reviewed in *Fraser's* (whatever the reasons) until *Catherine* had ended; the *Pickwick Papers* had been mentioned incidentally, and Dickens had been advised to turn his attention to the plight of the factory children.[88] Ainsworth, one of the original Fraserians, was never personally attacked. As for Bulwer, the completion of *Catherine* marked the end of a full decade of the campaign whose beginning has been described in connection with *Paul Clifford*. The absence of any Newgate novel by Bulwer after 1832 did not cause criticism to cease.

Thackeray's disapproval and dislike of Bulwer's work had begun long before he started to write for *Fraser's*. His private opinion of *Eugene Aram* was recorded on May 6, 1832, and a similarly unfavorable one of *Pelham* on September 9. Having commented on *Aram*, he went on with admirable candor and self-knowledge:

> The book is in fact humbug, when my novel is written it will be something better I trust—One must however allow Bulwer wit and industry. . . . Bulwer has a high reputation for talent & yet I always find myself competing with him—This I suppose must be vanity—If it is truth why am I idle?—Here is enough conceit for to night—[89]

"I always find myself competing with him"—this is the true key to Thackeray's attitude toward Bulwer, at least until the time when he achieved success with "his novel."

His first printed remark on Bulwer (if "Elizabeth Brownrigge" is excluded) must have appeared in the *National Standard*. Perhaps the earliest occurred in his Paris letter in the issue of June 22, 1833. Mere *Newgate Calendar* crimes, he reported, were "absolute drugs on the literary market"; and, apropos of a French collection of criminal stories, he said ironically that "this great nation excels us in genius and imagination, even though Bulwer and Disraeli still live and write." [90] In the issue of December 21, 1833, there was an article, "Importance at Home and Abroad," which did not touch on Bulwer's writing but satirized him for seeking to associate with persons of title.[91] A German paper had reported him in the company of Lord Hertford and of Lady Drummond.

From the beginning, then, of Thackeray's career as a practising writer one can trace a dislike of Bulwer, whether he had—as he often did have—critical judgment on his side, or whether he was going out of his way to strike a blow for his own pleasure. When Thackeray came to write rather steadily for *Fraser's*, in 1837, it is in his work that we find most of the satirical references to Bulwer. Maginn, who had a better reason for anti-Bulwerism, ceased to edit *Fraser's* after 1836; in effect, Thackeray took his place as the anti-Bulwer force in the magazine.

No one has taken the trouble to catalogue all the allusions to the other man that occur in Thackeray's work; the list would be longer than any casual reader could expect. About a third of his contributions to *Fraser's* from 1837 to 1840 contain some reference to Bulwer—always derogatory.[92] The Newgate campaign began in 1839; the first of Thackeray's attacks upon the Newgate novel appeared in "Horae Catnachianae," in the April number; *Catherine*, his satirical novel, ran its interrupted serial way from May 1839 to February 1840; and its last installment was accompanied in the same month by an article, "William Ainsworth and Jack Sheppard." This was the climax of the campaign in *Fraser's*.

"Horae Catnachianae: a Dissertation upon Ballads," deals ostensibly with the publications of James Catnach. Catnachian hours are only a springboard, however, by which Thackeray may come to his theme: the way high life and low life (especially the latter) are presented to the "middling" classes, to and for whom the writer of the article speaks. Go to first-hand sources of knowledge, he says, rather than trust "Bulwer's ingenious inconsistencies, and Dickens' startling, pleasing, unnatural caricatures." The "favorite, or Newgate parts" of *Paul Clifford* and *Oliver Twist* are misleading:

> Depend upon it, that Shire Lane does not in the least resemble Mr. Dickens's description of that locality; that the robbers' den

in *Pelham*, or the Bath rendezvous of the thieves in *Paul Clifford*, are but creations of the fancy of the honorable baronet who wrote those popular novels, and who knows as much about low life as he does of German metaphysics. As, indeed, how should he know? He never had half an hour's conversation with the thieves, cut-throats, old clothesmen, prostitutes, or pickpockets, described; nor can the admirable Boz be expected to have had any such experience.[93]

To this confident statement about their lack of knowledge Bulwer and Dickens could have replied only by asserting an embarrassing familiarity with low life. Thackeray makes it as hard as possible: surely, he goes on, neither Dickens nor Ainsworth nor Bulwer will be "insulted" by his accusation of ignorance. Fielding, by contrast, had first-hand experience.

After remarking on the perverted taste of the present (which likes virtuous sentiments from street-walkers, tragedy removed from the palace to the boozing-ken, and so on), Thackeray softens oddly to give personal commendation: he has read all of Dickens' works with delight and has "the strongest curiosity and admiration for Mr. Ainsworth's new work, *Jack Sheppard*."

At this point he makes use of Catnach's ballads—they represent the true vulgarity. He quotes a handful, with some humor and pleasure, and sets out to repeat his objections to the sham low, "altogether different from the honest, hearty vulgarity, which it pretends to represent."

Thackeray's campaign against Bulwer was accompanied in *Fraser's* by other anti-Bulwerisms that reflected no credit on the magazine. It would be interesting to know how often Maginn was consulted. In April 1838, it printed a sketch by Bulwer's estranged wife, "Artaphernes the Platonist, or the Supper at Sallust's," the hostility of which was a mere preliminary to that in her novel, *Chevely, or the Man of Honour*. Whatever the extent of Lady Bulwer's grievances, the novel was not worth more than a perfunctory notice; *Fraser's* gave it eleven pages, carefully transmitting the worst accusations it contained. "When this novel was announced," said the reviewer, "it was generally supposed that Sir E. L. Bulwer was intended to be the 'hero'; an idea quickly dispelled when its second title, 'The Man of Honour,' was given by his lady to the public."[94] When *Fraser's*, at this period, opened its pages to attacks on the Newgate novel, it did so not out of conviction but because the original Newgate author was an old enemy and because Thackeray was a growing influence as a writer.

Jack Sheppard began in *Bentley's Miscellany* in January 1839. By May the first installment of *Catherine* (under the name of Ikey Solomons, Esq., Jr.) came out in *Fraser's*; others followed in June, July, and August. The author and the other Fraserians must have enjoyed dogging Jack's footsteps with this month-by-month recurrence of a travesty intended to destroy both the crime novel and the public favor given to *Bentley's*. The three volumes of Ainsworth's completed book appeared in October, but the magazine serial went on through February of 1840. *Fraser's* omitted *Catherine* in September and October, printed a portion in November, omitted it in December, and carefully arranged the last two parts to coincide with the last two parts of *Sheppard*. (Although this serial form of attack suggests that part-by-part correspondences between the two novels might have been intended, no such plan is observable.) *Catherine* came between book covers only in 1869, in the author's posthumously collected works.

Thackeray had chosen, he said near the beginning of *Catherine*, certain characters and adventures which

> since they are strictly in accordance with the present fashionable style and taste; since they have already been partly described in the "Newgate Calendar"; since they are (as shall be seen anon) agreeably low, delightfully disgusting, and at the same time eminently pleasing and pathetic, may properly be set down here. . . . We give the reader fair notice, that we shall tickle him with a few such scenes of villany, throat-cutting, and bodily suffering in general, as are not to be found, no, not in—never mind comparisons, for such are odious.[95]

He was prepared to keep his word. He had successfully searched the *Newgate Calendar* ("to which excellent compilation," he said, "we and the *other* popular novelists of the day can never be sufficiently grateful") for a case bleaker than most in its lack of meaningful passions and grimmer than most in its physical horror. Catherine Hayes, wife of a London tradesman, plotted the murder of her husband and arranged that it should be carried out by two men, one a lodger and the other reputed to be her illegitimate son.

After making Hayes dead drunk they killed him with a hatchet, threw the severed head into the Thames, and disposed of the dismembered body in a pond. The head was soon found, and placed on display on a pole in a churchyard. Hayes' disappearance cast suspicion on his wife, the accomplices confessed, and Mrs. Hayes was convicted along with them. The men were hanged; the law, with interesting discrimination, set the wife's penalty as burning at the stake. (Murdering one's husband was petty treason.) Because the executioner failed to accomplish the preliminary strangling which was customary, she was in actuality burned alive, at Tyburn, on May 9, 1726.[96]

No reader of *Catherine* fails to observe that Thackeray carried out his plan for the use of the dismal story in a most equivocal way. By contrast one thinks of Fielding's *Jonathan Wild*, which he admired so greatly, and of his own *Novels by Eminent Hands*. In choosing from the *Newgate Calendar* Thackeray was making the decision not to write a direct parody, despite the fact that a month-by-month inversion of Ainsworth's tale, with close and recognizable parallels, would have been more effective as satire. But he chose new material; and, having chosen, he himself complicated the plain account with apparent interest, extending the whole to some seventy thousand words. No doubt he thought of himself as providing an elaborate demonstration in the large: approaching novel length, he would subject himself to the other novelists' temptation to arouse sympathy for the chief character—and he would avoid doing so.[97] Whatever the background of his intention, the plan turns out badly—one is constantly uneasy at the author's lack of single-mindedness.

The leisurely first chapter shows the young Catherine as maid in a country inn, eager to go away with a soldier or gentleman who can offer her a more exciting life than do her village suitors. This is the first of the eighteenth-century backgrounds which Thackeray developed so great a liking for. Century-old types of character, century-old manners delight him; one finds here, in this first historical essay, the same curious quality of nearness with distance that permeates most of his work. The figures are like those in a stereopticon; they move projected in depth from their correct surroundings, but one remembers always that they are contrived.

A Mr. Wood, who is one of the murderers in the *Newgate*

Calendar, becomes Corporal Brock–Captain Wood in *Catherine.* Because he is given a long career of roguery before the time of the murder, his affairs are partly responsible for the general expansion. A traditional picaresque figure, he illustrates Thackeray's extreme conventionality in working according to tried and popular literary formulas. Remembering *Barry Lyndon,* one is puzzled to know how to account for so much of this early work of a major writer. Even though he long conceived of himself as a working journalist, how can the journalist not have felt that the picaresque tradition was exhausted?

Thackeray continues his refurbishing of the story with sufficient credibility. To the characters mentioned in his source he adds a German military man of title, who keeps Catherine for a time and who leaves her with a child. She marries Hayes, but has long been weary of him when her seducer, von Galgenstein, reappears in London seventeen years later with the title of ambassador from his German court. Foolishly supposing that she can now persuade him to marry her, she is ready to put her husband out of the way. Thackeray's characterizations of the ambitious, deluded woman and her equally unpleasant son are remote but realistic. He is at his ironic best with the egotism and stupidity of Maximilian von Galgenstein, a forerunner—with the Earl of Crabs—of a whole series of contemptible aristocrats. In the Yellowplush series the essayist was tentatively making himself into a writer of fiction; in *Catherine* he reaches another stage in the process, which proceeds with tantalizing indirection until he arrives at *Vanity Fair.*

Thackeray's scattered satire on the styles of the Newgate authors furnishes some of the pleasantest moments of *Catherine.* When he has brought the vicious Mrs. Hayes and the stupid, bemedalled Count of Galgenstein face to face after many years, the nobleman says, "Madam, 'tis a charming evening—egad, it is!"; and the woman replies, "It is dreadful hot too, I think."

> Now I know what I could have done [Thackeray interrupts]. I can turn out a quotation from Sophocles (by looking to the index) as well as another: I can throw off a bit of fine writing too, with passion, similes, and a moral at the end. . . . [Here he proceeds to prove it with some lines from Aristophanes' *Clouds,* which he nonchalantly attributes to Cornelius Nepos.] Or suppose, again,

I had said, in a style still more popular:—The Count advanced toward the maiden. They were both mute for a while; and only the beating of her heart interrupted that thrilling and passionate silence. . . . Thus is it ever—for these blessed recollections the soul always has a place; and while crime perishes, and sorrow is forgotten, the beautiful alone is eternal.

"O golden legends, written in the skies!" mused De Galgenstein, "ye shine as ye did in the olden days! We change, but ye speak ever the same language. Gazing in your abysmal depths, the feeble ratioci—" [98]

Here the *Fraser* editor cut "six columns of the finest writing to be found in this or any other book." This part of the parody is aimed at Bulwer (who was fond of 'ratiocination' and of classical quotations); it hardly touches Ainsworth, who had an easy hand with clichés but was no master of the inflated style. However, Thackeray reaches Ainsworth neatly in a passage in the last chapter ("Here follows a description of the THAMES AT MIDNIGHT, in a fine historical style"), and he has his fun with all historical romancers who connect their fictional characters with actual persons:

we had a good mind to make Hayes philosophizing with Bolingbroke, like a certain Devereux; and Mrs. Catherine *maitresse en titre* to Mr. Alexander Pope, Doctor Sacheverel, Sir John Reade the oculist, Dean Swift, or Marshal Tallard; as the very commonest romancer would under such circumstances. But alas and alas! . . . the excellent Newgate Calendar . . . does not say a word of their connections with any of the leading literary or military heroes of the time of her majesty Queen Anne.[99]

By the time he came to write *Esmond*, Thackeray felt differently about such a practice. What we may call his special interest in Bulwer shows itself in the mention of Devereux, above, and in another place where he goes out of his way to ridicule Bulwer's efforts in verse.

The leisurely observations which were always a part of his prerogative are frequently turned to the special purpose of the occasion. "Who could meddle with dull virtue, humdrum sentiment, or stupid innocence," he says, "when vice, agreeable vice, is the only thing which the readers of romances care to hear?" Such gentle ironies often give way to the most specific attacks upon the authors and books he considers vicious; one of them must be quoted at length.

> And here, though we are only in the third chapter of this history, we feel almost sick of the characters that appear in it, and the adventures which they are called on to go through. But how can we help ourselves? The public will hear of nothing but rogues; and the only way in which poor authors, who must live, can act honestly by the public and themselves, is to paint such thieves as they are: not dandy, poetical, rosewater thieves; but real downright scoundrels, leading scroundrelly lives, drunken, profligate, dissolute, low; as scoundrels will be. They don't quote Plato, like Eugene Aram; or live like gentlemen, and sing the pleasantest ballads in the world, like Jolly Dick Turpin: or prate eternally about *to kalon*, like that precious canting Maltravers, [in Bulwer's *Ernest Maltravers*] whom we all of us have read about and pitied; or die white-washed saints, like poor "Biss Dadsy" in "Oliver Twist." No, my dear madam, you and your daughters have no right to admire and sympathize with any such persons, fictitious or real; you ought to be made cordially to detest, scorn, loathe, abhor, and abominate all people of this kidney. Men of genius like those whose works we have above alluded to, have no business to make these characters interesting or agreeable; to be feeding your morbid fancies or indulging their own, with such monstrous food.[100]

We shall find the sermon repeated in the final paragraphs of the story. Here is Thackeray's extreme insistence—that virtue and vice must not be confused; since not to be confused, they must not be mingled in the same character, and vice must not even be made interesting. It is an extraordinary doctrine.

In the final chapter of *Catherine*—entitled "Another Last Chapter"—Thackeray drops much of the playfulness which he has affected recurrently and strikes out with every weapon at hand. When the story was reprinted after his death, certain parts of the chapter were removed;[101] the original is a more serious polemic than this tactful version which has nearly always been followed ever since. (The Oxford edition, edited by George Saintsbury, gives the text as it was in *Fraser's*.)

Since Newgate novels are immediately dramatized, Thackeray

points out the usefulness of Catherine's story for the purpose, and offers a sample of a horrific bill to advertise it, for the benefit of such theatrical entrepreneurs as Yates, Davidge, and Crummles. (Crummles was an instrument of Dickens' satire in *Nickleby*; Yates and Davidge, managers of the Adelphi and the Surrey, had produced versions of both *Twist* and *Sheppard*.) There follows a specific account of the murder of Hayes, condensed from the *Annals of Newgate* and concluding with a quotation from the *Daily Journal* of May 10, 1726; in accordance with his purpose Thackeray diminishes none of the bloody hacking involved in the disposal of the corpse. This cold and gruesome account is preceded by a section of "the very finest writing," which includes everything from murder to madness, all in a delicate purple; thus the contrast in the original version is sadly missing when the later editor omits the newspaper writing which Thackeray calls "far more emphatic than any composition of his own could be." This preference for the plain style gives the author opportunity to speak of other novelists who have used the *Newgate Calendar*, and a joke intrudes upon the straightforward polemic:

> Mr. Aram's trial, as taken by the penny-a-liners of those days, hath always interested [the author] more than the lengthened and poetical report which an eminent novelist (who hath lately, in compliment to his writings, been gratified by permission to wear a bloody hand),* has given of the same. Mr. Turpin's adventures are more instructive and agreeable to him in the account of the Newgate Plutarch, than in the learned Ainsworth's "Biographical Dictionary." [102]

The story of Catherine, he continues, has not been pleasantly received, but the nausea which it has induced in its readers is merely the proper effect of a wholesome medicine. Apparently he feels, though, that the homeopathic dose has not been enough, for he closes with a direct attack upon the centers of the disease. These

---

* This parenthesis was removed when *Catherine* appeared in book form in 1869. The coat of arms which Bulwer took upon receiving the title of baronet in 1838 had a red hand at the center. This was, of course, the red hand of Ulster, commemorating the founding of the baronetcy in 1611, which every baronet was entitled to combine with his escutcheon.

considered complaints against Dickens and Ainsworth, not included in most of the editions of *Catherine* in book form, must be seen in their entirety:

> To begin with Mr. Dickens. No man has read that remarkable tale of *Oliver Twist* without being interested in poor Nancy and her murderer; and especially amused and tickled by the gambols of the Artful Dodger and his companions. The power of the writer is so amazing, that the reader at once becomes his captive, and must follow him whithersoever he leads; and to what are we led? Breathless to watch all the crimes of Fagin, tenderly to deplore the errors of Nancy, to have for Bill Sikes a kind of pity and admiration, and an absolute love for the society of the Dodger. All these heroes stepped from the novel on to the stage; and the whole London public, from peers to chimney-sweeps, were interested about a set of ruffians whose occupations are thievery, murder, and prostitution. A most agreeable set of rascals, indeed, who have their virtues, too, but not good company for any man. We had better pass them by in decent silence; for, as no writer can or dare tell the *whole* truth concerning them, and faithfully explain their vices, there is no need to give *ex-parte* statements of their virtue.
>
> And what came of *Oliver Twist?* The public wanted something more extravagant still, more sympathy for thieves, and so *Jack Sheppard* makes his appearance. Jack and his two wives, and his faithful Blueskin, and his gin-drinking mother, that sweet Magdalen!—with what a wonderful gravity are all their adventures related, with what an honest simplicity and vigour does Jack's biographer record his actions and virtues! We are taught to hate Wild, to be sure; but then it is because he betrays thieves, the rogue! And yet bad, ludicrous, monstrous as the idea of this book is, we read and read, and are interested, too. The author has a wondrous faith, and a most respectful notion of the vastness of his subject. There is not one particle of banter in his composition; good and bad ideas, he hatches all with the same gravity; and is just as earnest in his fine description of the storm on the Thames, and his admirable account of the escape from Newgate; as in the scenes at Whitefriars, and the conversations at Wild's, than which nothing was ever written more curiously unnatural. We are not, however, here criticizing the novels, but simply have to speak of the Newgate part of them, which gives birth to something a great deal worse than bad taste, and familiarises the public with notions of crime. In the

dreadful satire of *Jonathan Wild*, no reader is so dull as to make the mistake of admiring, and can overlook the grand and hearty contempt of the author for the character he has described; the bitter wit of the *Beggar's Opera*, too, hits the great, by shewing their similarity with the wretches that figure in the play; and though the latter piece is so brilliant in its mask of gaiety and wit, that a very dull person may not see the dismal reality thus disguised, moral, at least, there is in the satire, for those who will take the trouble to find it. But in the sorrows of Nancy and the exploits of Sheppard, there is no such lurking moral, as far as we have been able to discover; we are asked for downright sympathy in the one case, and are called on in the second to admire the gallantry of a thief. The street-walker may be a virtuous person, and the robber as brave as Wellington; but it is better to leave them alone, and their qualities, good and bad. The pathos of the workhouse scenes in *Oliver Twist*, or the Fleet prison descriptions in *Pickwick*, is genuine and pure— as much of this as you please; as tender a hand to the poor, as kindly a word to the unhappy as you will; but in the name of common sense, let us not expend our sympathies on cut-throats, and other such prodigies of evil! [103]

The article on *Jack Sheppard* which appeared in *Fraser's* (along with the final chapter of *Catherine*) was a planned effort to shape both the public attitude and the direction of Ainsworth's work. Unsigned, it has been attributed to Thackeray.[104] On the other hand it may have been a composite production, Thackeray being one of two or three who had a part in it.

The general tone of the article is serious. It begins by recalling an unfavorable review of a book about highwaymen some six years before—an attempt to show a consistent policy in *Fraser's*.[105] (It does not mention that at the same period no objection was made to *Rookwood*.) The magazine gravely regrets "the popular exhibition of Jack Sheppard metamorphosed from a vulgar ruffian into a melodramatic hero," and thinks that by the novel "and its manifold theatrical adaptations" boys will be turned to crime. The circumstances of the case of the real Jack are reviewed, with the conclusion that society was a "greater culprit" than the boy. This emphasis on social influences was a thoroughly modern one in 1840, and the writer makes his point well. The hanging of Jack Sheppard did not reform his class nor deter others from crime. It would have been creditable in the eighteenth-century wits, says the writer, "if they had thought of dispensing with such punishments."

Whoever wrote the words, the sentiment is in harmony with the conviction expressed six months later in Thackeray's "Going to See a Man Hanged," already quoted for its criticism of *Oliver Twist*.[106] Although the hanging was that of Courvoisier, the author did not mention *Jack Sheppard* in his account. He must have been aware of the report that the murderer had been influenced by reading the book, but he wisely avoided saying anything of it.

These February and August articles, though not the last word in *Fraser's* on crime and crime novels, mark the end of a period of concentrated attention in that magazine. The center of Thackeray's offensive was there, but he contributed to certain other periodicals in this year of his crusading enthusiasm.

Thackeray's dislike of *Jack Sheppard* did not extend to the work of the illustrator who helped make it popular and whose pictures were used by producers to set it on the stage. Four months after the close of *Catherine*, he reviewed with the highest praise all of Cruikshank's work up to that time.[107] He gave discriminating attention to the *Sheppard* plates and attributed to them the attractiveness of the novel: "With regard to the modern romance of *Jack Sheppard* . . . it seems to us that Mr. Cruikshank really created the tale, and that Mr. Ainsworth, as it were, only put words to it." Thackeray had high praise also for the *Oliver Twist* plates; but in this instance he did not exalt the illustrator above the writer.

In the autumn of 1840 Thackeray reviewed in the *Times* a new edition of the works of Fielding. *Sheppard* was far from being extinguished, and he made what was to be his last frontal attack.

> Vice is never to be mistaken for virtue in Fielding's honest downright books; it goes by its name, and invariably gets its punishment. See the consequences of honesty! Many a squeamish lady of our time would fling down one of these romances in horror, but would go through every page of Mr. Ainsworth's *Jack Sheppard* with perfect comfort to herself. Ainsworth dared not paint his hero as the scoundrel he knew him to be; he must keep his brutalities in the background, else the public morals will be outraged, and so he produced a book quite absurd and unreal, and infinitely more immoral

than anything Fielding ever wrote. *Jack Sheppard* is immoral actually because it is decorous.[108]

It is a clear statement and a fine commentary on Victorian taste. But Thackeray's real attitude toward this taste and his conception of its relation to literature are far from simple. Are writers to accept in every particular the current fashions in good manners? Or are they to try to influence them? In the same review Thackeray makes note of the change which has taken place since Fielding's time—and he is curiously quick to direct his application to sexual behavior:

> The world does not now tolerate such satire as that of Hogarth and Fielding, and the world no doubt is right in a great part of its squeamishness; for it is good to pretend to the virtue of chastity even though we do not possess it; nay, the very restraint which the hypocrisy lays on a man, is not unapt, in some instances, to profit him.

There—in the plainest terms—is a fragmentary truth. Overemphasized during the nineteenth-century extension of the middle-class virtues, it is still a logically defensible position. The significant and well-known passage carried on the theme:

> The same vice exists, only we don't speak about it; the same things are done, but we don't call them by their names. Here lies the chief immorality of Fielding, as we take it. . . . It is wise that the public modesty should be as prudish as it is; that writers should be forced to chasten their humor, and when it would play with points of life and character which are essentially immoral, that they should be compelled, by the general outcry of incensed public propriety, to be silent altogether. But . . . Fielding's men and Hogarth's are Dickens' and Cruikshank's, drawn with ten times more skill and force, only the latter humorists dare not talk of what the elder discussed honestly.

Such painful subservience to "incensed public propriety" goes far beyond what most Victorian writers felt necessary—Thackeray not only takes the bitter medicine but insists that it is good for him— but the mention of honesty betrays a stifled longing. The discussion ends in hesitation and bewilderment:

> Fielding gives a strong, real picture of human life, and the virtues which he exhibits shine out by their contrasts with the vices which he paints so faithfully, as they never could have done, if the latter had not been depicted as well as the former. . . . Are persons who profess to take the likeness of human nature to make an accurate portrait? This is such a hard question, that, think as we will, we will not venture to say what we think.[109]

Surely there has never been a more remarkable withdrawal from a dilemma: "we will not venture to say what we think."

What is Thackeray's conception of the public taste? A restricted one, certainly. At this point and many others he not merely accedes to custom—as any man may who is not a born rebel —but over-refines it. This unnecessary eagerness to apologize for Fielding (and other eighteenth-century writers) has often been remarked. He becomes even more severe in 1851, in his lectures on the English humorists. "I cannot offer or hope to make a hero of Harry Fielding," he says, as if about to seek some virtue in a very nearly lost soul. Indeed many of the lectures, with all their charm, sound like a man giving an explanation to guests about a disreputable person they have been forced to meet at his house. As for Fielding's Tom,

> I can't say that I think Mr. Jones a virtuous character; I can't say but that I think Fielding's evident liking and admiration for Mr. Jones shows that the great humourist's moral sense was blunted by his life, and that here, in Art and Ethics, there is a great error. If it is right to have a hero whom we may admire, let us at least take care that he is admirable: if . . . it is propounded that there exists in life no such being, and therefore that in novels, the picture of life, there should appear no such character; then Mr. Thomas Jones becomes an admissible person, and we examine his defects and good qualities, as we do those of Parson Thwackum or Miss Seagrim.[110]

With those strictures upon the character of Tom Jones, we have come back to the question raised in the 1840 review of Fielding's works. Thackeray now ventures to say a part of what he thinks: minor characters may be flawed, but a hero must be thoroughly admirable. At the same time, we have come back to the implication raised in *Catherine*—that good and evil are not to be mingled in the same character. There is a kind of consistency in it all; but as the lecturer proceeds to praise Fielding we are reminded that he never seems happy with his conflict and its compromise. We remember the odd paradox in "Horae Catnachianae": "We could 'hug the rogues and love them,' and do—in private. In public it is, however, quite wrong to avow such likings, and to be seen in such company." [111] By 1851, Thackeray was more accustomed to speaking as a public character.

It must be evident that the Newgate novel controversy brings to light some of Thackeray's most significant attitudes and points up the chief conflict in a literary man, who, as a writer, seems for the most part extraordinarily serene and integrated.

The external controversy in which he quite deliberately involved himself was unquestionably the parallel of an internal one. The question seemed to be one of truth versus the inhibition of truth. The two positions in the public argument roughly coincided with the two sides of a problem he became aware of as his own. He gave an answer, but the problem did not cease to trouble him —dozens of remarks touching upon it could be gathered from his later works. Better known than any of the others is the statement which he put in the preface to *Pendennis*:

> Even the gentlemen of our age—this is an attempt to describe one of them, no better nor worse than most educated men—even these we cannot show as they are, with the notorious foibles and selfishness of their lives and their education. Since the author of "Tom Jones" was buried, no writer of fiction among us has been permitted to depict to his utmost power a MAN. We must drape him, and give him a certain conventional simper. Society will not tolerate the Natural in our Art. Many ladies have remonstrated and subscribers left me, because, in the course of the story, I described a young man resisting and affected by temptation. My object was to say, that he had the passions to feel, and the manliness and generosity to overcome them. You will not hear—it is best to know it—what moves in the real world, what passes in society, in the clubs, colleges, mess-rooms,—what is the life and talk of your sons. A little more frankness than is customary has been attempted in this story; with no bad desire on the writer's part, it is hoped, and with no ill consequence to any reader. If truth is not always pleasant, at any rate truth is best. . . .

But he had already written, as we have seen, more than one manifesto espousing hypocrisy, or at least a limitation of truth. One great morality seemed to be in conflict with another.

However, in 1840 we find him saying, with not quite a whole heart, that virtue and vice must not be interwoven in a single character; and that vice must not appear interesting to any reading dullard. In practice he did not keep this mistaken rigor, but the unhappy error was in the texture of his character, to connect itself with his major work as an artist. For Thackeray, among the most sensitive of all authors to the qualities of personality, was deliberately denying his own perceptions. He must have felt uneasily that he was avoiding a truth, evading what he well knew of the complexity of human beings. Even *Catherine*, for all its burlesque impulse, was a first, an original novel, in which the author set himself to do novelist's work. What other great writer of fiction has begun his career with a book seriously asserting the proposition that human motives are reasonably simple and that our opinions of character may be reasonably simple too?

The reception of *Catherine*—which means a fairly general lack of attention to it—must have been disappointing to Thackeray, but his remarks to his mother about it indicate resignation and modesty rather than the unimpressive show of confidence which he wrote into the last chapter. While the writing was still in progress he had worked up a substantial belief in it; he wrote to his mother in mid-December, "This horrid book will be finished in 6 weeks please God, and now for the 1st time I begin to fancy that it will be tolerably pleasant." By the middle of January, when all but the last installment had been printed, he felt otherwise; he then wrote her, "It is not generally liked and I think people are quite right." When the final part had appeared, he wrote of it again: "The Judges stand up for me: Carlyle says Catherine is wonderful, and many more laud it highly, but it is a disgusting subject and no mistake. I wish I had taken a pleasanter one. . . ." [112] In the next month, however, his mother's compliments brought out a different comment:

> Your letter with compliments has just come to hand; it is very ingenious in you to find such beauties in Catherine w^{h} was a mistake

all through—it was not made disgusting enough that is the fact, and the triumph of it would have been to make readers so horribly horrified as to cause them to give up or rather throw up the book and all of it's [sic] kind, whereas you see the author had a sneaking kindness for his heroine, and did not like to make her utterly worthless.[113]

VI

NEWGATE AND ANTI-NEWGATE, 1841–47

CRIME NOVELS AND CRITICS

Ainsworth being occupied with historical fiction, the remainder of the story of the Newgate novel belongs to Dickens and Bulwer—indeed, chiefly to Bulwer and the opposition. There were, however, a few other writers of literary standing who essayed criminal themes and a considerable number who exploited crimes and horrors in the sub-literary press. Cheap serialization became a prominent feature of the eighteen-forties.

Bentley's, the vehicle of both *Oliver Twist* and *Jack Sheppard,* continued to provide exciting romances (and short pieces) often flavored with crime. Bentley was aware of the value of having a new serial begin before a current feature ended. As *Guy Fawkes* had overlapped *Jack Sheppard,* so Charles Whitehead's romance about Richard Savage followed *Fawkes. Richard Savage,* far better than the same author's *Jack Ketch,* was published in book form in 1842. After this story of the eighteenth-century poet who killed a man in a tavern brawl, Whitehead accomplished no more work of any substance.

There were crime and mystery in the books of G. P. R. James: for example, *The Gipsy* (1835), *The Robber* (1838), and *Charles Tyrrell* (1839). But he is mentioned only to be excluded, for the chief figures in these books were of the middle or upper classes. James did not seem a Newgate novelist to anyone, not even to Thackeray, who was later to include a parody of him in *Novels by Eminent Hands.* William Mudford, whose Gothic *Five Nights of St. Alban's* (1829) had been popular, presented in *Stephen Dugard* (1840) criminal scenes marked by violence of language as well as action. Though the book is dull, the general crudity of Mudford's low characters is more convincing than the facile slang in *Jack Sheppard*; his criminals are unpleasing. The *Spectator*, neither attracted nor alarmed by fictional crime, said that Mudford's novel

> may be strongly recommended to those whose taste is for the Newgate Calendar romanticized as well as it admits; for neither Bulwer nor Ainsworth, nor even Boz, has come up to its author in the powerful delineation of criminals and crime. . . . Nor is there any incongruous attempt at excusing their crimes through circumstances, or veiling them by attributes of romantic feeling, or touches of generosity: they are painted as criminals and nothing more.[1]

Frederick Marryat was never tagged as a Newgate author, although there were episodes of crime and violence in his oddly individual novels of this period: *Japhet in Search of a Father* (1836), *Snarleyyow, the Dog Fiend* (1837), and *Joseph Rushbrook, or the Poacher* (1841). In *Japhet*, the criminal Ogle is acquitted on perjured evidence—and then confesses to the crime, in order to "prove how little there is of justice." He asserts that "Many a man is hung for what he never has been guilty of." [2]

With *Joseph Rushbrook*, serialized in a newspaper, Marryat was attempting to write a moral tale for readers not used to buying books or even the novels in shilling parts. Ainsworth tried the newspaper, and Dickens was to try weekly publication with *Master Humphrey's Clock*, for those who might find it easier to part with threepence, though somewhat oftener, than with a whole shilling at one time. All of this effort was in competition with the really cheap literature of the forties, the penny serials of Salisbury Square. Although there were earlier efforts, the large volume of these dates from 1841, when Edward Lloyd began publishing cheap periodicals and novels in penny weekly parts. He had the largest enterprise and employed many writers, but there were others who did well in the business. This popular literature has been described by E. S. Turner, by Margaret Dalziel, and by Richard D. Altick.[3] Many of the titles are to be seen in Andrew Block's bibliography of the novels of the period, though not specially identified. The penny serials have almost no merit as literature, though they have considerable interest for the sociologist or the historian of popular taste. Many were innocuous, but crime and Newgate material were always popular; the proportion of crime and other sensational material increased, probably, in later decades. Among the prolific and popular writers were James Malcolm Rymer, Henry D. Miles, Pierce Egan, Jr., and Thomas Peckett Prest, the plagiarizer of Dickens and the inventor or importer of Sweeney Todd. Though Prest is perhaps unequalled for horrors the most sensational writer of the serials in the forties was G. W. M. Reynolds, author of *Mysteries of London* (1844–48) and *Mysteries of the Court of London* (1848–56), and many later works.[4] Reynolds, a Chartist, combined in his extraordinary narratives complicated action, crime, political radicalism, sadistic violence, and an unabashed emphasis upon sex. The vice of the wealthy, ostensibly deprecated, is at the same time presented as enviable; one effect of their horrid oppression is that the poor have not the same opportunities for indulgence. Before undertaking serials, Reynolds had written a book on modern French literature. In 1846, he set up his own paper, *Reynolds's Miscellany*.

Most middle-class readers knew nothing of the cheap serials at first-hand, but anyone with a knowledge of the London scene would be aware of their existence. Their use of crime had something to do with the attitude taken by serious-minded critics of the expensive Newgate novel.

The year 1841 saw the publication of novels by both Bulwer and Dickens containing scenes of crime, and between them, chronologically, the appearance of "The Newgate Garland," verses which satirized the taste for such things. Bulwer, in the nearly nine years since *Eugene Aram*, had turned from the criminal to other subjects. In the course of the thirties, he had written an excellent book of social comment, *England and the English*. He had been highly successful with historical novels, *The Last Days of Pompeii* and *Rienzi*, moderately successful with others: *Ernest Maltravers* (which had in it a tincture of ruffianly crime) and *Alice, or the Mysteries*. He had written a series of successful plays, and some poetry as well. In this feverishly productive period, he had passed through a tempestuous separation from his wife. Since 1830, he had been in parliament, where he concerned himself with copyright protection for authors. Although constantly criticized in some places, he was one of the most important figures in contemporary literature.

It was after such an interval that he returned to the theme of crime in *Night and Morning*, published in January 1841. The greater part of it was straight romance, with many sentimental and some lurid episodes. Because a secret marriage cannot be proved, two boys are cut off from a rightful inheritance and thrown upon the world as orphans, while their father's brother enjoys possession of the estate. Despite the worthy efforts of the older boy, the younger brother is taken from him and settled in a comfortable home; the elder seeks his fortune abroad. After some years, he returns to make a search for the evidence which will restore his mother's honor and his own rights. The lost witness to the secret marriage appears, documentary evidence for it is discovered in a secret drawer, and the younger brother is found. The property is restored, and the two brothers are both to be happily married. This standard plot is tricked out with much busy coming and going and with shameless contriving by the author. In a climactic scene near the end, Bulwer brings together the illegal holder of the Beaufort property and his brother-in-law, the cynical and vicious Lord Lilburne. (The latter is a type of character Bulwer used in several novels, always effectively.) To their colloquy, the author brings the heroine, to listen at the door. She is able to rush in to pull a precious document out of the fire, and a moment later the hero bursts in to save the paper and the girl. In the confrontation which ensues, the hero reveals the girl's identity: Lord Lilburne learns that he has been trying to seduce his own granddaughter.

The part of the story that involves crime forms a section of the first half of the book. Philip Beaufort, the hero and the dispossessed heir, tries to earn an honest living in England; when he is unable to do so, he goes to Paris, to take employment with one William Gawtrey, a chance acquaintance who has shown him kindness. Philip has seen the good side of Gawtrey's nature, and does not suspect that Gawtrey is really one of a gang of counterfeiters. He observes that others have an obscure control over his patron. Somewhat uneasy, he nevertheless accepts Gawtrey's assurances that the employment to be given him is innocent; after a period of waiting, Philip, still in ignorance, is taken to the secret workshop to be inducted into full complicity. At this moment, Gawtrey and the others find they have been betrayed: the police are at the doors and have surrounded the building. Gawtrey kills the police spy, Favart, and the treacherous associate, Birnie, who has betrayed them. (Birnie is the one whose power has prevented Gawtrey from leaving the gang.) Gawtrey then throws a rope and hook from a window to the building across the way. Philip goes first and escapes; Gawtrey is shot while on the rope and falls dead into the street.

That is the extent of Philip's connection with the criminals. It is also the end of the underworld scenes in the novel, though a convict enters briefly at a later time. He has learned the secret of the Beaufort marriage, and tries to blackmail Robert Beaufort, illegal holder of the property. Lord Lilburne, assisting Robert Beaufort, employs a Bow Street officer and learns the blackmailer's identity. Since the convict has returned before his time is up, he is easily frightened off by the threat of being sent back to the colonies.

The parallel which Bulwer drew between Gawtrey, the coiner, and Lilburne, the nobleman who cheated at cards, distinctly favored Gawtrey. It was especially pointed, in that Gawtrey had preserved little Fanny from the danger of a vicious life, whereas Lilburne would have destroyed her virtue. As in Eugene Aram, Bulwer had tried to present a character in which good and evil were mingled; he did not expect, apparently, that he would again be accused of showing approval of criminal acts.

The point was raised, though, and—of all places—in the Examiner. The review, an extraordinarily long one, contained high praise, but the praise was qualified. The reviewer (Forster, of course, as everyone knew) found some of the characters, and the writing, finer than anything Bulwer had previously done. But—

> The hero never quite recovers his position after he has been con-
> nected with the man of crime who figures in the second volume
> and in whom the limits between good and evil are scarcely marked
> throughout with sufficient clearness and precision. Upon these
> points there should be no possible doubt, for they imply the ex-
> treme danger of suggesting a false sympathy with crime.[5]

Gawtrey had murdered two men, the review went on, but the reader was expected to maintain some sympathy for him.

These objections, cautiously stated, occupied a small part of a friendly review, in which, incidentally, the modern reader is likely to disagree as much with the praise as with the censure. But they were there—and Forster, Bulwer's sympathetic friend, had never said such things before; Bulwer had been regularly praised in the *Examiner*. Only six months earlier, when *Paul Clifford* had been reissued, newly dedicated to Albany Fonblanque, it had been cited as a novel in which vulgar materials were rightly handled.[6] Bulwer was more disturbed than he should have been about the effect of the review, but he was also surprised and hurt. Forster must have anticipated the feeling, for he took care to send a letter. Bulwer's reply is dated January 18, the day after the appearance of the paper:

> Many thanks for your note, which I am glad I received before reading the review.—In regard to Fonblanque's opinion—I regret to hear it is so unfavorable—. . But of course he has a right to it. I am not aware of any "girding" at the Liberal Party. It was necessary to my story that Philip should be a Carlist—. In order to be an exile from France; it was natural as a Foreigner, & a soldier from the East, that he should take that side. . . . [After further remarks on the naturalness of Philip's joining the Carlists, Bulwer turns to his own affairs, recounting his services to the Liberal Party and complaining that he has been rewarded with abuse.]
>
> I thank you sincerely and cordially for the friendly spirit in your review which it is quite impossible to misconceive—I regret only that the point only selected for blame should be on the score of *immorality:*—This charge coming first from the Examiner—, supposed, & truly, to be kindly disposed, both by political agreement and private friendship will encourage and hound on the attacks of others—. on a score the most painful and where the accusation will be less tempered.[7]

In the next part of the letter, which appears in the *Life* of Bulwer by his grandson, Bulwer argued against the principle that one must never excite any sympathy for or interest in a criminal; such an attitude, he said, would do away with *Othello* and *Macbeth*. In none of his books had he ever shown approval of crime. The letter went on:

> Nay, so strongly did I mark the reprobation of Gawtrey's darker crimes so broadly and sternly did I draw the limits "between the

good and the evil"—that *you* thought the distinction too emphatic and too strong and at your wish I altered it.

Then follow some lines which have been crossed through and are partially unreadable, though the substance is apparent. Forster had quoted in his review a dictum that it is wrong to give a generous principle to atrocious actions. Where, Bulwer asks, has he given any generous principle to Gawtrey's detestable actions? But a man who commits great crimes may have some good qualities. After the stricken passage, the letter goes on:

> I have been wearisome on this head—especially as it can lead to no conviction or result—But it is vain to deny that the charge from such a quarter pains me deeply—& while the pain is fresh—. the remonstrance is prolix.—.

He next defends the realism of certain details in the story not connected with crime, and finally brings himself to round off the subject:

> And here closes the ungracious task of Defense—. more ungracious where it appears agst so much of kindness—. But had the flower been of any other Nature whatsoever than that; (so hailed & gloated over as it will be)—. of dangerous and immoral tendency—there would be sufficient myrtle round the Thyrsus to flatter away any smart from the point of steel beneath.

The letter shows Bulwer to be both sensitive and vain. At the same time, he was largely in the right—he was being criticized for the wrong things, and his weaknesses went unreproved, at least by Forster. And had not Bulwer reason to be surprised? Apparently Forster had seen the manuscript of *Night and Morning* and had pronounced, on the point of the black and white in Gawtrey, a judgment exactly the opposite of that he expressed in the review. "*You* thought the distinction too emphatic and too strong and at your wish I altered it," says Bulwer. Although this sentence may spring from unconscious distortion or from a misunderstanding, it arouses a conjecture: that Forster, originally approving, found his editor, Fonblanque, so strongly opposed that he felt constrained to write Fonblanque's opinion into the review.

And the source of Fonblanque's disapproval? Fonblanque,

whose paper had always supported Bulwer on the handling of the criminal theme? Apparently he saw a deviation from the liberal cause in Bulwer's making the hero of *Night and Morning* an officer under Charles X of France and a supporter of the monarch after the July revolution. Once more, then, political considerations—this time, fortuitously—seem to have caused a crime novel to be criticized on moral grounds.

Bulwer's fears about the effect of the *Examiner* review turned out to be exaggerated. If his critics gloated, they did so in private. *Fraser's* did not mention *Night and Morning*, nor did *Blackwood's*. The *Times* did not review it. The impartial *Athenaeum*, as so often happened, gave the soundest criticism: recognizing Bulwer's abilities, it described the book "not so much a work of art, as a work of artifice." Gawtrey's character was called improbable, but nothing was said against Bulwer's treatment of the criminal theme.[8] The book was noticed in the new *Ainsworth's Magazine* and in the *Monthly Review*, but not in the *New Monthly Magazine*. The reviewer in *Tait's*, in March, had tolerant admiration for *Night and Morning*: despite exaggeration and overstrained energy, the book was one which would make the reputation of a new author. The character of Gawtrey was original and powerful, though it was one "to which those critics who look strictly to moral tendencies, may take exception."[9] After the great *Jack Sheppard* hysteria, the dangers of *Night and Morning* did not excite much concern.

There was a newspaper attack in November of the same year, aimed not at *Night and Morning* but at Bulwer's work in general. It was a *Times* article, political in essence but with an appropriate screen of morality. The *Morning Chronicle* came to Bulwer's defense; its reply was political too. The *Examiner* commented on both, in a way that should have consoled Bulwer for the temporary disappointment of the review of *Night and Morning*:

> The *Times* has discovered in Sir Edward Bulwer's writings the great demoralising agency of the time. It seems that "false moral principles" have made much progress in this country; that one evidence of so deplorable a fact is a morbid sympathy with criminals; and that the evil thus superinduced upon our national character is, in no slight degree, to be ascribed to the novels of Sir E. L. Bulwer.[10]

Grouped as Newgate writers in Thackeray's *Catherine*, Bulwer, Ainsworth, and Dickens were linked again, in *Tait's Magazine*, in the spring of 1841, in the first of the popular Bon Gaultier papers. It contained a set of good-natured parodies, "Flowers of Hemp, or, the Newgate Garland." [11] The author was a young Scot, Theodore Martin, then at the beginning of a successful career in law and letters.

The professional thief who sent his manuscript to Bon Gaultier dedicated it "to the Authors of Eugene Aram, Paul Clifford, Rookwood, Jack Sheppard, Oliver Twist, &c." The ten poems included in it were intended to assist in gilding the gibbet and the hulks and in securing "for the boozing-ken and the gin palace that hold upon the general sympathies which has been too long monopolized by the cottage and the drawing-room." The first piece follows the pattern of Wordsworth's sonnet, "Great men have been among us"; its roster of great men includes Duval, Turpin, Blueskin, and Sheppard. The second, like Wordsworth's address to Milton, apostrophizes: "Turpin, thou shouldst be living at this hour! England hath need of thee." Others pleasantly imitate poems or songs at least as well known in 1841, if less familiar now. "The Nutty Blowen," paralleling T. H. Bayley's "She wore a wreath of roses," begins:

> She wore a rouge like roses, the night when first we met,
> Her lovely mug was smiling o'er the mugs of heavy wet.

Ann Taylor's "My Mother," always a favorite for parody, gives the framework for another:

> Who, when a baby, lank and thin,
> I called for pap and made a din,
> Lulled me with draughts of British gin?—
> My mother.

Most of the verses, like these, celebrate underworld life, but do not aim at the novelists. "The Faker's New Toast" is the only one that mentions them by name:

> Come, all ye jolly covies, vot faking do admire,
> And pledge the British authors who to our line aspire.

· · ·

> If they goes on as they've begun, things soon vill come about,
> And ve shall be the upper class, and turn the others out;
>
>   .   .   .
>
> 'Tis ve as sets the fashion now; Jack Sheppard is the go,
> And every word of "Nix my dolls" the finest ladies know.

At last it calls amiably for a toast:

> To them as makes the cracksman's life the subject of their
>   story,—
> To Ainsvorth, and to Bullvig, and to Reynolds be the glory,
>   Jolly trumps!

Here, and in the dedication already quoted, "Flowers of Hemp"
gives us a roll-call of the Newgate authors. In the poem, G. W. M.
Reynolds has been substituted for Dickens; Ainsworth and Bulwer
thus are jokingly linked with an author of cheap and violent serials.
Reynolds' best-known titles, the *Mysteries* already mentioned, were
yet to come, but *The Drunkard's Progress* was probably appearing
at the time.[12]

The jesting of "The Newgate Garland" was mildly satirical
and by no means hostile. Martin had had a friendly correspondence
with Ainsworth some two years before, and had written a highly
complimentary letter about *Jack Sheppard*.[13] In the later Bon
Gaultier papers, where Ainsworth is mentioned more than once,
there is no indication that the friendship was impaired. Bulwer,
however, did not enjoy the same immunity. "Lays of the Would-be
Laureates," printed in *Tait's Magazine* in 1843, shortly after
Wordsworth had been appointed poet laureate, included the contributions of all those who (so the jest ran) had applied for the
post.[14] Everything else is good-humored, but "A Lucullan Meditation by Sir E— B— L—" is written with acid. The purported meditation of Bulwer touches on his dandyism, with

> and oh, what head
> More fit with laurel to be garlanded
> Than this, which, curled in many a fragrant coil
> Breathes of Castalia's streams, and best Macassar oil?

and includes this stanza about *Aram*:

> Yes, I am he who sang how Aram won
> The gentle ear of pensive Madeline!

How love and murder hand in hand may run,
Cemented by Philosophy serene,
Who breathed the melting sentiment of crime
And for the assassin waked a sympathy sublime!

The pseudonym, Bon Gaultier, by this time represented two writers; the changed tone was perhaps due to the influence of the collaborator, W. E. Aytoun, author of the "Lucullan Meditation." [15]

THE NEWGATE THEME OF *Barnaby Rudge*

Dickens' 1841 work, *Barnaby Rudge*, serially belonging to the *Master Humphrey's Clock* project, has a right to the title of Newgate novel, though it did not suffer from being so labeled by reviewers. In accounting for its beginnings, Kathleen Tillotson gives importance to "the direct inspiration of Newgate itself, both as place and symbol." [16] It is a story of the Gordon riots of 1780, during which the prison was attacked and set on fire.

Without undertaking to tell the whole complicated story it is possible to review briefly the Newgate element. There is Rudge, an escaped murderer, who is finally apprehended and hanged for his crime. It is in Newgate that he meets face to face his son, the half-witted Barnaby, whom he has not seen for twenty-eight years. Innocent Barnaby, who has joined the rioters as if in a game, has been imprisoned; his life at the last is spared. There is Hugh, hostler at the Maypole Inn, uncouth and violent, who loves the rioting, and finally there is Dennis, the hangman. In the story, it is to release Barnaby that Hugh and the others storm and set fire to Newgate. Dennis assists, but he will not set free his prospective clients in the condemned cells, who are let out against his will. The prison itself is the focal point of the last half of the book.

Ainsworth, looking at Newgate, had concocted an essentially cheerful romance of escape. Dickens incorporated Newgate into a fairly grim story with a message, and so restored the explicit reformer's attitude toward the criminal law which had been absent from Newgate novels since *Paul Clifford*.

He deliciously shocks himself and us with the violence of the rioters, but he passionately warns their oppressors. These are, as everybody recognizes, not the ruling classes of 1780, but those of the hungry forties, the time of the two nations. They are the same rulers Carlyle had warned in *Chartism* and the *French Revolution.* Edgar Johnson says:

> The mob scenes of *Barnaby Rudge* . . . are a strange fusion of the exultation and fascinated horror that gives them a curious emotional ambiguity. But there is no ambiguity in the social attitudes the book implies. The only possibility of misreading it would be to assume that the evils of 1780 had been completely eradicated by a more humane and enlightened world. Dickens gives no encouragement to that misapprehension.[17]

The message has been described by other writers. What is necessary here is to emphasize the attitude of Dickens toward the criminal law and the extremely topical nature of *Barnaby Rudge* in 1841.

Like Bulwer in *Paul Clifford*, Dickens sees oppressive laws as the instruments of an oppressive social system—his novel may be called a document of the struggle between the classes. The privileged have the gallows as their ultimate instrument in maintaining their power over the disinherited. To show the wickedness of such a system, Dickens uses the same device Bulwer used: comfortable father against neglected son. Rough Hugh, to whom society has never given a family name, is privately employed by Sir John Chester, elegant and supercilious, whom Dickens bids us despise. (The similarity to the name of Lord Chesterfield is obviously intentional.) Finding that Hugh has stolen a bracelet, Sir John has a firm hold upon him: "So long as you deserve it, my good fellow, as I hope you always will, you have a friend in me, on whose silence you may rely." To Sir John, Hugh has spoken of his mother, whom he saw hanged at Tyburn when he was six years old. As we come near the end of the book, that interview is, in retrospect, tinged with horror, and "on whose silence you may rely" takes on an added meaning. The riots over, Hugh is condemned to death for his leadership in them. It is then discovered that he is Sir John's son by a gipsy woman. Sir John pretends not to believe the fact; he will make no effort to aid his son, nor even visit him. He has indeed been "silent." Hugh dies hating all the world except his dog and the fool, Barnaby, and cursing "that black tree of which I am the ripened fruit." The aristocrat self-destructively cuts off all his progeny; for he also curses and dis-inherits his acknowledged son, Edward. Irresponsibility and ir-rationality, spread from the upper to the lower classes, are counter-pointed throughout the book.

5. Hablot K. Browne, Hugh's Curse. Chapter 77, *Barnaby Rudge*, 1841.

The mean employee of the oppressors, Dennis the hangman, who is in love with his work, is an emblem of corruption and is important in Dickens' plan. There was a real hangman, Edward Dennis, who was convicted of helping to burn a house in the riots but was not executed; it was Dickens' inspiration to have him help burn Newgate instead and to make him into the grim absurdity he is.[18] Mrs. Tillotson suggests that Dickens has drawn something from Whitehead's *Autobiography of Jack Ketch*. This is likely enough, but a closer parallel is with the Jack Ketch of the puppet drama, who by his own gullibility finds himself dangling in the noose he intended for Mr. Punch. Dickens elaborates to the utmost the pleasure which was always afforded by that spectacle. Dennis, like Ketch, is stupid. Sentenced to death, he cannot believe that they will actually hang *him*; he expects a reprieve. When it does not come, he begs and pleads abjectly; he is described as held between two men, "with his legs trailing on the ground," and trembling so, "that all his joints and limbs seemed racked by spasms." When the last preparations are made, he sinks down, "a mere heap of clothes between the two attendants." The little puppet hangman has been expanded to a life-size grotesque and placed in Dickens' history.

Dickens' irony, at other points too extravagant for most tastes, is at its best when the hangman reflects in prison:

> When he remembered the great estimation in which his office was held, and the constant demand for his services; when he bethought himself, how the Statute Book regarded him as a kind of Universal Medicine applicable to men, women, and children, of every age and variety of criminal constitution; and how high he stood, in his official capacity, in the favour of the Crown, and both Houses of Parliament, the Mint, the Bank of England, and the Judges of the land; when he recollected that whatever Ministry was in or out, he remained their peculiar pet and panacea, and that for his sake England stood single and conspicuous among the civilized nations of the earth: when he called these things to mind and dwelt upon them, he felt certain that the national gratitude *must* relieve him from the consequences of his late proceedings, and would certainly restore him to his old place in the happy social system.[19]

"Whatever Ministry was in or out" is a phrase that evokes not the time of the riots, but 1841, when the serial was appearing. The general election had been held in July, after which Peel formed his ministry; this passage, in Chapter 74, appeared near the end of October.

Barnaby's death sentence is the occasion for direct comment:

> It is not the least evil attendant upon the frequent exhibition of this last dread punishment, of Death, that it hardens the minds of those who deal it out, and makes them, though they be amiable men in other respects, indifferent to, or unconscious of their great

responsibility. The word had gone forth that Barnaby was to die. It went forth every month for lighter crimes. It was a thing so common, that very few were startled by the awful sentence, or cared to question its propriety. Just then, too, when the law had been so flagrantly outraged, its dignity must be asserted. The symbol of its dignity,—stamped upon every page of the criminal statute-book,—was the gallows; and Barnaby was to die.[20]

In describing the situation of the condemned men, Dickens emphasizes their mental condition. (Here, as in *Oliver Twist*, some of his phrasing suggests that he knew Hugo's *Le Dernier jour*.) He wishes to combat the familiar notion that the prospect of death induces spiritual repentance; most men, he says, show defiance, like Hugh, or self-pitying fear, like Dennis, and can fix their minds firmly on nothing.

Barnaby Rudge thus spoke persuasively against capital punishment and against public executions, but it cannot be said to have had any immediate effect. Certain capital penalties were repealed in 1841, as we have already seen, and if Dickens' book had appeared earlier, it might be thought to have had some direct influence. In particular, how neatly the story would have coincided with the removal of the death penalty for destruction of buildings in riots! But what parliament did with the criminal law was concluded in June, before the election; in the short session of early autumn, it did not deal with these matters. In the first half of the year, Dickens' serial had not reached the scenes which convey his message.

Dickens was again to declare himself forcefully against capital punishment in *Daily News* articles in the spring of 1846; and with equal force, against public executions, in letters to the *Times* in 1849, when he had seen the Mannings hanged.[21] Widely discussed, these utterances must have contributed to the state of public opinion, but they too were followed by no immediate legal change.

Barnaby Rudge, though not a legal influence, was in theme and emotion keyed to the period of reform. Dickens had begun to think of it before *Oliver Twist* was written and had kept the project before him during those years when the major reductions of capital punishment were completed. The first readers of *Barnaby Rudge* also had recollections of how great and how recent the changes were—could they not read with special feeling the story of the hangman hanged? For them, Dickens' story, filled with scorn for the bad old days and with pity for all the wretched, must have sounded not merely a warning against violence, bad as it is shown to be, but a paean of exultation and release. Newgate had been assaulted, condemned cells had been emptied. Dickens' riotous gaol-delivery seems symbolic, and the energy of his writing seems an overflow of the great current of popular feeling.

Lucretia: THE "ARSENICAL" NOVEL CONDEMNED

During the early forties, there was a considerable amount of crime in minor fiction, but it aroused no special attention; usually it was in an upper- or middle-class setting. Charles Ollier did a fictional account of the notorious Earl Ferrers, hanged in 1760 for the murder of his steward. More representative was a novel by Catherine Sinclair, *Flirtation, or a Month at Harrowgate,* which included murder by arsenic poisoning.[22] Catherine Crowe's novel, *Susan Hopley, or Circumstantial Evidence* (London, 1841) was popular enough to be reissued by William Tait (Edinburgh, 1842) as a cheap serial. An ambitious but incompetent mystery tale, which showed that the author was trying to learn the methods of Dickens, it contained deception, intrigue, murder, and suicide; but the people are middle-class, and though one character is imprisoned in Newgate, the book hardly qualifies as a Newgate novel. Eugene Sue's *Mysteries of Paris,* a serial in Paris in 1842–43, became popular in translation in London.

In the middle forties both Dickens and Bulwer made use of the story of a living criminal, this time a poisoner. The case itself had aroused great interest and had helped to create a believing public for stories of poisoning. Dickens' use of the matter was limited, Bulwer's considerably greater. In *Martin Chuzzlewit,* 1843–44, as in later works, Dickens was able to maintain his special interest in crime without incurring the Newgate label. Bulwer, after an interval in which he wrote successful novels on other themes, put poisoners in the foreground in *Lucretia, or the Children of Night,* published in December 1846. Like Dickens, he avoided scenes of low life; unlike Dickens, he allowed evil to bulk large in the story, and gave his readers too little to admire. Perhaps for this reason, and certainly because the author was Bulwer, *Lucretia* became the final object of attack in the war against the Newgate novel.

Thomas Griffiths Wainewright (1794–1847) was an artist of considerable talent who had been acquainted with a number of literary men; he was also a murderer. Much has been written about him, and his case has been used in fiction more than once. The most extensive biography is that by Jonathan Curling, which has been drawn upon here, though the later one by Charles Norman includes some additional material.[23] Wainewright's work was included in Royal Academy exhibitions for five successive years, 1821 to 1825. Between 1820 and 1823, he wrote for the *London Magazine* under pseudonyms, of which the best known was Janus Weathercock; and he did other literary work. In essays, he dramatized himself as an aesthete and dilettante; he claims modern respect for being aware of Blake's work and admiring it. He became acquainted with Thomas Noon Talfourd, John Clare, H. F. Cary, DeQuincey, Hazlitt, and Lamb; of these, it was Lamb who wrote of him most warmly and who lamented not seeing him when the *London Magazine* group were dispersed. Other well-known persons dined at Wainewright's house during the period when he lived most extravagantly.

His tastes, however, ran beyond the very limited income which he had inherited. He married in 1821. In 1822 and again in 1824, he forged powers of attorney, by means of which he obtained £5,000 of his inheritance so that he might live upon his capital instead of merely the interest. He expected a larger fortune upon the death of his uncle; when the uncle died, in 1828, the disappointed Wainewright got a few thousand pounds and a big house which he could not afford to keep up. It is probable that he had poisoned the uncle; and he probably poisoned his wife's mother, who died some two years later. She had no fortune to leave, but she may have been inconvenient. In the spring of 1830, Wainewright apparently decided he must do something to meet the variety of financial obligations he had incurred. His wife had two half-sisters, of whom the elder, Helen Abercromby, was just turning twenty-one. Wainewright paid the premiums for her to insure her life with several companies for a period of two or three years. She got policies amounting to some £16,000, and would have got more but for several refusals. Why was she willing to do this? Several writers have speculated that the plan, as Helen Abercromby knew it, was that the family would soon go abroad and that fraudulent proof of her "death" would procure the large sums of money to be enjoyed by them all.[24] This was not what happened. She grew ill in December 1830, and, despite the attention of a doctor, died within seven or eight days. The doctor performed an autopsy, though not from suspicion; he found water on the brain, as he had expected, but saw nothing unusual in the condition of the stomach. Later studies of all the evidence indicate that she had first been dosed with antimony, then finally killed by strychnine in a quantity small enough to escape observation.

The insurance companies, though lacking the information which was later gathered, were understandably suspicious. Collaborating, they refused to pay the death benefits, on the ground that falsehoods had been told when the policies were obtained. Wainewright went to France to escape his creditors; he probably never again saw his wife, who had, presumably, participated in the plot. From France, he undertook to sue the insurance companies; the second of two such efforts failed by the end of 1835. The suspicion that Helen Abercromby had been murdered hung darkly over both trials; but there was no indictment of Wainewright, and the jury was not called upon to decide the point. The insurance companies were upheld in their refusal of payment, chiefly because Helen Abercromby's assignment of policies to Wainewright placed him, illegally, in a position to benefit by her death.

Earlier in 1835, the Bank of England had discovered the forgeries which Wainewright had committed in 1822 and 1824, and prepared to prosecute him whenever the opportunity might arise. (Legal reform had not yet proceeded to the point where it was someone's official duty to investigate the open suspicion of murder.) Wainewright inexplicably returned to England in May 1837 —no one knows why. He was found and taken into custody on June 9.

At this time the forgery he had committed was one of the few types which remained capital offences, although a bill then in parliament and not yet passed (mentioned above, p. 26) was to change the matter. Of several counts in the indictment of Wainewright, those for uttering the forged instruments were not capital. At first saying Not Guilty to all, he was induced at the last moment to plead guilty to these two. As he would probably have been transported even if he had been convicted of all the charges, he was resentful when on July 5 he was sentenced to transportation for life. This was his punishment for obtaining, fraudulently, his own money; he was never legally charged with murder.

In the newspapers and in Newgate itself, he was a sensationally interesting prisoner. Former acquaintances and friends came to see him; Lamb, however, had died in 1834 without knowing any evil about him. There is one reliable statement that he confessed the poisoning of Helen Abercromby.[25] Some accounts of his speaking factually out of court do not seem to be based on contemporary documents. Apparently, though, he did adopt the pose of an unrepentant and jesting murderer. Within less than a month after the verdict, Wainewright was on the convict ship, bound for Van Diemen's Land. He died there ten years later, in 1847.

Dickens visited Newgate, as has been said, in preparing to write one of the Sketches by Boz. He and John Forster and Hablôt Browne were present when the fourth member of the group, William Macready, suddenly recognized the man he had known and dined with twenty years before: "My God! there's Wainewright!" [26] After such an episode, it was inevitable that Dickens should make some use of the case. Probably the Jonas Chuzzlewit element in Martin Chuzzlewit is as it is because of Wainewright. Curling points out the likeness of the names, Jonas and Janus. Jonas obtains two types of poisons; one acts quickly and one slowly. He plans to poison his father and believes himself to have done so. When he seeks to insure the life of his wife, another poisoning is obviously in preparation, though ultimately he must give himself the fatal dose. He has not the artistic accomplishments, but he has the cold villainy universally attributed to Wainewright; in this, Dickens did not exceed what he had heard of his model. But the novelist knew better than to imitate life too far and allow a villain to escape, as Wainewright had. In the world he creates, evil is punished, and the deeds of Jonas are no exception. He knew better, also, than to make a Jonas Chuzzlewit the central figure of a book; he kept the monster in the sub-plot and gave his readers a great deal else to think about. When *Martin Chuzzlewit* was reviewed in 1844, there was no clamor that Dickens was again trafficking in crime.

Dickens used Wainewright again, but at a time when the Newgate novel agitation was long past. One or two minor bits from the Wainewright story went into the Rigaud Blandois of *Little Dorrit*, and considerably more into his story, "Hunted Down," done in 1859.[27]

One does not know exactly why Bulwer decided to try a novel involving poison. With an eye to popular notice, he may have been influenced by the notoriety of the Tawell case, the best-known one of the forties. *Punch* complained about the indignity of the preparations for Tawell's hanging—and also about poisoning in fiction:

> Tawell, the Quaker, is at the present moment a very powerful rival to the makers of Newgate volumes. Folks are apt to turn from a novel, though wholly composed of French sentiment and French arsenic, to study the living animal charged with poisoning.

After quoting from a newspaper account of the many curious visitors, *Punch* continued:

> In the first place—to say nothing of the feelings of the prisoner—this practice is highly prejudicial to the interests of the Newgate novel-monger. How, for instance, is Mr. Bentley, the publisher, to continue to sell his monthly doses of literary arsenic—or rather, arsenicated literature—treating the gentle public as he would treat rats,—if a crowd of magistracy can take a crowd of friends and show a man suspected of being a poisoner for nothing? Bentley should protest to the Home Office that as he endeavors every month to make poisoning familiar to the meanest understanding . . . as formerly he taught housebreaking by *Jack Sheppard*—he ought not to be thus unfairly competed with by gratuitous exhibitors.[28]

Punch had not objected to *Martin Chuzzlewit*.

Dickens disguised rather than advertised his use of Wainewright. Bulwer did not identify his original by name, but his preface almost invited readers to do so. He became acquainted, he wrote, "with the histories of two criminals, existing in our own age," whose perverted characters "became a study full of intense, if gloomy interest."

> Incredible as it may seem, the crimes herein related took place within the last seventeen years. There has been no exaggeration as to their extent, no great departure from their details—the means employed, even that which seems most far-fetched (the instrument of the poisoned ring), have their foundation in literal facts. Nor have I much altered the social position of the criminals, nor in the least overrated their attainments and intelligence. In those more salient essentials, which will most, perhaps, provoke the Reader's incredulous wonder, I narrate a history, not invent a fiction.[29]

On the whole, the claim is true. He had studied Wainewright: he had obtained from one Henry P. Smith, of the Eagle Insurance Company, all the papers collected in the investigation of the case, and the poisonings in *Lucretia* are indeed no worse than the supposed facts about Helen Abercromby.[30]

The mention of *two* criminals is puzzling at first, because of Bulwer's additional note that he had "no authority to suppose that the one was known to the other." The preface, that is, asked readers to believe that he had combined in his story two quite separate cases. Bulwer's grandson, however, wrote explicitly, "The character of Varney in *Lucretia* is based upon Thomas Wainewright, and that of Lucretia Clavering upon his wife." [31] If we accept that statement, as I believe we must, why did Bulwer assert that the two poisoners were unknown to each other? Why did he make the woman even more brilliant than the man, as no one could suppose Mrs. Wainewright to be? And, to glance ahead at the story itself, why did he avoid making the poisoners husband and wife, as they originally were? There can be only one answer: Bulwer was protecting himself against the possibility of a suit for libel. He wished Wainewright to be recognized; and the convict, though still living, was in no position to cause trouble. But Mrs. Wainewright also still lived, and was in England. A novel which unmistakably pointed her out, even under a fictional name, as a vicious murderer might very well be taken as libellous; her poverty might not prevent her from taking action. The chances of her success in a suit, if it were undertaken, are hard to calculate, but the possibility of it—a very real possibility, if Bulwer had not disguised her—is enough to account for his statements in the preface and for the changed relationship of the poisoners in the story. The novel was so generally accepted as factual that some parts of it entered into the Wainewright legend, to the confusion of later researchers.

In making use of the case, Bulwer kept its cardinal features and its central character. Wainewright becomes an artist named Gabriel Varney, whose likeness to the real criminal was attested by some who had known him. He poisons his uncle to obtain the uncle's £6,000, he commits forgeries to obtain capital, he insures a young girl's life, collaborates in poisoning her, and is transported for the forgeries. Helen Abercromby becomes Helen Mainwaring, beautiful and innocent, who dies of the poison. The other poisoner, aunt rather than half-sister of the victim, is Lucretia Clavering, intellectal and ambitious. While Gabriel Varney is still a boy, she marries his father, whose name is Olivier Dalibard. Thus there is no counterpart for Mrs. Wainewright; at the same time, it seems quite clear that Bulwer considered her guilty. Readers who knew of the case no doubt saw her in the book. Many years later, the editor of Wainewright's essays relied upon his memory and spoke of Lucretia, mistakenly, as Varney's wife.[32]

To all these factual elements Bulwer added more events, more characters, and birth mysteries from the stockpile. He formed the story in two sections. The events of Part the First (which fills the first volume) take place shortly after the turn of the century; after a lapse of twenty-seven years, the story is resumed in Part the Second, the events of which culminate in 1832, a time close to but not exactly matching the date of Helen Abercromby's death.

Among Bulwer's additions is the villain Olivier Dalibard, who possesses great intellect but also selfish ambition unattended by compunction. He takes his little son to see his mother die by the guillotine. He rediscovers the secret poisons of the Borgias, about whom Bulwer seems to believe all the most lurid stories—hence the name of Lucretia, who in the story is an English heiress. Under Dalibard's tutelage, she becomes as ambitious and as selfish as he; she reads medical books to try to estimate how long her rich bachelor uncle may withstand his infirmities. But we must pass over the details of the story—or the synopsis will get out of hand. She loses her estate, loses her suitor, and marries Dalibard. Having gone to France, Dalibard rises in wealth and power; he poisons a relative and begins to poison Lucretia, who, as his wife, is now in the way. She has her husband murdered by one of his political enemies and returns to England with his son, Varney; she possesses Dalibard's cabinet of poisons and his secret formulas. She marries again; this husband, dying, hates her so much that he contrives to spirit away their little son. Only at this point do we come to the events which parallel the Wainewright case.

Varney, now a gay bachelor artist, has poisoned an uncle, got a bequest, forged powers of attorney—all as in the Wainewright story—and is about to be discovered in his forgery. He enlists the aid of Lucretia, who gives it in return for assistance in seeking her lost son, who can inherit—if she poisons the right people—the estate she was cut off from. They begin with Helen Mainwaring, all heart and kindness, who has happily taken up the idea that she ought to be insured in favor of her noble Aunt Lucretia, who appears to be a bedfast invalid. The author builds up to a crashing climax, the excitement of which can hardly be suggested by this fragmentary account. Events begin to tighten; all the characters converge upon the country house where Helen lies dying. Lucretia is observed putting poison in Helen's medicine by a servant, Beck, formerly a crossing-sweeper. She punctures his wrist with her poison ring, and goes to await the news that her long-lost son is found. She has persuaded herself that the son will prove to be a handsome young lawyer whom she knows. Helen dies. Before witnesses, Beck accuses Lucretia of poisoning her; then he himself dies in fearful pain. His sleeve is pulled up: on his wrist near the poison puncture is the infant brand which reveals *him* as her missing son. Lucretia goes violently mad, but miserably lives on in custody; Varney is transported. It is an ending that would be easier to match on the stage than in Victorian fiction. This summary, devoted chiefly to the villains, omits a bewildering variety of other characters, of ordinary, or even extraordinary goodness. These outnumber the three villains several times over. Nevertheless, the villains do stand out, perhaps because of their cold domestic treachery.

As a thriller, the book ought to be called a success, despite

Bulwer's plentiful use of coincidence, which is not to modern taste. The makers of motion pictures seem not to know that they have missed an extraordinary script; the romantic interest is blighted by the death of the heroine, but that death, resulting from the interference of fact, is remediable, as Bulwer himself was to show. Seven years later, in preparation for a new edition, he decided that the ending was too dreadful. In a preface dated December 7, 1853, he announced that he had diminished "the gloom of the catastrophe" and saved the life of "the victim whose fate in the former cast of the work most revolted the reader, as a violation of the trite but amiable law of Poetical Justice." In the revised work, Helen Mainwaring, now spared the final and fatal dose of poison, recovers and marries Percival St. John, and they live happily ever after. This change required numerous alterations, and Bulwer made others of mere detail. So reprinted since 1853, the novel is a little further from the Wainewright source, but that is all. It is the defect of such plot-making that a heroine can die or live by the author's whim. One cannot say that the book was damaged by the change.

But Bulwer, though he wished to be popular, wished a great deal else. No novelist, it must be repeated, has ever been more ambitious. Without asserting equality with Shakespeare and Euripides, he draws upon them for comparison. Obviously he thinks of *Lucretia* as being, like *Eugene Aram*, in the tradition of tragedy, and he believes that the catastrophes wrought by evil passions can be made rewarding objects of contemplation. One can say again, as of *Eugene Aram*, that such ambition deserved more success in the accomplishment, but it is not easy to say why Bulwer failed. In part, the difficulty lies in the nature of prose fiction, which is easily made analytical or expository or journalistic, but which is not easily imbued with the poetic and symbolic energy of tragedy. Bulwer is not a good enough poet. In part, the difficulty lies in the confusion of taste during the period when Bulwer came to maturity. In this confusion, criticism was as capable of vagaries as was public taste and gave little help to a writer whose natural judgment did not serve him adequately. And, in part, the difficulty lies in Bulwer's style. Style is perhaps inseparable from the whole of taste, but it is not quite the same thing. Bulwer's style is often admirable, but his liking for purple betrays him. If his books could have been revised by a sympathetic and talented editor, his standing in the twentieth century would be very different from what it is.

Amid the general waste of *Lucretia*, there is still the excellence of Bulwer's moral and social analysis. In the preface and in the last chapter of the novel, he remarks that one part of his purpose is to present the power of the inducement of wealth in modern civilization. The theme was important and timely, and he was right to see it in the Wainewright story, but he does not really grapple with it —as some reviewers quite justly complained. There is more explicit emphasis on another theme: the evil which results when intellect is relied upon without ethical guidance. This was the theme of *Eugene Aram*; it was Bulwer's warning to those who espoused analysis such as Bentham's and were inclined to enthrone Reason. At an early point in the story, Lucretia says to her tutor:

> In the knowledge you have communicated I felt a charm that, at times, seems to me to be only fatal. You have confounded in my mind evil and good, or, rather, you have left both good and evil as dead ashes, as the dust and cinder of a crucible. You have made intellect the only conscience.[33]

Bulwer points the moral again when the story is over. He who cultivates only the reason runs the risk of Dalibard; he who lives only for the senses runs the risk of Varney. The tale was not written "for the coarse object of creating an idle terror. . . . We recover from the dread, the awe, the half incredulous wonder, to set closer watch upon our inner and hidden selves."

Among the earliest reviews of *Lucretia* were those in the *Athenaeum*, the *Examiner*, and the *Literary Gazette*, on December 5. The *Athenaeum* condemned it flatly: "a bad book of a bad school." Many of the reviewer's specific objections—to the improbabilities of the inflated dialogue—were sound; a patchy work of art, he called it, to come from one who loves to lecture on the Art of Fiction. Bulwer should "consult the permanence of his reputation—which is perilled by the present work." [34] The judgment was severe but without malice. In the *Examiner*, Forster dealt with the book sympathetically, in a review of unusual length, more than two pages. *Lucretia* gives the reader a thrill of interest from beginning to end, he said, "but it leaves us without morbid thoughts or unhealthy fancies, in no danger of mistaking Night's children for those of Day, without the least desire to play ingenious tricks with our consciences." Those who had known literary and artistic society twenty-five years ago would remember the original of Varney:

> They have but to recall, for example, from the group that sur-rounded the London Magazine, one man; a Janus with more than two faces; the gaudy, violent, flaring artist; the insolent, bullying, double-voiced critic; the profuse and extravagant entertainer; the shabby cheat; the swindler and forger; the unscrupulous and un-sparing murderer; and to the last, even when loaded with a felon's chains, the daring and impudent braggart.[35]

With this assistance, Forster's readers would be sure to find out about Wainewright if they did not already know of him. The same kind of assistance came from William Jerdan, friendly to Bulwer through the years and habitually generous or over-generous to new books. "The principal characters are limned with terrible force," he said, and went on to recall the criminal Wainewright by name.[36]

During the period when *Lucretia* was being reviewed, Bulwer's letters to Forster, most of them unpublished, reveal his response to criticism; they show why this book became the last of the Newgate novels. They are best seen along with the reviews, which Bulwer seems to have read extensively. On December 7, he wrote to Forster, who had advised him about the preface to *Lucretia*, thanking him for the friendly *Examiner* review. "I foresee a storm against *Lucretia*," he said.[37]

He wrote again on December 9; his prediction had been borne out already. Portions of this letter—it became voluble and repeti-tive—are quoted by Bulwer's biographer: "The press, as far as I have seen it, sings one chorus of attack as if it was Jack Shep-pard out-shepparded." He feared the loss of a lawsuit because of the outcry. Then, below the signature of the letter, he burst out again:

> No. I was not prepared for such attacks. I do not see why my sub-ject should provoke them. Surely great crime is the highest province of fiction—it has always been so considered—from the Greeks to Shakespeare. It is the analysis of the prodigies thus startling that is the true work of the Master—is it not so?—And then I am told I

have no characters in Lucretia but Criminals—So Helen, Percival, John Ardworth, Sir Miles, Mr. Fielding all the contrasts to crime go for nothing.—I have heard from Mr. Smith [who had furnished the documents] who says Varney is Wainewright to the life—only the lust softened.—This I did not anticipate.[38]

In response to these letters, Forster printed an additional note about *Lucretia* on December 12, for which Bulwer was grateful.[39] But December 12 also brought a review in the *Spectator*, which had praised Bulwer's novels of the thirties; this one contained little praise, and condemnation was both stated and implied. The author of *Lucretia* was said to have "mortal unhealthiness of mind," being like some Elizabethan poets "in the nature, if not the extent of his genius." [40] No one else in modern English literature had so consistently made use of revolting crime.

The next important attack against *Lucretia* was a review in the *Times*—perhaps the most damaging attack of all, in view of that newspaper's large circulation and leading position among the London dailies. The article was a long one: more than two columns on the six-column page. The author of *Lucretia*, it said, had committed "a grave offence." As a scholar and a legislator, he knew "the risk of tampering with a trustful mind, easier to instruct in good than to guide when well informed of evil." The reviewer, with the patronizing air of the *Fraser* articles of the preceding decade, went on: "He is neither young in years nor strange to his work. He has been admonished; and wholesome truths, in time of need, have not been withheld from him. To some remonstrance comes in vain." [41] Mothers and fathers should not bring murderers to their hearths; and never, except in the Newgate Calendar itself, were so many murders seen within so few volumes. None in the Calendar was so monstrous.

> Parents, you are surprised! We are not! Four years ago Sir Edward Bulwer Lytton wrote a novel, and promised he would write no more. We did not believe him. We looked for this production. He had dallied so long with crime and criminals, had thrown so sickly a halo around the forms of vice, had taken such pleasure in the tricking out of naturally repulsive thoughts, that we knew it to be impossible for the man to depart for ever without some crowning work of hideousness and strangely morbid fancy. It is here, unre-

deemed and unredeemable,—a disgrace to the writer, a shame to us all!

The book was founded on fact? That was no excuse, for prisons and hospitals reeked with such melancholy truth; the newspaper knew how much truth was to be found in the annals of the police, and for good reason had to exclude from its reports "the sad humiliating evidence of natural corruption."

> Is it because Jack Sheppard lived that we are to be made the associates of a thief? Are we to shrink with horror from Thurtell paying the penalty of his crime on the scaffold, and yet shall our daughters become fascinated over the volume that in glowing language and glittering metaphor reveals "his great nobility of soul?"

Since the review gave no synopsis, *Times* readers who came upon nothing else about *Lucretia* must have inferred that Thurtell was in the novel and that Bulwer applied to him the quoted words. At the end, the reviewer struck a patronizing note:

> As you love your reputation and the privilege to be useful to your generation, Sir Edward Bulwer Lytton, avoid for the future all novels "founded upon fact." Or if you must needs indite them, apply to Miss Smith for her innocent notes on the Great Ferrers case and spare us horrors good for neither precept nor example.

On first reading it, at least, Bulwer attributed the review to his most persistent attacker. He wrote to Forster:

> Many thanks for your Note & sympathy as to the attack in the Times which greeted me at Breakfast this morning. It appears evidently Thackerys, & is written with the animus to do *me*, as well as the Book, as much harm as possible.—Certainly it has an injurious effect more or less—appearing in a journal so influential as the Times—He has frightened Saunders [*Lucretia* was published by Saunders and Otley] very much who is always a coward in these matters. Do you think that Fox, provided always he does not disapprove of the Book would write something of a counterblast in the Chronicle?—It would not do much perhaps—but it might do something— [42]

Two days later, on December 20, he wrote to Forster again, wishing to know whether public opinion was really on the side of the

Times. He had been working on a version of Sophocles' *Oedipus* for the stage and had commissioned original music to be composed for the production. Ought he to drop the plan? "True that this Drama is not mine but Sophocles's—. still I may be liable to the charge of having selected & revived that, of all the range of Greek Drama, for horrid & perverted purposes of my own." [43] Still capable of humor, he was nevertheless disturbed. The same letter continues:

> Can you inform me if I am right in ascribing the Art: in the Times to Thackery. And can you inform me also, how far you honestly and frankly (for I really want not to delude myself it is most important that I should not)—. how far I say, the general sentiment in the Times is shared by the Public—I see cause to fear, that, right or wrong, the feeling of reprobation is more wide and deep than I supposed—.& however unjust this may be it is well that I should know the truth—. in order to guide me, as to future publications & as to the best modes of removing the impression[.]

Bulwer's letters do not again mention Thackeray (or any other person) as author of the attack in the *Times*. Forster may have avowed ignorance, or he may have answered that Thackeray was innocent. The article certainly was not in Thackeray's manner.*

In a letter of December 24, Bulwer discussed Forster's suggestion about some kind of reply to the *Times* article, and because of Forster's letter was more uneasy about its public effect than he had been before. "To say truth, I did not read the Art. in the Times attentively—It gave me so much rage & pain that I hurried over it, without eye to a reply which at the moment I thought impossible." [44]

There was a review in *John Bull* on December 26; on the whole unfavorable, it made a distinct effort to be balanced. It found "ex-

---

* The last sentence of the *Times* article makes one think of Thackeray because of the humorous device it employs: "apply to Miss Smith for her innocent notes . . ." In 1841 he published *The Second Funeral of Napoleon, in Three Letters to Miss Smith, of London.* (*Works*, IV, 673ff.) The fictional Miss Smith of the title, variously addressed within the little book as my dear, madam, Amelia, and my love, is likewise innocent. But nothing else sounds like Thackeray, and the article as it stands cannot have been written by him. The remark about Bulwer near the beginning, "wholesome truths, in time of need, have not been withheld from him," has the old Fraserian tone. The *Times* article seems to have been written by one who remembered the controversy.

traordinary power and talent perverted from their legitimate uses"
and yet was able to call the book "a work of high genius." It found
too much fine writing but none of the author's earlier foppery. The
review made no personal attack.[45]

On January 1, 1847, two more of the London papers dealt with
Lucretia in extended reviews of some three and a half columns
each. Both told something of the story. Without attacking the author in the personal manner of the *Times*, these articles nevertheless hammered the book without restraint. That in the *Morning
Chronicle*, the daily next in importance after the *Times*, began by
remarking that if *Lucretia* came from an unknown author, a brief
rebuke would be enough; its inherent dullness would counteract its
inherent vice. There followed numerous complaints about inconsistencies in the story and in the delineation of character. Some of
them were trifling; the review did not do well at finding Bulwer's
really vulnerable spots. The heartless young Lucretia was quoted,
at the time when she looked forward to her uncle's death, and thus
commented upon: "Is it not painful to reflect upon the mischievous
influence which such monstrous sentiments as these may have upon
the weak-minded classes of society who are the chief supporters of
circulating libraries?" [46] Lucretia and Gabriel talked over their plans
"with a coarse open freedom which is perfectly revolting." Allowing that the novel may be founded on fact, were the facts fit for
poetic treatment? We have not written in vain, the reviewer concluded, if a single person has been deterred from investigating
"these unwholesome and tedious volumes." So ran the review in the
paper in which Bulwer had fondly hoped someone might be got to
speak in his favor.

The *Morning Herald* was somewhat harsher. Writers had had
a share in depraving the public mind, "as the sublime contempt for
law and decency exhibited by the Cliffords and Maltraverses can
testify." To those among the patrons of the circulating libraries who
bought their creed and their principles by the quarter, *Lucretia*
would be "as mischievous as those other works of the same author"
which avoided presenting the worst of crimes. Founded on fact?
Yes. But it was a mistake to try to use such a case as a moral example: "The great body of the people are too apt to sympathize with

criminals." The crude souvenir-hunting populace were described as readers of Bulwer and Ainsworth:

> Those readers of "Paul Clifford" and "Jack Sheppard" who carried off the bricks of the wall at Belsize Park, last year, as mementos, are too numerous a class to teach by such inadequate examples as are given in this book, and far too likely to admire what the author desires to make odious. . . . There is far too much of the slaughterhouse in the last two volumes not to revolt any reader whose taste would not also lead him to hire a window at the Old Bailey.[47]

After some comment on other matters, including a justified complaint about the coincidences, the *Herald* reviewer concluded by saying, "It would be hard to point to a worse novel than *Lucretia*."

Having read the papers, Bulwer wrote to Forster on the same day:

> This morning brought me the congratulations of the New Year in the shape of 2 Reviews in the Chronicle & the Herald for January 1st.—. This wholesale and general attack—. from so large a portion of the Press, drives me into thinking either that there is some concerted plan in certain quarters to scare me from writing—or that after all I am mistaken in Lucretia & myself—& that we are both bad & stupid alike—. . . It would be a great point of relief to my mind, not for the sake of retaliation but for my clearer judgment of myself and works—to know who wrote these sundry yet seemingly concerted attacks—Surely you must know & can inform me.— [48]

The coincidence—if it was a coincidence—of two reviews on the same day more than three weeks after publication of the book would be enough to cause any writer to wonder what was happening. (That this was also the day the first number of *Vanity Fair* was published can be nothing but a neat historical accident: Thackeray presents a mature novel at the moment the quietus is delivered to the type he has been jealously attacking.) Hitherto always confident, Bulwer was tortured into seriously questioning the validity of his own judgment and motives, and into doubting the rightness of his literary efforts. After a remark about the essay in defence, on which he is working, the same letter goes on with anguished inquiry. It need not be reproduced in full; its very length indicates the depth of the disturbance. He feels begirt with foes, as if he had walls around him, at a time when he would like to undertake larger and more varied experiments. Without the spur of poverty, can he force himself to make his way?

> Is there any mode by which this evil might be abated—whether in any amendment in myself whether by any plan of meeting my opponents—. Not having lived much among the literary masses, I want really insight into their motives, or their rationale of self-defence— But something there is evidently peculiar to my own case—

He cannot think of any other modern writer who has met with such malignity. Is there a remedy? A postscript, grasping at a straw, speculates upon the unequal influence of publishers.

The element of self-questioning in this letter, along with the public rejection which induced it, is an adequate explanation of why Bulwer wrote no more novels about criminals. He was yet to defend himself and to be attacked again, but one feels sure that the moment of decision has been reached with this letter.

Bulwer probably never saw the notice of *Lucretia* in *Reynolds's Miscellany* on January 2 which praised the novel and at the same time impudently accused Bulwer of imitating Reynolds' own *Faust* (which contained a tale of poisoning) and *Mysteries of London*.[49] The activities of Reynolds, the mere existence of the cheap serials, help to explain the reaction in the newspapers against *Lucretia*. Its notoriety, unlike that of *Jack Sheppard*, seems not to have been enhanced by the theatre; no one mentions plays based upon it.[50]

As for the magazines, the *New Monthly* for January carried a laudatory notice, and *Bentley's Miscellany* for February had a judicious and appraising one.[51] Ainsworth was then editor of the *New Monthly*. He or his reviewer, observing the storm, took the trouble to comment on the poor quality of the reviewing accorded to *Lucretia* and gave examples of the "tone of malevolence" of the detractors.

Fraser's did not review the novel, but the January number contained "A Grumble about the Christmas Books," by M. A. Titmarsh, *i.e.*, Thackeray. In the course of a genial and humorous complaint about a sad story by Mrs. Gore, there comes a comment on *Lucretia*:

> No, No! I am not jolly at a funeral. I confess that it does not amuse me. I have no taste for murders, or measles, or poison, or black jobs of any sort. We will have a word or two with Sir Edward Lytton Bulwer Lytton, Bart., presently, by the way, who for his infamous and murderous propensities, as lately shown in his most appalling and most arsenical novel of *Lucretia*, deserves to be brought up with a tight hand. But of this anon.[52]

A little later, Titmarsh remarks that "a poet does not take his inspirations from the copy-book or his pictures from the police-office."

When he comes to Mrs. Norton's *Drawing-Room Scrap Book*, he deals with Bulwer again: this time it is not *Lucretia* but some impossible verses which Bulwer had contributed to go with a picture of the editor of the volume. Thackeray quotes some of the lines:

> No human beauty ever bore
> An aspect thus divine:
> The crown the brows of seraphs wear
> Has left its mark on thine;—
> The unconscious glories round thee, bear
> The stamp divine,
> Of One divine,
> Who trod the spheres of yore.

Then come his urbane comments. At the end of them, Mrs. Norton has been praised, and Bulwer bears a razor-thin incision, showing blood:

> No! No! There's some error in the Bard's (or, to speak more correctly, the Bart's) description. This sort of writing, this flimsy, mystical, namby-pamby, we hold to be dangerous to men and reprehensible in Barts. When Irreverence puts on a sanctified look, when Mayfair begins to have revelations, when—but let us restrain our beautiful and outraged feelings, and return to the matter in hand.[53]

Thackeray's standard jest at Bulwer's title never came off so neatly; sentimental verse was never better disposed of. A page or two further on, Mrs. Norton's own verses become his subject: "What a mournful, artless beauty is here! What a brooding, tender woman's heart!"

It was apparently this article in *Fraser's* which roused Bulwer to desperation. Thackeray's playful needling very nearly resulted in catastrophe. Bulwer wrote asking to see Forster at once:

> The fact is I have seen Thackery's article & since it is published in the name he has acknowledged it enables me, of course, to call him out. I do not see how he can refuse it after using such expression [s.] But your kindness makes me inform you of this, before I act on it.—I trust, that you will approve my course.[54]

At first glance Thackeray's article seems an absurd ground for a challenge to a duel, but I know of no other offensive article of this month which bears a pseudonym known to belong to him. Bulwer's response, in the circumstances, is understandable. He knew the old sneers in *Fraser's*, the more recent jests in *Punch*. Without doubt, he still suspected Thackeray of being the author of the *Times* article; he probably thought him the instigator of the New Year's day attacks—and now he found with relief a signed article to lay hold of. What expression there would serve? "Irreverence," perhaps. It was not enough—what would be?—but Bulwer had been goaded too long.

He was prevented from carrying out the rash impulse. Perhaps, at bottom, he wished to be dissuaded—perhaps that was the unconscious reason for the note to Forster. Nevertheless, the record of strain in these letters makes a duel seem entirely possible, if strong advice had not been given. The next letter suggests that Forster's advice alone was not enough to prevent the challenge— Bulwer had gone on to Albany Fonblanque: "1st. As to Thackeray. Fonblanque is so decidedly of your opinion & even to a degree much more emphatic, that I submit, without further consultation." [55] The crisis was past.

Bulwer's urge to defend himself took shape in the pamphlet published under the title *A Word to the Public* on January 23 and later included with *Lucretia* as an after-piece. On January 28 he wrote to Forster that the pamphlet had been issued, but apparently without its most outspoken parts:

The preliminary part which you liked so well, has been almost wholly omitted, at the urgent instance of Fonblanque which was backed by the representative of the publishers themselves—The whole is toned down into one calm logical argument.[56]

He had given in reluctantly, he said, to the omissions.

His advisers, no doubt, served him well. Certainly the tone of the pamphlet was unexceptionable, Bulwer's attitude was dignified, he said nothing that could give cause for regret. It was a personal defence, but he gave a considerable portion of his space to the theory that crime had a proper place in literature and to illustrious examples of the fact. He listed his sixteen novels, mentioning also the plays, poems, essays, and history, and pointed out that in only three of them had a criminal occupied the position of hero: *Paul Clifford*, *Eugene Aram*, and *Lucretia*. He defended these in some detail, though he said little that had not already been said in prefaces. To those who approved the use of ancient crimes but protested going to Newgate and Tyburn, he had several appropriate replies; one of them was that the newspapers were the true literature of Newgate, and that the novel must do what was impossible for the newspaper. In Greek tragedy, he argued, Fate was the chief instrument of woe and crime; modern man found the source of guilt or woe within himself. Hence the greater need, in modern works, for mental analysis which would look into "the links between the thought and the sin."

Placed on sale in the bookshops, the pamphlet was also to be sent to all the hostile critics. It cannot have changed the opinions of any of them. The *Athenaeum* had the grace to answer it, somewhat inconsistently, in a short review; Jerdan gave it a long review and placed himself heartily on Bulwer's side, though he thought the provocation hardly worthy of an answer.[57] The attitude of Bulwer's friends may be represented by that of Macaulay, who had praised *Lucretia* in a letter and who wrote of *A Word to the Public*:

> It was not needed as far as I was concerned. . . . I utterly detest and despise that cry of immorality which was raised against you.
> The names of those who raised it I do not know, but I cannot doubt that they wrote under the influence of personal enmity. Your

vindication is undoubtedly well written and with great temper and dignity. But I am not sure that I should not have recommended silence as the best punishment for malignant scurrility.[58]

Vanity Fair AND "GEORGE DE BARNWELL"

Thackeray's potentially catastrophic article in the January *Fraser's* was not the end of his efforts; the campaign went on into the spring. The article was, however, the last of the long series of anti-Bulwerisms in *Fraser's*; indeed, none had appeared for an interval of five years although *Fraser's* had continued to disapprove of Newgate novels.[59] The gibes at Bulwer were gone because Thackeray, relying more and more upon *Punch*, had been writing little for *Fraser's*.[60]

In the early and middle forties, to go back a little in time, *Punch* had taken up the battle against Newgate fiction and become the vehicle for Thackeray's occasional Bulwer jokes. There were other squibs besides those known to be Thackeray's; one does not know how much his influence was responsible for bringing them forth. Often they were good-humored, like the "Literary Recipe for a Startling Romance," which appeared in 1841, the year *Punch* was founded. The first sentence of the "Recipe" alluded to *Oliver Twist*, Mrs. Trollope's *Michael Armstrong* (despite its lack of Newgate matter), and *Jack Sheppard*:

> Take a small boy, charity, factory, carpenter's apprentice, or otherwise as occasion may serve—stew him well down in vice—garnish largely with oaths and flash songs—boil him in a cauldron of crime and improbabilities.[61]

A series of valentines, in 1842, included one to The Literary Gentleman: a cartoon showed a writer at his table surrounded by the materials of his craft—a model of a gallows, a dagger, volumes of the *Newgate Calendar*. There was not much humor in the lines of verse below, which included an allusion to Dickens as well as to Ainsworth and Bulwer. They read, in part:

> But you, great scribe, more greedy of renown,
> From Hounslow's gibbet drag a hero down

Embue his mind with virtue; make him quote
Some moral truth, before he cuts a throat. . . .
Or would you picture woman meek and pure,
By love and virtue tutored to endure,
With cunning skill you take a felon's trull,
Stuff her with sentiment, and scrunch her skull! [62]

6. Artist Unknown, The Literary Gentleman, *Punch*, February 12,
1842

No more humorous was a pair of items, also in 1842, on the novelists' heroes in fiction and in fact. "Murderers as They Are and Murderers as They Ought to Be" dealt with Eugene Aram; in parallel
columns, short passages about him from Bulwer's novel were
printed alongside contradictory quotations from factual sources.
The second of the pair, "Felons . . ." did the same for Jack Shep-

pard. As late as 1845 Ainsworth's novel was still good for a scolding.[63]

Between 1844 and 1846 *Punch* contained a number of allusions to or jests at Bulwer, though not for his Newgate work; for example, *The Last of the Barons* was mentioned as "The Last of the Baronets." Most of them were Thackeray's, but not all have been so identified.[64] Those of 1845 were chiefly in his Jeames de la Pluche papers, and were not necessarily marked with Bulwer's name —as when Jeames entertains dukes, viscounts, and "barnits as many as I please." Different from these, however, was the angry rebuke Thackeray wrote when Ainsworth, taking over the *New Monthly*, advertised authors "eminent not only for talent, but for high rank." [65] Bulwer is to be discerned behind the visible target here, but Thackeray's scorn for such sycophancy was genuine. "The Snobs of England," which ran in *Punch* through most of 1846 and ended early the next year, contained no reference to the Newgate controversy.

The most interesting of the anti-Newgate articles in *Punch*, Thackeray's famous "George de Barnwell," was to come in the spring of 1847. This parody of Bulwer was to be the first of a series, "Punch's Prize Novelists." We shall return to it, but for the sake of chronology we must at this point consider *Vanity Fair*, already mentioned as beginning on January 1. Thackeray's campaign against the Newgate writers was linked again—but far more effectively than in *Catherine*—with an effort to establish his own book in public favor and to establish his own realistic attitude in the public taste. Gordon Ray, commenting on the revolutionary character of *Vanity Fair*, reminds us that the novel and the parodies were together an assault on popular conventions of fiction:

> Everywhere in *Vanity Fair*, indeed, he displays his awareness of how different his book is from what Victorian readers had come to expect, and his determination that they shall be brought to realize the superiority of what he has to offer. Perhaps these objectives are seen most clearly in the part-issue text of Chapter 6, which opens with burlesques of the Newgate and silver-fork styles of novel-writing. These pages also serve as a reminder that Thackeray's series, "Punch's Prize Novelists," appeared in that periodical concurrently with the early numbers of *Vanity Fair*. Obviously he

had planned his attack with care, bringing to bear at once the sixteen-inch guns of his great novel and the forty-millimeter artillery of his magazine parodies.[66]

In fact several early chapters of *Vanity Fair* contain echoes of the Newgate controversy. (They were not inspired by *Lucretia*, for they exist in slightly different form in the manuscript which dates from 1845.) "I know that the tune I am piping is a very mild one," he begins in Chapter VI, and deliberately reminds the reader that the tale deals with people in common life. Will Jos Sedley marry Rebecca? "That is the great subject now in hand." The next paragraph, the second of the chapter, suggests how it might sound if differently treated.

> We might have treated this subject in the genteel, or in the romantic, or in the facetious manner. Suppose we had laid the scene in Grosvenor Square, with the very same adventures—would not some people have listened? Suppose we had shown how Lord Joseph Sedley fell in love, and the Marquis of Osborne became attached to Lady Amelia, with the full consent of the duke, her noble father: or instead of the supremely genteel, suppose we had resorted to the entirely low, and described what was going on in Mr. Sedley's kitchen;—how black Sambo was in love with the cook (as indeed he was), and how he fought a battle with the coachman in her behalf; how the knife-boy was caught stealing a cold shoulder of mutton, and Miss Sedley's new *femme de chambre* refused to go to bed without a wax candle; such incidents might be made to provoke much delightful laughter, and be supposed to represent scenes of "life." Or if, on the contrary, we had taken a fancy for the terrible, and made the lover of the new *femme de chambre* a professional burglar, who bursts into the house with his band, slaughters black Sambo at the feet of his master, and carries off Amelia in her night-dress, not to be let loose again till the third volume, we should easily have constructed a tale of thrilling interest, through the fiery chapters of which the reader should hurry, panting. But my readers must hope for no such romance, only a homely story, and must be content with a chapter about Vauxhall, which is so short that it scarce deserves to be called a chapter at all. And yet it is a chapter, and a very important one too. Are not there little chapters in everybody's life, that seem to be nothing, and yet affect all the rest of the history?

At that point, in most editions of the novel, we are asked to "step into the coach with the Russell Square party" and be off to Vauxhall Gardens.

In February 1847, the burlesques so briefly suggested in that one paragraph were amplified; the terrible and the genteel were each illustrated at more length. The terrible runs thus, following immediately after *panting* in the quotation above:

Fancy this chapter having been headed

THE NIGHT ATTACK

The night was dark and wild—the clouds black—black—ink-black. The wild wind tore the chimney-pots from the roofs of the old houses and sent the tiles whirling and crashing through the desolate streets. No soul braved that tempest—the watchmen shrank into their boxes, whither the searching rain followed them—where the crashing thunderbolt fell and destroyed them—one had been so slain opposite the Foundling. A scorched gaberdine, a shivered lantern, a staff rent in twain by the flash, were all that remained of stout Will Steadfast. A hackney coachman had been blown off his coach-box, in Southampton Row—and whither? But the whirlwind tells no tidings of its victim, save his parting scream as he is borne onwards! Horrible night! It was dark, pitch dark; no moon. No, no. No moon. Not a star. Not a little feeble, twinkling, solitary star. There had been one at early evening, but he showed his face, shuddering, for a moment in the black heaven, and then retreated back.

One, two, three! It is the signal that Black Vizard had agreed on.

"Mofy! Is that your snum?" said a voice from the area. "I'll gully the dag and bimbole the clicky in a snuffkin."

"Nuffle your clod, and beladle your glumbanions," said Vizard, with a dreadful oath. "This way, men: if they screak, out with your snickers and slick! Look to the pewter-room, Blowser. You, Mark, to the old gaff's mopus box! and I," added he, in a lower but more horrible voice, "I will look to Amelia!"

There was a dead silence. "Ha!" said the Vizard, "was that the click of a pistol?" [67]

The description of the stormy night parodies the storm scene in Chapters VI and VII (First Epoch) of *Jack Sheppard*; the remainder suggests in part Ainsworth and his underworld slang but is aimed equally at Eugene Sue.

Then follows the silver-fork passage, of nearly a page, after which Thackeray comes to his point:

> Thus you see, ladies, how this story *might* have been written, if the author had but a mind; for, to tell the truth, he is just as familiar with Newgate as with the palaces of our revered aristocracy, and has seen the outside of both. But as I don't understand the language or manners of the Rookery, nor that polyglot conversation which, according to the fashionable novelists, is spoken by the leaders of *ton*; we must, if you please, preserve our middle course modestly, amidst these scenes and personages with which we are most familiar.[68]

So it was in 1847. In 1853, however, the Newgate controversy was a thing of the past, and Thackeray removed what was no longer of current interest.[69]

Chapter VII, in the same February number, ends with a paragraph of Dickensian nostalgia for the days of the stage-coach, in which is an easy-going remark about novels.

> To those great geniuses now in petticoats, who shall write novels for the beloved reader's children, these men and things will be as much legend and history as Nineveh, or Coeur de Lion, or Jack Sheppard. For them, stage-coaches will have become romances—a team of four bays as fabulous as Bucephalus or Black Bess.[70]

The next chapter, which appeared in the following number, included a passage which not only recalls the controversy but is significant for the technique of the whole novel. Thackeray is now presenting a central figure from whom he must dissociate himself quite as much as he had from Catherine Hayes. In the interval since *Catherine*, he had also met the problem in *The Luck of Barry Lyndon* (1844); in that story, told in the first person, he separated himself from the rogue and domestic bully by means of editorial footnotes. Now in *Vanity Fair* he develops to the fullest extent the method of the author-showman, in full view of the audience, whose comments on the characters are interlaced with the third-person narrative. In Chapter VIII, which opens the March number, Rebecca writes a long letter to Amelia Sedley describing the crudities

of Sir Pitt and life at Queen's Crawley. It is followed by a discursive
address from author to reader, announcing that disagreeable matter
must be expected when the truth is told about Vanity Fair. The
closing paragraphs are these:

> I warn my "kyind friends," then, that I am going to tell a story
> of harrowing villainy and complicated—but, as I trust, intensely
> interesting—crime. My rascals are no milk-and-water rascals, I
> promise you. When we come to the proper places we won't spare
> fine language—No, no! But when we are going over the quiet coun-
> try we must perforce be calm. A tempest in a slop-basin is absurd.
> We will reserve that sort of thing for the mighty ocean and the
> lonely midnight. The present Number will be very mild. Others—
> But we will not anticipate *those*.
>
> And, as we bring our characters forward, I will ask leave, as a
> man and a brother, not only to introduce them, but occasionally to
> step down from the platform and talk about them: if they are good
> and kindly, to love them and shake them by the hand: if they are
> silly, to laugh at them confidentially in the reader's sleeve: if they
> are wicked and heartless, to abuse them in the strongest terms
> which politeness admits of.
>
> Otherwise you might fancy it was I who was sneering at the
> practice of devotion, which Miss Sharp finds so ridiculous; that it
> was I who laughed good-humoredly at the reeling old Silenus of a
> baronet—whereas the laughter comes from one who has no rever-
> ence except for prosperity, and no eye for anything beyond success.
> Such people there are living and flourishing in the world—Faith-
> less, Hopeless, Charityless: let us have at them, dear friends, with
> might and main. Some there are, and very successful too, mere
> quacks and fools: and it was to combat and expose such as those,
> no doubt, that Laughter was made.[71]

Gordon Ray, having examined the manuscript form of these
early chapters, points out that the whole address after Rebecca's letter, including the paragraphs just quoted, was added late in 1846,
when Thackeray set to work again on the novel after an interval
when he was occupied with other things. In October or November
he hit upon the title *Vanity Fair* (the chapters previously written
had gone under the name of "The Novel Without a Hero"), made
revisions, and continued the writing with enthusiasm.

The chapters that Thackeray wrote in 1845 were very much in the vein of "The Luck of Barry Lyndon" [the irony of which had not been understood by some readers]; they form a detached, non-committal narrative in which the reader is told what happened, but rarely what to think about it. In revising his story Thackeray added a number of passages of moral commentary to supply this lack; and having fallen into this habit, he remained close at the reader's side during the rest of the book in his new capacity of "Manager of the Performance." [72]

Without denying the influence of the reception of *Barry Lyndon*, one can see another influence at work in the passage quoted from the novel: the Newgate controversy. It is clear that Thackeray has thought of it; in that context, we do not find it odd that he should announce "a story of harrowing villainy and complicated—but, as I trust, intensely interesting—crime." The faults of Bulwer's style are recalled: "When we come to the proper places we won't spare fine language." It is after this reminiscent paragraph that Thackeray says he will not only introduce the characters but occasionally "step down from the platform and talk about them"; and thereafter gives his reason: "Otherwise you might fancy it was I" who sneered at devotion and took evil lightly. Mr. Ray reminds us that *Eugene Aram* was reissued in 1846 and that Thackeray's revulsion against it was renewed.[73] Thackeray was soon to write the parody of it, "George de Barnwell." Both the substance and the timing, therefore, of Thackeray's address to the reader suggest that he had been thinking of the problem of the Newgate authors as well as of his own in *Barry Lyndon*. Indeed, the problem of that story was identical, technically, with that of *Eugene Aram*: Thackeray's rascal gives his own monologue, and Bulwer's murderer wrote his confession. Separating author from fictional mischief-maker would seem to be much more easily accomplished in the third-person *Vanity Fair*. Thackeray, however, about to deal extensively in worldly evil, took no chances; and he proceeded to make a virtue out of what he saw as necessity. His commentary flavors the novel throughout; the effect is like that which Joseph Conrad, for example, was later to achieve with Marlow as a narrator. There seems every reason to suppose that the experience of the Newgate controversy impelled Thackeray toward this development in *Vanity Fair*.[74]

One other question raised by the Newgate controversy lurks in the early chapters of *Vanity Fair* and demands at least to be recognized. Sir Pitt Crawley, introduced in Chapter VII and further described in Chapter VIII, is a baronet; his rank and title are much emphasized there and in other chapters where he appears, though in some places the title merely serves to distinguish him from his son of the same name.

In view of Thackeray's frequent satirical thrusts at Bulwer's title, one is forced to ask whether Sir Pitt Crawley's baronetcy itself is another stroke in the duel. Bulwer and Sir Pitt have nothing in common but the title; Sir Pitt is a member of parliament, but at the time of *Vanity Fair* Bulwer no longer held a seat there. However, of perhaps six hundred baronets listed in Debrett, Thackeray had previously attacked only one. Sir Pitt a baronet because Bulwer is one? The question has become necessary, but the answer is No.

The introduction of Sir Pitt is hugely comic. Young Rebecca, before she sees him, is dazzled by the prospect of being governess in a baronet's family; she will be lowly, but she will no longer be among vulgar City people. She is taken to his house, and is incredulous: he is ill-dressed, ill-educated, ill-mannered, miserly—he is everything, in short, that an aristocrat should not be, and the shocked reader despises him while laughing at Becky's discomfiture. Some contemporary readers were incredulous also; Thackeray's reply was that Sir Pitt was an exact portrait.[75] As we go on reading, we find, of course, that this is an anti-society novel: lords and their ladies—especially their ladies—are shown to be snobbish wasters; baron and marquis are treated no better than baronet. Sir Pitt's crude lack of pretence becomes almost a virtue; he is not a hypocrite. Moreover, Thackeray's broad social criticism attacks not merely the whole aristocracy but the materialism of the middle class; Mr. Osborne's false values are dealt with as severely as the myth of aristocracy. Against both, Thackeray's passion is bitter and deep.

Sir Pitt is a baronet presumably because the baronetage, most recently established of the orders, politically created and not anciently rooted in the feudal system, had been criticized occasionally from its beginning. Until the eighteenth century, there was no serious attempt at registry of it; baronetcies had been assumed improperly. Among the nobility, baronets were most vulnerable and hence a fit choice for first place in Thackeray's satire. Baronets rather conscious of place and title are not uncommon in mid-Victorian fiction.

In context, nevertheless, these early chapters about the elder Sir Pitt Crawley must have been seen by contemporary readers as part of a succession of satirical remarks about baronets, in which one baronet had figured by name. There were the jests for several years past in *Punch*; there was the article in *Fraser's* in January ("dangerous to men and reprehensible in Barts"); Sir Pitt appeared in February; Rebecca's letter reporting life at Queen's Crawley came in March. Here (Chapter VIII) she mentions that the hall bears "the dove and serpent of the house." Possibly Thackeray was not aware that Bulwer's crest and coat of arms included doves; they are, however, rare among the heraldic emblems of baronets. (There are eagles and falcons in numbers, as one flips through Debrett, but doves are few indeed—there are more Cornish choughs.) In the same March number, in Chapter IX, was a slanting reference to the red hand of Ulster, which every baronet was entitled to display:

> in a word, the whole baronetage, peerage, commonage of England, did not contain a more cunning, mean, selfish, foolish, disreputable old man. That blood-red hand of Sir Pitt Crawley's would be in anybody's pocket except his own; and it is with grief and pain, that, as admirers of the British aristocracy, we find ourselves obliged to admit the existence of so many ill qualities in a person whose name is in Debrett.[76]

Despite the thousands of words he had written since the end of 1840, can one suppose that Thackeray had quite forgotten his remark in *Catherine* that Bulwer "hath lately, in compliment to his writings, been gratified by permission to wear a bloody hand"? In April came "George de Barnwell" in *Punch*, prominently marked as being by "Sir E.L.B.L.BB.LL.BBB.LLL., Bart." And in Chapter XV of *Vanity Fair*, in May, Sir John Redhand is used briefly to signify any baronet, whose favor untitled persons may covet.

In this continuing obsession with baronets, the very chronology constitutes a sort of link between the real baronet and the fictional. Contemporary readers familiar with the magazine world of 1847 and ten years preceding, readers who had observed the Newgate hostilities, would see the association. When Sir Pitt first appeared, the question of whether another attack on Bulwer was imminent must certainly have occurred to Forster, to Fonblanque, to Ainsworth, to Dickens, and to Bulwer himself if he read the serial.

The extension of the commentator's technique and the topical allusions of these early chapters are not the only elements of *Vanity Fair* which recall the Newgate involvement. There is also the concluding event of the plot itself, in which Rebecca murders Joseph Sedley and returns to England to live a life of gentility, presumably with his money. The narration, in the last pages of the last chapter, is gracefully muted and very brief; Thackeray uses the method of hints and equivocations which he has used earlier to tell of the adultery with Lord Steyne. Some readers seem hardly to notice the murder; on the other hand, several twentieth-century critics have objected violently that it is out of character and an unbelievable fault in the book. The objectors have a case, and perhaps the murder shows Thackeray's lingering involvement in a literary effort he ought to have left behind. Nevertheless, there is a case for him too, and the murder is not to be seen as the last-minute impulse of a writer hastily winding up the affairs of his characters. A careful reading discloses that Rebecca's ultimate evil is at least prepared for. Thackeray does not make her first an unfortunate outsider whose peccadilloes we can forgive because we delight in her ingenuity—and then turn her suddenly into an amoral criminal who will stop at nothing.

In Chapter VIII, the author promised a story of harrowing villainy and complicated crime, with "no milk-and-water rascals." Present-day readers may take this as all jest; Thackeray's contemporaries, with a recollection of Newgate novels, must have expected something from it. Apart from Becky's miscellaneous cold deceptions, the specific anticipation of the murder occurs in Chapter LI, where she acts triumphantly in the charades at Gaunt House. She is magnificent as Clytemnestra murdering her husband; Lord Steyne, shouting applause, also mutters, "By —, she'd do it too." A member of the royal family is impressed. Thackeray's illustration shows Becky, deferential, receiving the congratulations of His Royal Highness, with the huge dagger still in her hand. The scene is highly

7. W. M. THACKERAY, Becky's Second Appearance in the Character of
Clytemnestra. Final chapter, *Vanity Fair*, 1848.

suggestive: the dagger symbolizes the means—unscrupulous and even violent—which she is willing to use to break into society. Let her use the weapon well enough, and she may hold it naked in her hand at the moment of highest social success.

The final chapter, if we remember Lord Steyne's words, ought not to surprise us unduly. Joseph Sedley, now constantly accompanied by Becky, has insured his life; Dobbin goes to Brussels to see him. They suppose themselves alone, but Thackeray's illustration shows a dark, hideously glowering Rebecca listening behind a curtain. It is entitled, "Becky's second appearance in the character of Clytemnestra"; her first, we now see, was no charade but a chilling prediction of fact. Joseph insists that he is not in financial trouble, that Becky's character is spotless, that she has nursed him like a daughter. At the same time, he is horribly afraid of her. She must not know of their private talk: "She'd—she'd kill me if she knew it." Dobbin would take him away that moment, but Jos will not go. He dies at Aix-la-Chapelle three months later, leaving nothing substantial except the two thousand pounds of insurance, to be divided equally between his sister and Mrs. Rawdon Crawley. The insurance is at first refused, but Becky comes to London and overwhelms the company with her histrionic innocence and the legal pressure of her solicitors, Messrs. Burke, Thurtell, and Hayes. (Could any three names sound more professional?) Thackeray says with casual, bitter irony, "the money was paid, and her character established." Dobbin returns Amelia's share. Becky, who seems to have more wealth than Joseph's insurance and an allowance from her son, finds sympathy in some quarters; her new life includes a busy round of public charities. In Vanity Fair, in the eighteen-thirties, the criminal "goes to church, and never without a footman. Her name is in all the Charity Lists. The Destitute Orange-girl, the Neglected Washerwoman, the Distressed Muffin-man, find in her a fast and generous friend." Dobbin and Amelia see her at a booth in a charity fair, and Thackeray's picture, like the story itself, emphasizes Becky the actress. In contrast with the dark Clytemnestra figure in the preceding one, Becky on public display is fair and smiles demurely.

Within two short pages, then, Thackeray writes a little parallel to Bulwer's Lucretia—a poisoner versus an insurance company—and to his own Catherine. Vanity Fair almost becomes the last of the Newgate novels. Perhaps this strains credulity, perhaps murder is too far outside the range of the probable in ordinary life, but Thackeray must have been well aware of this hazard. That he chose to do as he did shows not only the intensity of his desire to challenge and surpass Bulwer but—more importantly—the benign rage he felt against selfishness, materialism, and hypocrisy. His attack upon the society which denies goodness and the heart must be as violent as he can make it: therefore, Becky's ultimate wickedness followed by her tranquil success.

To return at last to *Punch*, the "Prize Novelists," later called *Novels by Eminent Hands*, included Disraeli, Mrs. Gore, G. P. R. James, Charles Lever, and Fenimore Cooper. Before the series began, we find it mentioned in a letter, which, in view of what has appeared from Bulwer's letters (above, pp. 194–201) takes on additional interest. Thackeray wrote to Albany Fonblanque, January 27, 1847 (only a few days, incidentally, before the publication of the second number of *Vanity Fair*, containing the impossible baronet, Sir Pitt):

> My dear Fonblanque.
>
> A great qualm has just come over me, about our conversation this morning. I am going to do a series of novels by the most popular authors for Punch and Bulwer's is actually done, the blocks designed and the Story in progress it is George Barnwell. He will quote Plato speak in Big Phrases, and let out his Nunkys old &c— numbers of others are to follow Cooper, James, Dickens, Lever &c. but they will all be good natured—and I cant afford to give up my plan. It is my bread indeed for next year.
>
> I am bound to tell you this (How the deuce did I forget it in our talk this morning?) lest you should be putting your hospitable intentions into execution, and after having had my legs sub iisdem trabibus with Bulwer I sh^d seem to betray him—I cant leave him out of the caricatures—all that I promise is to be friendly and meek in spirit.[77]

The conversation mentioned took place perhaps three weeks after Fonblanque and Forster had persuaded Bulwer not to call Thackeray out. They undoubtedly hoped that a personal acquaintance would bring some measure of understanding or at least would dampen hostility. One can imagine Fonblanque saying to Thackeray that he was thinking of a dinner . . . and naming, casually, some of those he hoped to have at his table, including Thackeray and Bulwer. Thackeray had not refused the hospitable overture— and then thought better of it. If we accept his determination that the parody must appear, we must approve his avoidance of meeting Bulwer, with legs under the same board. Nevertheless, we feel a touch of regret. In 1858, Thackeray wrote, "Why, when I used to lampoon a certain Bulwer, I had never seen him but in a public place, and had no kind of animosity to him. If I had I should never have attacked him." [78] The remark, "If I had . . . ," is less than candid.

"George de Barnwell" was not forestalled, then; it appeared in *Punch* in the issues of April 3, 10, and 17. Like the others which came after it, it was a delicious exercise in parody, but good-natured only in comparison with what had preceded it, and not meek in spirit. Thackeray chose for his target not the recent *Lucretia* but the more vulnerable *Eugene Aram*, published fifteen years earlier.[79] It had been republished in 1846, as we have already observed. Thackeray had shown in the March number of *Vanity Fair* that he knew how to deal with moral delinquency in fiction; he had even complicated the matter by having Rebecca report on Sir Pitt, after which he had exposed both of them. He now proceeded to make fun of Bulwer for not knowing so much. He knew very well— it is impossible to suppose that he did not know—what was the matter with *Eugene Aram*: that the author had not properly separated himself from the character. But who wanted to read a technical criticism? Thackeray set himself instead to exploiting the novel satirically and to alienating its readers.

Taking up Lillo's familiar play—an inspired choice—he retold the story in a mockery of Bulwer's worst style, with all its mannerisms exaggerated for display. The Greek and Latin phrases were there; the fine abstractions, the Ideal, the Beautiful; the general magniloquence of Bulwer's purple. *Eugene Aram* was not the only book to which Thackeray put the knife; his second section delightfully mocked Bulwer's historical inconsistencies in *Devereux*. Thackeray's serious point, in the midst of all the gaiety, was that Eugene Aram had been portrayed as virtuous and noble; so much, we can agree, Bulwer deserved. The satire cheerfully omitted Bulwer's serious point: that the intellect might delude and that Eugene Aram had made himself the victim of a selfish rationalization. Thackeray retained some of the old tricks he had used so many times before: the playing with Bulwer's name, and the constant addition of the title Bart. He even added a subtle allusion to Bulwer's dressing his hair with oil. These are trivial weaknesses in a sharp and entertaining deflation of pomposity.

Without doubt, "George de Barnwell" was chiefly responsible for Bulwer's revision of *Eugene Aram*, already described in connection with that novel.[80] Whether the parody alone would have turned Bulwer permanently away from criminal themes it is impossible to say. The self-scrutiny and the appraisal of his literary fortunes induced by the *Lucretia* disturbance were a sufficient cause.

Attended by animosities from its beginning, the Newgate story could not end without one more outburst of tempers. At this distance in time, it can be read as high comedy. Thackeray, told that Forster had called him "as false as hell," refused to shake Forster's hand when he next met him in company. There followed letters, conferences through intermediaries, more letters, and finally reconciliation.[81] Forster's anger and his phrase seem best explained by his reading the new attack on Bulwer, "George de Barnwell" (without even the publication of a new book to excuse it)—and his remembering what had happened some three months before. He may well have been thinking of the challenge nearly sent, of the invitation to Fonblanque's peace-making forestalled—may well have said "false" about the writer with a new novel then appearing who had described the satires as his "bread" for next year.[82] After this occasion, Thackeray in his turn had moments of self-searching; a letter of great intimacy (dated July 2) shows how deep the inquiry went:

> Jerrold hates me, Ainsworth hates me, Dickens mistrusts me, Forster says I am false as hell, and Bulwer curses me—he is the only one who has any reason—yes, the others have a good one too as times go. I was the most popular man in the craft until within ab^t 12 months—and behold I've begun to succeed. It makes me very sad at heart though, this envy and meanness—in the great sages & teachers of the world. Am I envious and mean too I wonder? Those fellows think so I know. Amen. God knows only. I scarcely understand any motive for any action of my own or anybody else's—[83]

The novelist who came to be admired for his largeness of spirit was the man who had learned to ask the hard question, "Am I envious and mean too I wonder?" and to wonder, at least for a little time, about his own motives.

As the Newgate novels came to an end with *Lucretia*, so Thackeray's attacks upon Bulwer, in which he had indulged from his twenty-eighth to his thirty-eighth year, came to an end with "George de Barnwell." Thackeray had won his battle. Would he have continued it if Bulwer and Ainsworth had written more crime novels? Probably not, for the end of the battle coincided with his success as a novelist. (We ought to keep in mind that it coincided also with his questioning of his own motives.) He had discovered his powers; he could teach by example rather than precept. He was recognized, he was successful in the eyes of the world. No longer dissatisfied with his own achievement, he could look with a more comfortable spirit upon the obviously smaller work of others, which had galled him when the world seemed determined to grant its favors to wrong-headedness and bad taste. At times, after 1849, he uttered explanations and regrets. Those in private had a patronizing tone and were accompanied by self-exculpation. On the other hand, the public apology printed in a New York preface was unmarred and graceful; it came, if not from the heart, at least from a personal center of good feeling and good taste.

Among the magazine pieces reprinted by the American publisher were two Yellowplush papers Thackeray now found regrettable; in his preface, he wondered at "the recklessness of the young man who could fancy such satire was harmless jocularity, and never calculate that it might give pain." He wrote Bulwer, on June 21, 1853, to inform him of this "cry of peccavi." [84] The letter was perhaps a little too confident that the apology was adequate, but until he was sure of himself as a novelist Thackeray could not have made the apology.

Thackeray's campaign against Newgate fiction was confined to the "literary" novelists—it never extended to Salisbury Square. Why did he not make some satirical effort, even though the penny serials were too low to be treated as literature? He condemned the *Mysteries of Paris* in an article and later did a *Punch* cartoon depicting Sue and Dumas as the cabmen's favorite reading, but he did not deal similarly with G. W. M. Reynolds.[85] There is a playful satirical allusion to Reynolds' work in the 1853 lecture, "Charity and Humour." The author is not named, and the target of the jest is the repetitive attack on the vices of the aristocracy. Perhaps Reynolds' immunity was the result of his having employed Thackeray briefly in Paris in 1836; he was the first publisher, Thackeray once said, who paid him for his writing.[86] Whatever the reason for the restraint, the inclusion of Reynolds would have given more consistency to Thackeray's warfare. He did not concern himself with the morality of what was offered to the lower classes.

The omission was soon to be remedied by other hands. Some six months after "George de Barnwell," near the end of October 1847, the *Daily News*, full of the crusading enthusiasm first instilled in it by its founders, began a series of three articles by Hepworth Dixon, "The Literature of the Lower Orders," describing the cheap literature as vicious in its influence.[87] The articles were much talked about and were noticed in other publications. The first dealt chiefly with Lloyd's publications; on these, Mrs. Dalziel considers Dixon too severe. The second included comment on *Reynolds's Miscellany*, *Mysteries of London*, and the publications of G. J. Holyoake, regarded as pernicious for his anti-religious attitude. *Mysteries of London* was described as worse than Eugene Sue. Of certain others, including the stories in *Reynolds's Miscellany*, Dixon wrote a comment which reflected upon other authors than those of the cheap serials:

> Their looseness, warmth of colouring in the criminal scenes, and of the false glow cast round guilty indulgencies, are their bane; but, unfortunately, these qualities are hardly sufficient to separate them from much of the literature of the day, which aspires to different rank, and proposes to itself a higher kind of audience.[88]

He did not name any titles from "the literature of the day"; the articles kept to their subject. They added weight, however, to the attacks that had been made upon the literature of crime. The *Examiner* called sympathy with criminals a disease in the courts; it saw a love of mischief, of wanton cruelty, springing up among the people: "We want a Sanatory Commission to explore the foul reading to which we owe so much disease."[89] No immediate change resulted from the newspaper attack, but this one was not the last. Mrs. Dalziel points out that Reynolds' work in the later fifties reduced its emphasis on sex and violence so much as not to give offence.

The age of newspaper sociology had begun. It arrived at a remarkable maturity with the series of articles which Henry Mayhew began to write for the *Morning Chronicle* in the autumn of 1849 and which were later collected into *London Labour and the London Poor* (1851). These accounts of the street folk and the laborers in unrecognized occupations were an astonishing revelation. They are astonishing still in their patience, their sympathy, their overwhelming detail. As one reads Mayhew's description of the costermongers—the barbarian nomads of England, he calls them, in contrast with the civilized persons of settled lives and habitations—and all the teeming underlife of London, it does not appear that even *Jack Sheppard* could have had significant influence upon them. They lived the life they were brought up to; no other sort of life presented itself as possible, and poverty enforced what custom transmitted. Apart from poverty, Mayhew shows whole classes of people little touched by any influence from outside or above. He deplores the immoral influence of the penny gaffs, where the songs were lewd, the jokes obscene; he speaks again and again of the vicious cheap lodging houses, the only places where many street children could stay at night. The fourth or "Extra" volume does indeed mention some familiar names. Bracebridge Hemyng, author of the section on "Prostitution in London," deploring the immorality of the young, speaks of the cheap serials:

> Another very fruitful source of early demoralisation is to be looked for in the quantities of penny and halfpenny romances that are sold in town and country. One of the worst of the most recent ones is denominated, "Charley Wag, or the New Jack Shepherd, a history of the most successful thief in London." To say that these are not incentives to lust, theft, and crime of every description is to cherish a fallacy.[90]

John Binny, author of the "Thieves and Swindlers" section of the same volume, quotes a sneak thief as follows:

> On Sunday evenings the only books read were such as "Jack Sheppard," "Dick Turpin," and the "Newgate Calendar" they got

out of the neighboring libraries by depositing 1 s. These were read with much interest; the lodgers would sooner have these than any other books.

The 'Jack Sheppard' which is named may have been Ainsworth's book, but it may have been a cheap imitation. Even in the one-volume reprint, could the street-boys have borrowed the Ainsworth book on a one-shilling deposit? Binny tells of a former pick-pocket, son of a Wesleyan minister, who had read Paine, Volney, Holyoake, Bulwer, and Dickens, but there is no assertion that his reading took him into crime.

A burglar told Binny of going to the Victoria theatre to see plays about Oliver Twist and Jack Sheppard. Having gone with a friend to the Sheppard play a second time, "We were both remarkably pleased . . . and soon after determined to try our hand at housebreaking." This seems to be a genuine piece of evidence in its way, but its import is very limited. As an orphan of nine, the burglar-to-be had gone to work, and had been taught by his older brother to commit petty thefts; through the older brother he had become acquainted with bad companions, with the result that he was well on his way before the Sheppard drama made him think of house-breaking.

In 1852, a House of Commons inquiry into the situation of Criminal and Destitute Juveniles also obtained information on such matters. Many kinds of facts were entered in the report, but the frequency with which Turpin, Sheppard, and the theatre were mentioned—and knowledge of them tabulated—is a proof that the perturbation caused by Ainsworth spread far and lasted long. The informants were magistrates, prison inspectors, a prison chaplain, a secretary of the Ragged School Union, and the like, as well as interested volunteers. Unquestionably they spoke with ample knowledge. All who had seen the penny theatres, sometimes called singing or concert rooms, called them pernicious; in London the audience consisted chiefly of boy thieves and young prostitutes. Some sort of Jack Sheppard performance was a favorite in them. Large numbers of juvenile offenders were found to be familiar with the lives of Turpin and Sheppard; it seems fairly obvious, however, that their condition turned them toward these heroes—not that an interest in Turpin and Sheppard made them into offenders.[91] On the other hand, the favorable representation of such "heroes" may well have been a further inducement to boys already delinquent. Some of the men who reported to the Committee had undoubtedly asked leading questions; the alacrity with which boys affirmed that the theatre had influenced them for the worse ("I am certain that the theatre has been my ruin") shows how pleased they were to lay hold of an acceptable excuse. The Select Committee's *Report* includes among its appendices the report of an inspector of prisons compiled in 1841, when the Sheppard craze was at its initial height.[92] Making a heavy allowance for the predisposition of the inspector, one still cannot explain away his evidence: some boys were indeed made worse by the admiration they conceived for the Sheppard they saw on the stage.

One comes to the conclusion that the novels of Ainsworth—much less those of Bulwer and Dickens—did not lead ragged boys into crime, if only because in their regularly published forms they did not reach those who might seriously have thought Jack Sheppard a hero to be imitated. There is ground for believing, on the other hand, that imitations and derived versions, including those on the stage, did sometimes exert an undesirable influence upon boys whose condition made them susceptible, boys who already had had a taste of petty crime or who were already subject to corrupting influences in their daily environment. In the way of direct incitement to bad behavior this is all that can be alleged. If it touches any of the three writers, the criticism touches only Ainsworth, who is also the least when considered as artist or thinker.

CONCLUSIONS

In summary, the Newgate novels extend over a period of seventeen years—as it happens, from just before the Reform Act to just after the repeal of the corn laws. The Newgate novel began as an instrument of protest against the severity of criminal law and against the structure of class privilege which that law represented. Its political and social alignment was set by Bulwer and later taken up by Dickens; in the struggle between the haves and the have-nots (a phrase which Bulwer coined), the crime novel was on the side of the dispossessed. Both writers advanced the proposition that crime is in part the creation of harsh law and social injustice. Only one novel which preached legal reform came early enough to permit it to have effect on the climactic reductions in capital punishment—reductions which were certain to occur, regardless of what might be said of them in fiction. The other novels reflected the general interest in crime and criminals, which Ainsworth exploited in romances of sheer entertainment. So great was the legal change—and other social changes were equally great —that from 1837 on Dickens and Bulwer addressed themselves not primarily to the condition of the law but to the vicious effect of public executions, to social injustice, and to the psychology of crime.

Besides involving individual prejudices, which did much to sharpen controversy from beginning to end, the Newgate novel was opposed on both political and moral grounds. The opposition ceases with the forties, when two of the writers have quit the field. Crime novels of later decades were received when the social and literary scene had changed—when no one had any fear of revolution in England and when middle-class dominance had removed the parallel fear of an extension of low manners and morals. We need look no further ahead than 1855 to illustrate how differently a crime novel could be received. In that year came *Paul Ferroll*, by Caroline Clive, the story of a gentleman who murders his wife in order to marry an earlier true-love. He successfully conceals the crime and lives an exemplary life for some eighteen years, admired by all his acquaintances, loved by his family, and apparently untroubled by his conscience. He has had the delicacy to return the murdered wife's property to her family. Ultimately a revelation of the crime is forced, but the author contrives to have Ferroll escape. In spite of absurdities, the story has a certain power, part of which is due to the author's chilling amorality; the book was popular enough to call for a sequel. Paul Ferroll is almost as great a genius as Eugene Aram; unlike the fictional Aram, he makes no apologies when he is discovered. All the objections to the earlier novel might have been raised even more forcefully against Mrs. Clive's, which was quite without Bulwer's moral aim. Some objection there was;

but respect outweighed sarcasm in the reviews, and there was no storm. (What would have happened if Bulwer's name had been signed to *Paul Ferroll* is fascinating to conjecture.) The fifties took the book in their stride, and Thackeray did not campaign against Mrs. Clive.

Thackeray, the leading opponent of the Newgate novelists, was not different from them in opinion; he too disliked capital punishment, public executions, and the social conditions which nurtured crime in the young. In addition to the personal elements in the controversy, the two serious novelists and their critic had the emotional attachments of three different social classes. Thackeray, whose temperament—not his opinions—might be described as Whiggish, stood posed against Dickens and Bulwer in an array which paralleled, perhaps accidentally, the class alignments felt in politics at the same time. Gordon Ray comments that when Thackeray went into society he was "attracted and welcomed by the Whigs." Bulwer, by inheritance owner of land and an ancient name, and Dickens, by birth not far removed from the servant class, understood each other well; but to Thackeray, Bulwer seemed an anachronism in the republic of letters and his books an extravagant denial of middle-class taste and judgment. It would be as misleading, however, to think of the opposition primarily in those terms as to think of it solely in terms of personal conflict. The novels were quite as controversial when they attempted art as when the first one began with propaganda; Thackeray's opposition ensued partly because he was a different kind of artist from Bulwer and Dickens.

What interests them most is not the situation of the criminal in the law, but his situation as a member of the human family. In *Eugene Aram* Bulwer takes up a psychological and ethical problem of motivation. Both he and Dickens are interested in the criminal as representative of black evil erupting from the depths of a human nature which is shared by all. At the end of *Lucretia*, Bulwer says we "set closer watch upon our inner and hidden selves." In the *Oliver Twist* preface, speaking of Nancy, Dickens uses the phrase, "our common nature." Bulwer can imaginatively identify himself with Eugene Aram; Dickens can do the same with Sikes. (The Newgate novels are more concerned with the image of the murderer than with its associate, the prison image, which Lionel Trilling says "haunted the mind of the nineteenth century.") Bulwer and Dickens—the one with talent, the other with genius—worked from springs of intuition which made them sometimes aware of the shocking affinity with the enemy. The man who opposed them was a daylight temperament; for his art, he had not yet drawn from his own depths. In his onslaught upon the other two, in 1840, he was reason chastising the irrational. He could not sympathize with what they were doing, nor could they explain it to him. Their artistic effort, despite its fabric of realism, was symbolic and myth-making; Thackeray's effort was realistic. Bulwer and Dickens could, therefore, plot wildly and could admit coincidence freely, amid the furnishings of the visible world; Thackeray must insist that fiction remain within the probable. With Thackeray's success, realism triumphed. Dickens, seeming to be realistic too, went on with his myth-making. Bulwer gave up his murderers, but Dickens did not.

The effort of the Newgate novelists met with too many obstacles in the thirties and forties to achieve artistic success. Some of the tangles require no further comment—the mingling of politics and literature, the indulgence in personality in literary dispute—but certain others may be remarked. The Newgate novelists, particularly Bulwer, suffered from the confusion of taste, or from the presence of several reading publics with conflicting tastes. In this uncertainty, the writers lacked the aid of any criticism of sufficient intellectual stature. Reviewing was everywhere, but there was almost no disinterested criticism which devoted itself to literature as craft and art. R. H. Horne undertook in 1844 to supply the deficiency; *A New Spirit of the Age* was notable in its attempt to judge by high standards and to avoid personal bias. Horne's judgment of Dickens was reasonably good, in view of what Dickens had written up to that time; he did not include Thackeray, who had not yet published a novel. He thought *Jack Sheppard* "reprehensible" but wisely avoided discussing it; instead, he simply denied that Ainsworth could be considered a serious novelist. He showed the same sound judgment in dealing with the popular *Ingoldsby Legends*. He praised all three of Bulwer's crime novels. He understood the aim of *Eugene Aram*; the author, he said, exposed "the casuistries of the brain." Bulwer needed this interpretation, but Horne's general estimate of him was too high and did not furnish the assistance of a sympathetic analysis of his mistakes. Horne's effort, altogether, was admirable, especially in its lack of bias, but he lacked originality and scope of mind. He could be a valuable teacher of the public, but he had not the intellectual qualities necessary in an instructor of the writers.

A more advanced criticism would have been of service not only to taste but to the specialized problems of the craft of fiction, which was in a rapid adolescence. The numerous efforts at narrative or epic poetry dwindled; the opportunities, financial or artistic, of prose narrative attracted a greater portion of the total of literary endeavor. In spite of all that had been done in it, prose fiction was still not a standard subject for literary criticism, and its potentialities, even when the novelists were trying to explore them, were seldom discussed.[93] *Paul Clifford* was one kind of experiment, *Oliver Twist* another. Each of Bulwer's and Dickens' Newgate books had some novelty of theme or method. (Mr. Jack Lindsay, in his book on Dickens, has appreciative words for the little-noticed *Night and Morning*.) In form, in technique, in subject matter, whole ranges of possibility awaited exploration.

Since the opponents in the Newgate conflict had antipathies as artists, a critic with sufficient insight—a later-born Coleridge, perhaps—might have explained the contenders to each other as well as to their readers. Everyone suffered from the limited under-standing of the modes of representation available to prose fiction. Very few recognized that the imaginative and symbolic methods which were known (if not always appreciated) in poetry could also enrich the novel. Realism had not yet been fully exploited, and its triumphant advance was so exclusive that for seventy-five years after *Vanity Fair* every new effort was presented as a realism made fuller and truer. Suggestive and symbolic devices did make their way, but somewhat deviously, clandestine and frequently un-recognized.

The Newgate novels faced certain problems of technique which were relatively new. One example which has continued to be interesting is the role or posture of the creator. For a long time we have been familiar with the invisible author, a being not invented by the Naturalists, but favored by them. In the eighteen-thirties and -forties, this familiar convention was not well understood; yet the role of the author was a crucial problem. One hundred years later, this invisibility was to become a tyrannical convention, which ought to be breached more often than it has been —but that is irrelevant for the historical moment under consideration.

Dickens was almost uniformly successful in communicating with readers; minor difficulty with *Oliver Twist* made him the more careful. He conveyed his own disapproval when he dealt with what his public abhorred, and so was regarded as one who could touch pitch and not be defiled. Ainsworth failed, at least with some of his audience, but his failure was not wholly technical: when disapproving readers felt that he despised thief and whore somewhat less than they did, perhaps they were right. Thackeray's success was complete: he took his place as author in plain sight and made his opinions known. His practice as we see it in *Vanity Fair*, flexible and delicate in its tonal control, is one of the significant features of his art. His "intrusion" has repelled some twentieth-century readers, but it continues to charm others, and it made him unassailable among his contemporaries. It goes hand in hand with a self-conscious, selective, limited omniscience: at one time he writes, "Becky thought," or "the novelist . . . knows everything"; at another, "Amelia did not answer, yes or no; and how do we know what her thoughts were?"

In this matter of point of view, as in others, Bulwer presents the interesting failures. *Eugene Aram* could be honestly misunderstood or wilfully misrepresented because Bulwer had not met his readers on the ground of a convention they perfectly understood; nor had he followed with consistency one of his own establishing. Although he never affected the cozy intimacies of Dickens and Thackeray, he was quite willing to intrude as author at many points in his narrative; but he did not always address his readers when he should have done so. He wrote Aram's rationalization of murder without sufficient comment; he was then accused of believing the sentiments he had written as dramatically appropriate for his central character. He had a little of the same trouble with *Night and Morning*. He undertook to avoid this defect in *Lucretia*, and largely succeeded; that novel left little room for a critic to argue that the author approved of murder by poison. There were still some readers not willing to have these somber crimes described by an author who did not say "Fie" on every page, but *Lucretia* was not battered by the same ram used against *Eugene Aram*. Despite the existence—and annoyance—of his comments as author, Bulwer was fumbling for the method of the omniscient author who has withdrawn from the book and made himself invisible. In this, as in his grand ambitions for fiction as art, he pointed toward developments which others were to bring about in later times.

At a time when Bulwer and Dickens and other writers would have extended the author's prerogative of omniscience as a technique for psychological exploration, Thackeray's achievement constituted in some degree a hindrance. His moral complaints against *Eugene Aram*, since they avoided technical analysis, obscured the view and for a time prevented other authors from instructing readers in the fictional convention which was in need of development. The spectacle of the Newgate controversy contributed, surely, to the generally cautious attitude of mid-Victorian novelists, such as Trollope, most of whom avoided taking risks with technique. "Otherwise you might think that it was I . . ." The effect of the controversy on observers was enhanced by Thackeray's personal example—his success in a technique that, supreme development though it was, looked back toward Fielding rather than ahead.

We turn finally to that exciting prospect of the thirties and forties, the new subjects open to novelists. The Newgate controversy was ostensibly about this problem. Was there any material not permissible for fiction? We have seen the replies the writers gave. The twentieth century has very nearly ceased to ask the question. The related one, of how the debatable matter was to be treated, they also considered; and this question our generation has raised again and again, in literary forums and in courts of law. It involves the nature of the writer's responsibility. Responsible to his own vision? Responsible to society? To whom in society? Irked though they were by unsympathetic responses, the crime novelists never denied a dual or multiple responsibility—not only for truth but also for the effect of their books on "the most jolter-headed juvenile." Modern critics do not demand so much. Nevertheless the problem has continued to perplex the societies which, having produced *Ulysses*, *Lady Chatterley's Lover*, Henry Miller, and Mickey Spillane, have not always known how to regard them, and frequently treat them differently on the two sides of the Atlantic. The perplexities may change their terms, but are not likely to diminish. The Victorians, who sometimes seem to have subordinated art unworthily, furnish an example which interests us: they respected art enough to be a little afraid of it. Some modern discussions of the freedom of the artist imply, by avoiding any consideration of the matter, that literature exercises no real influence upon thought and action. Such an attitude belittles the importance of imagination and of art. There is this to be said for Thackeray, Dickens, Bulwer, and all the Victorians, after an imbroglio deplorable, painful, and sometimes comic: they never doubted that the art of literature was an art of power.

APPENDIX A

COMMITMENTS AND PENALTIES, 1805–41
England and Wales *

Year	Committals	Convictions	Death Sentences	Executions	Executions for Murder
1805	4,605	2,783	350	68	10
1806	4,346	2,515	325	57	5
1807	4,446	2,567	343	63	16
1808	4,735	2,723	338	39	8
1809	5,330	3,238	392	60	9
1810	5,146	3,158	476	67	9
1811	5,337	3,163	404	45	7
1812	6,576	3,913	532	82	16
1813	7,164	4,422	713	120	25
1814	6,390	4,025	558	70	23
1815	7,818	4,883	553	57	15
1816	9,091	5,797	890	95	21
1817	13,932	9,056	1,302	115	25
1818	13,567	8,958	1,254	97	13
1819	14,254	9,510	1,314	108	15
1820	13,710	9,318	1,236	107	10
1821	13,115	8,788	1,134	114	22
1822	12,241	8,209	1,016	97	18
1823	12,263	8,204	968	54	11
1824	13,698	9,425	1,066	49	15
1825	14,437	9,964	1,036	50	10
1826	16,164	11,107	1,203	57	10
1827	17,924	12,567	1,529	73	11
1828	16,564	11,723	1,165	58	17
1829	18,675	13,261	1,385	74	13
1830	18,107	12,805	1,397	46	14
1831	19,647	13,830	1,601	52	12
1832	20,829	14,947	1,449	54	15
1833	20,072	14,446	931	33	6
1834	22,451	15,995	480	34	12
1835	20,731	14,729	523	34	21
1836	20,984	14,771	494	17	8
1837	23,612	17,090	438	8	8
1838	23,094	16,785	116	6	5
1839	24,443	17,832	56	11	10
1840	27,187	19,927	77	9	9
1841	27,760	20,280	80	10	10

* Figures taken from a table given by G. R. Porter, *The Progress of the Nation in Its Various Social and Economical Relations from the Beginning of the Nineteenth Century to the Present Time* (London, 1843), III, 178.

APPENDIX B

DATE OF THE ACTION OF *Oliver Twist*

Certain events of the decade before Dickens wrote *Oliver Twist* enable one to fix the time of the action, despite minor anachronisms. Two circumstances set terminal dates for the London part of the story. First, when Mr. Brownlow's pocket has been picked, Oliver is taken up by a policeman; the time, therefore, is 1828 or after. Second, near the end of the story, when Nancy meets Mr. Brownlow and Rose on London Bridge, it is "the ancient bridge," which was demolished after the new London Bridge was opened in August 1831. Everyone knew about the police; most of Dickens' London readers must have been aware of the replacement of the old bridge.

The time span within the story can be accommodated to these narrow limits. Oliver, ten years old when he is placed in Sowerberry's funeral establishment, stays there "many months" before he runs away to London; thus he may be eleven (a little less or a little more) when he is taken to the police-office. He is twelve years old in Chapter XXXVII, when we approach the series of closing events, including the meeting on the bridge.

Such a dating, closing not later than the first half of 1831, also coincides with the requirements of the final chapter, in which Dickens traces the subsequent lives of the characters. What is told there demands an interval of at least six or seven years between the real end of the action and the time of publication, 1837–38. Incidentally, Fagin's career thus ends fairly close to the time when the real fence, Solomon, was removed from the London scene.

Several other circumstances, though they do not restrict the date so closely, belong to a time before the Reform Act rather than to the immediate present of the time of writing. The most important of them is that fear of the noose constitutes Fagin's hold over his gang, a state of affairs less easily arranged after 1833. After that date, for example, Fagin could not have threatened Noah Claypole with hanging (as in Chapter XLIII) for the twenty-pound note from Sowerberry's till.

Two items involve inconsistency; one is too late, the other too early. The judge sentences Fagin immediately after the jury return their verdict; but in the Old Bailey, before the establishment of the Central Criminal Court in 1834, it was the custom to sentence the prisoners in groups, at the end of the session.* Dickens knew this, and remembered it years later, as we see in the sentencing of Magwitch, in *Great Expectations*. The other anachronism is Dr. Losberne's fictitious spring-gun. To prevent Oliver from being connected with the attempted robbery, the doctor explains to Blathers and Duff, from Bow Street, that the bullet-wound came from a spring-gun while Oliver was engaged in "some boyish trespass." But spring-guns were illegal after 1827.** Perhaps Dickens did not know the date of the spring-gun prohibition (he was only fifteen then), or perhaps he decided that no one would be disturbed by the discrepancy. No objection seems to have been raised that he put into the same story policemen and a spring-gun.

To place the date of the greater part of the action between 1828 and 1831 presents another contradiction. The workhouse scenes in the early chapters commonly cause readers to assume that the fabric of the whole story belongs to the era of the new poor law, after 1834. In the satire of these chapters—on the diet, indoor and outdoor relief, and the philosophical members of the parish vestry—Dickens was indeed commenting on the immediate present, although orphan children were cared for as badly under the old law as under the new.*** It might be supposed, therefore, that Dickens did not plan his chronology: that at the age of nine Oliver was in a workhouse administered under the new poor law, and that Dickens, in the grip of magazine publication, actually moved the time of the story back as he discovered what he needed for his plot. On the other hand, it is far more likely that Dickens knew from the start the period he meant to deal with, and that he simply decided to attack new-poor-law injustice through the device of an economy-minded parish of slightly earlier date.

* Theodore Hook's *Gilbert Gurney*, first published in 1835, contains a satirical scene showing Old Bailey procedures as they were about 1811. Here the sentences seem to be determined at the end of the day. *Gilbert Gurney* (London, 1850), p. 192.

** Sir William Holdsworth, *A History of English Law* (London, 1950–52), XIII, 390.

*** See Humphry House, *The Dickens World* (Oxford, 1941), pp. 94–99. *The Edinburgh Review*, LXVIII (October 1838), 75–97, assumed Oliver's workhouse to have been under the old system.

NOTES

CHAPTER I

1. *Annual Register*, 1807, pp. 381–82.
2. W. Eden Hooper, *History of Newgate and the Old Bailey* (London, 1935), p. 110. The party of Lord Tomnoddy, in R. H. Barham's once popular verses, was extraordinary only because Tomnoddy slept during the execution. "The Execution—Mr. Sucklethumbkin's Story," *Ingoldsby Legends* (Oxford, 1921), pp. 181–85. For the 1850's, see James Payn, *Some Literary Recollections* (New York, 1884), p. 157.
3. John Thomas Smith recalled being taken by Nollekens to the execution of Jack Rann, a famous highwayman, at Tyburn. It was in 1774, when Smith was eight years old. *A Book for a Rainy Day*, ed. Wilfred Whitten (London, 1905), p. 38. In Mrs. Sherwood's *History of the Fairchild Family*, papa showed the children, who had quarreled, the gibbeted body of a man who had killed his brother. *Works* (New York, 1834), II, 54–59.
4. Sigmund Spaeth, *Read 'em and Weep* (New York, 1935), p. 178. Another version may be seen in John A. and Alan Lomax, *American Ballads and Folk Songs* (New York, 1934), pp. 133–34. An actual instance of the nineteenth century is recorded by Hepworth Dixon, in *John Howard and the Prison World of Europe* (New York, 1850), p. 276.
5. Charles Pollitt, *DeQuincey and the Westmorland Gazette*, as quoted in Horace A. Eaton, *Thomas DeQuincey* (New York, 1936), p. 240.
6. Charles Hindley, *The Life and Times of James Catnach (Late of Seven Dials), Ballad Monger* (London, 1878), p. 142.
7. William Ballantine, *Some Experiences of a Barrister's Life* (New York, 1882), p. 3.
8. Sir Samuel Romilly, *Memoirs* (London, 1840), I, 11–12.
9. Edmund Yates, *Memoirs of a Man of the World* (New York, 1885), p. 109. The original singer was W. G. Ross.
10. Albany Fonblanque, "The Diseased Appetite for Horrors," *Examiner*, December 11, 1831, p. 787. Reprinted in his *England under Seven Administrations* (London, 1837), II, 194–95.
11. John Thomas Smith made many drawings for the duke (*A Book for a Rainy Day*, p. 176); Sir James Thornhill, known chiefly as a court painter, made a portrait of Jack Sheppard (Horace Bleackley, *Jack Sheppard* [Edinburgh, 1933], pp. 68–69). William Mulready, R. A., made sketches of the accused in a famous case, but apparently kept them for himself; Sir Thomas Lawrence wished to make a cast of Thurtell's head. Eric R. Watson, *The Trial of Thurtell and Hunt* (Edinburgh, 1920), pp. viii, 29.
12. After its opening in 1728, the *Beggar's Opera* was performed during every year of the eighteenth century; and less, but still frequently, in the nineteenth. William Eben Schultz, *Gay's Beggar's Opera; Its Content, History and Influence* (New Haven, 1923), pp. 63, 87; 226–29.

13. Martin Madan, *Thoughts on Executive Justice*, 2nd ed. (London, 1785), pp. 243, 247–48.
14. *Punch's Real History*, illustrated by George Cruikshank, 3rd ed. (London, 1844). A similar description of the action occurs in Henry Mayhew, *London Labour and the London Poor* (London, 1864), III, 56–66.
15. John Gay, *Poetical Works*, ed. G. C. Faber (Oxford, 1926), pp. xxvi–xxvii, 186; Jonathan Swift, *Poems*, ed. Harold Williams (Oxford, 1937), III, 1111–15. For another, Swift, *Poems*, II, 399.
16. James Boswell, *The Hypochondriack*, ed. Margery Bailey (Stanford, 1928), II, 279; *Life of Johnson*, ed. George Birkbeck Hill, rev. L. F. Powell (Oxford, 1934), II, 93, and IV, 329; *Private Papers of James Boswell from Malahide Castle*, ed. Geoffrey Scott (Mt. Vernon, N. Y., 1928–34), VII, 163.
17. William Godwin, *Fleetwood* (London, 1832), Preface, pp. vii, xii.
18. *Memoirs of Bryan Perdue* (London, 1805), III, 127–28.
19. Walter C. Phillips, *Dickens, Reade, and Collins, Sensation Novelists* (New York, 1919), p. 166.

CHAPTER II

1. Sir James Fitzjames Stephen, A *History of the Criminal Law of England* (London, 1883), I, 470–71; II, 215–16.
   A magistrate's summary of the chief punishable offences, major and minor, at the end of the eighteenth century is to be seen in Patrick Colquhoun, *Treatise on the Police of the Metropolis*, 6th ed. (London, 1800), pp. 437–44.
   A careful summary of capital statutes may be seen in Leon Radzinowicz, *A History of English Criminal Law and Its Administration from 1750*; Vol. I: *The Movement for Reform*, 1750–1833 (New York, 1948), pp. 611–59. Radzinowicz's volumes have individual subtitles; this one will be cited hereafter as Vol. I.
2. Stephen, III, 108.
3. Detailed evidence of this practice in the early nineteenth century, 1814–29, may be seen in the *Report from the Select Committee* of the House of Commons *on Capital Punishment*, 1929–30 (London, 1931), p. ix. See also Radzinowicz, I, 95, n. 52.
4. Colquhoun, p. 411.
5. *Old Bailey Experience* (London, 1830), p. 59; *Westminster Review*, XX (January 1834), 147–49.
6. Radzinowicz, I, 575–78.
7. Radzinowicz, I, 579–84.
8. Radzinowicz, I, 600–605. The bill dealing with theft was brought in by a young member, William Ewart, who continued to be active against capital punishment. W. A. Munford, *William Ewart, M.P.* (London, 1960), pp. 60–61.
9. Radzinowicz, I, 733–34. Appendix 5, Table of Capital Statutes in 1839.
10. Stephen, I, 475; G. R. Porter, *The Progress of the Nation in Its Various Social and Economical Relations from the Beginning of the Nineteenth Century to the Present Time* (London, 1843), IV, 181–82.
11. *Quarterly Review*, LXIX (December 1841), 1–51; *Letters of William and*

Dorothy Wordsworth: The Later Years, ed. Ernest de Selincourt (Oxford, 1939), III, 1094, 1098.
12. Porter, IV, 183.

CHAPTER III

1. Richard D. Altick, *The English Common Reader* (Chicago, 1957), pp. 322–23.
2. Thomas Skinner Surr, *Russell, or the Reign of Fashion* (London, 1830), I, 81.
3. W. M. Thackeray, "Solitude in September," *National Standard*, September 14, 1833, as quoted in H. S. Gulliver, *Thackeray's Literary Apprenticeship* (Valdosta, Ga., 1934), Appendix B, p. 195.
4. Ballantine, p. 85.
5. Simon Maccoby, *English Radicalism, 1832–1852* (London, 1935), pp. 415–16.
6. Thomas Gaspey, *The History of George Godfrey* (London, 1828), II, 184.
7. Blanchard Jerrold, *Life of George Cruikshank* (London, 1883), p. 20.
8. On the Thornton case, see Stephen, I, 249–50; the conditions of battle may be seen in an appendix to *The Complete Newgate Calendar*, ed. G. T. Crook (London, 1926), V, 325–26. The play which used the case was William Barrymore's *Trial by Battle, or Heaven Defend the Right*, listed by Allardyce Nicoll in *Nineteenth Century Drama, 1800–1850* (Cambridge, 1930), II, 251.
9. The phrases are from *Old Bailey Experience*, which contains a serious-minded but not puritanical description of the attachment of poor boys to the theatre and of its influence upon delinquents. Pp. 297–98; 307–13.
10. *New Monthly Magazine*, February 1822. Hazlitt, *Works*, ed. P. P. Howe (London, 1932), XVII, 72–85.
11. G. M. Trevelyan, *British History in the Nineteenth Century* (London, 1922), p. 170.
12. James Grant, *The Great Metropolis*, 2nd ser. (London, 1837), II, 285.
13. Eric R. Watson, *The Trial of Thurtell and Hunt* (Edinburgh, 1920), Preface, p. vii.
14. Nicoll, II, 455–56. The play at the Coburg was called *The Gamblers, or the Murderers at the Desolate Cottage*. This was followed on December 1 by another melodrama at the Coburg, *The Hertfordshire Tragedy, or the Victims of Gaming*. Nicoll, II, 468.
15. Watson, pp. 26–27; but Watson does not mention the Coburg performance or action against it.
16. Hindley, p. 143. See also Altick, pp. 287–88.
17. Watson, pp. 33–34.
18. *The Romany Rye* (London, 1907), p. 269; *Letters of Charles and Mary Lamb*, ed. E. V. Lucas (London, 1912), II, 681.
19. Though probably the jury regarded this as punishment for his assistance to Thurtell. Ballantine, p. 188.
20. Charles Dickens, "The Out-and-Out Young Gentleman," *Sketches by Boz*, New Oxford Illustrated Dickens (Oxford, 1957), p. 506.
21. Borrow, *Celebrated Trials*, ed. Edward Hale Bierstadt (London, 1926), II, 988–89.
22. Thurtell's name appears in the manuscript of *Lavengro*. Clement K. Shorter, *George Borrow and His Circle* (London, 1919), p. 117.

23. Watson, p. 46, n.; *Quarterly Review*, XXXVII (Jan. and March 1828), 15.
24. Thomas Burke, *Murder at Elstree, or Mr. Thurtell and His Gig* (London, 1936).
25. Michael Sadleir, *Bulwer: A Panorama*, Vol. I: *Edward and Rosina, 1803–1836* (Boston, 1931), p. 175.
26. This aspect of *Pelham* is recognized by A. E. Murch, *Development of the Detective Novel* (New York, 1958), pp. 36–38. Unfortunately, the part of the work dealing with crime fiction up to 1845 cannot be relied upon; there are both omissions and inaccuracies.
27. Edward Robert Bulwer, first Earl Lytton, *The Life, Letters, and Literary Remains of Edward Bulwer, Lord Lytton*, by His Son (London, 1883), II, 193. This work will be cited hereafter as Lytton, 1883.
28. *Pelham*, New Knebworth Ed. (London, 1895), p. 318.
29. Lytton, 1883, I, 308–9; II, 193.
30. *London Magazine*, XXII or II of 3rd series (October 1828), 388. See also *Athenaeum*, May 14, 1828, 735–36; *Westminster Review*, X (January 1829), 179; *Monthly Review*, CXVII or IX n.s. (September 1828), 50–53; *Blackwood's Magazine*, XXVI (October 1829), 562; *Examiner*, September 14, 1828, 595–97, and September 21, 613–14.
31. *Pelham*, p. 205.
32. This brief account is based upon Horace Bleackley, *The Trial of Henry Fauntleroy and Other Famous Trials for Forgery* (Edinburgh, 1924).
33. Bleackley, p. 10.
34. Bleackley, pp. 25, 26, 37; and Appendix II, "Fauntleroy and the Newspapers," pp. 144–53.
35. Perhaps as a result of the legal action on the Thurtell play, the Lord Chamberlain refused a license to a melodrama about Fauntleroy, *Forgery, or, Le Roy*. Nicoll, II, 453.
36. In the *London Magazine*, April 1828. Reprinted in Charles and Mary Lamb, *Works*, ed. E. V. Lucas (London, 1912), I, 333.
37. Sadleir, *Bulwer*, p. 192.
38. Ballantine, pp. 259–60.
39. Bleackley, pp. 54–58.
40. Ballantine, p. 259.
41. Radzinowicz, I, 195, n. 6.
42. See below, p. 50.
43. Thomas Love Peacock, *Crotchet Castle*, Halliford Ed. (London, 1924), pp. 134–35.
44. Bleackley, pp. 238–39.
45. *Crotchet Castle*, pp. 62–63.
46. Information about the case is drawn from James Curtis, *The Murder of Maria Marten*, ed. Jeanne and Norman Mackenzie (New York, 1948). Concerning Curtis, author of this contemporary account, see Grant, II, 199–205.
47. *Bell's Life in London*, May 24, 1829, quoted in Hindley, pp. 186–90.
48. Jeanne and Norman Mackenzie, Epilogue to James Curtis, *The Murder of Maria Marten*, pp. 249–51, 255. Another play, perhaps written later than 1828, has been published: John Latimer, *Maria Marten, or, The Murder in the Red Barn*, ed. Montagu Slater (London, 1928).
49. Sixth Report of Inspectors of Prisons, Northern and Eastern District, 1841,

as quoted in Appendix 2 of *Report from the Select Committee on Criminal and Destitute Juveniles*, ptd. by order of the House of Commons, 24 June, 1852, p. 420.

50. London: Knight and Lacy, 1828. Reissued in 1831 by another publisher. Certain bibliographies list also the *Red Barn, a Tale of Truth*, 1828, which may or may not be the same work.

The Knight and Lacy publication has been attributed to William Maginn. (Hindley, p. 189.) Without supporting evidence, this must be laid aside as gossip. The pedestrian seriousness of the *Red Barn, a Tale Founded on Fact*, does not belong to the man who in the same year collaborated in *Whitehall*.

See also Michael Sadleir, *Nineteenth Century Fiction, A Bibliographical Record Based on His Own Collection* (London, 1951), I, 222.

51. Huish, *The Red Barn, a Tale Founded on Fact*, pp. 388–89.

52. There are bibliographies in William Roughead, *The Trial of Burke and Hare*, 3rd ed. (Edinburgh, 1948).

53. Radzinowicz, I, 220, n. 70.

54. *The Murderers of the Close: A Tragedy of Real Life* (London, 1829).

55. *The Burkers*, concerning Bishop and Williams, at the Shakespeare, an unlicensed theatre. E. L. Blanchard, "Vanished Theatres," *Era Almanack*, 1877, cited by Hindley, p. 234.

In this century, Burke and Hare appear, along with Dr. Knox, in James Bridie's play, *The Anatomist*. (In *A Sleeping Clergyman, and Other Plays* [London, 1934]).

56. Thomas DeQuincey, *Collected Writings*, ed. David Masson (London, 1897), XIII, 43.

57. London, 1827. I call it the first detective novel, for I have not come upon an earlier one, but Gaspey's book would still be noteworthy even if it should prove not to be the first. Published anonymously, the book has also been attributed to T. S. Surr, but it does not resemble Surr's other work. To judge by the content, there are better reasons for ascribing it to Gaspey.

The title is mentioned by John Carter in his article on collecting detective fiction in *New Paths in Book Collecting* (London, 1934), p. 51, n., and is alluded to—not named—by Howard Haycraft in *Murder for Pleasure* (New York, 1941), p. 7. *Richmond* is included in Fritz Wölcken's *Der Literarische Mord* (Nürnberg, 1953), p. 55, but not in any other history of detective fiction that I have seen. Patrick Pringle mentions it in his introduction to Henry Goddard, *Memoirs of a Bow Street Runner* (London, 1956), p. xxx.

58. Radzinowicz, *A History of English Criminal Law and Its Administration from 1750*, Vol. II: *The Clash between Private Initiative and Public Interest In the Enforcement of the Law* (New York, 1957), 321–25, 333 f.

59. *Memoirs of Vidocq, Principal Agent of the French Police until 1827, and now Proprietor of the Paper Manufactory at St. Mandé* (4 vols.; London, 1828–29).

60. Vidocq, II, 244–55.

61. Jean Savant, Introduction, *Les Vrais mémoires de Vidocq* (Paris, 1950), pp. 20–25.

62. Samuel Halkett and John Laing, *Dictionary of Anonymous and Pseudonymous Literature*, ed. James Kennedy, W. A. Smith, and A. F. Johnson (Edinburgh, 1926), VI, 396. With even less likelihood, the translation has been claimed

for George Borrow, William I. Knapp, *Life, Writings and Correspondence of George Borrow* (New York, 1899), I, 115. An editorial "Sequel" concerning Vidocq, at the end of the English version, is signed "H.T.R." This may or may not be the translator.

Maginn has been proposed mainly because he did translate (*Blackwood's*, XXIV [July 1828], 131–33) one of the flash songs which appeared in French in the English version (III, 56–58), and because this translation was reprinted, among others, in an appendix at the end of the fourth volume. However, the song as it appeared in Vol. III had English notes—a translation, in effect—which do not coincide with the easy slang of Maginn's verse translation. Moreover, the translator of the memoirs, differentiating himself from O'Doherty (Maginn's pseudonym), proceeds to give in the appendix his own translations of other songs. It seems most unlikely that Maginn was either sole or chief translator and editor. But since Vidocq's book undoubtedly appealed to him, he might have had some connection with the project without undertaking the labor of the whole.

63. Vidocq, I, 206, n.
64. Vidocq, III, 197–98.
65. Vidocq, II, 261–62. Other books followed in the wake of Vidocq's memoirs. For example, *Le Livre noir de MM. Tranchet et Delaveau, ou répertoire alphabetique de la police politique* (Paris, 1829), filled with gossipy records of a few years earlier.
66. Vidocq, IV, 3.
67. Vidocq, IV, 2.
68. "Merton" was a rewriting of an early attempt, *The Man of Sorrow*, 1808. Myron S. Brightfield, *Theodore Hook and His Novels* (Cambridge, Mass., 1928), p. 224.
69. "Le Revenant," *Blackwood's Magazine*, XXI (April 1827), 409–16.
70. Letter to William Hone, who followed Lamb's suggestion to make an extract for the *Table Book*. Charles and Mary Lamb, *Letters*, ed. E. V. Lucas (London, 1912), II, 773.
71. *History of George Godfrey*, II, 184–85.
72. *Foreign Quarterly Review*, IV (April 1829), 233; *Foreign Review*, III (July 1829), 540–42; *Westminster Review*, XI (July 1829), 164; *Blackwood's Magazine*, XXVI (August 1829), 209; *Edinburgh Review*, LVII (July 1833), 348–49; *Quarterly Review*, LVI (April 1836), 77.
73. *Le Dernier jour d'un condamné*, Preface, p. 233. In *Bug Jargal, Le Dernier jour, Claude Gueux* (Paris: Nelson, n.d.).
74. Kenneth Ward Hooker, *The Fortunes of Victor Hugo in England* (New York, 1938), p. 25.

CHAPTER IV

1. Louis Cazamian, *Le Roman social en Angleterre, 1830–1850*, nouvelle edition (Paris, 1934), I, 65 ff.
2. *Paul Clifford*, in *Complete Works*, Knebworth Ed. (London, 1874), p. ix. This edition is used in further citations of *Paul Clifford* except where some other is noted.

3. *Paul Clifford*, p. 415.
4. Michael Sadleir, *Bulwer: a Panorama*, Vol. I: *Edward and Rosina, 1806–1836* (Boston, 1931), p. 133.
5. The Mills gang, broken up in Gloucestershire in 1826, had had a large subterranean hiding place. Harriet Martineau, *History of England during the Thirty Years' Peace* (London, 1887), II, 82–83.

There was a Captain Clifford in 1683 who was sentenced to Newgate for a year; his offence was the abduction and forced wedding of a widow of property. Arthur Griffiths, *The Chronicles of Newgate* (London, 1884), I, 180.
6. *Paul Clifford*, p. 80.
7. *Paul Clifford*, pp. 392–93.

The idea expressed here suggests Rousseau, who is probably the ultimate if not the immediate source. The idea is to be found in the *Contrat Social*, but there is an even closer likeness of phrasing in the Encyclopedia discourse, "De l'économie politique": "La sûreté particulière est tellement liée avec la confédération publique, que, sans les égards que l'on doit à la foiblesse humaine, cette convention seroit dissoute par le droit, s'il périssoit dans l'État un seul citoyen qu'on eût pu secourir, si l'on en retenoit à tort un seul en prison, et s'il se perdoit un seul procès avec une injustice évidente; car, les conventions fondamentales étant enfreintes, on ne voit plus quel droit ni quel intérêt pourroit maintenir le peuple dans l'union sociale, à moins qu'il n'y fût retenu par le seule force qui fait la dissolution de l'état civil." Jean Jacques Rousseau, *Oeuvres Complètes* (Paris, 1856), II, 561.
8. *Paul Clifford*, p. 77.
9. *Paul Clifford*, p. 156.
10. *Paul Clifford*, p. 123.
11. *Paul Clifford*, p. 200.
12. *Paul Clifford*, p. 233.
13. *Paul Clifford*, pp. 202–3.
14. William Godwin, *An Enquiry Concerning Political Justice*, ed. and abr. Raymond A. Preston (New York, 1926), I, 17–18.
15. William Godwin, *Caleb Williams* (New York, 1926), p. 270.
16. G. Kegan Paul, *William Godwin, His Friends and Contemporaries* (Boston, 1876), II, 302, 307; second Earl Lytton, *Life of Edward Bulwer, First Lord Lytton* (London, 1913), I, 399, 401. The latter will be cited hereafter as Lytton, 1913.
17. The Dedicatory Epistle itself was addressed to Bulwer's Cambridge friend, Alexander Cockburn, who likewise was not named in it. When reissued in 1840, the book was inscribed to Albany Fonblanque.
18. Dedicatory Epistle, *Paul Clifford* (London, 1830), I, xvi–xvii.

The friend has formerly been identified as William Godwin, upon the authority of Bulwer's son (Lytton, 1883, II, 245–46), but the statement of William Jerdan should be credited. (*Autobiography* [London, 1853], IV, 195–96.) See my discussion of the question in *Modern Language Notes*, LXIII (November 1948), 489–91, and LXVI (April 1951), 288.
19. Sadleir, *Bulwer*, pp. 206–7.
20. *Paul Clifford*, p. 101.
21. Sadleir, *Bulwer*, p. 207.

22. *Paul Clifford*, p. 104.
23. *Paul Clifford*, p. 416.
24. *Paul Clifford*, p. 104.
25. One of Lord Eldon's enemies, perhaps as disgusted with his stable as with his litigation, named his racehorses Old Bags, Upright Judge, etc. Ralph Milbanke, Earl of Lovelace, *Astarte*, ed. Mary, Countess of Lovelace (New York, 1921), p. 29, n.
26. Romilly, *Memoirs*, II, 421.
27. *Paul Clifford*, p. 182.
28. Jeremy Bentham, *Indications Respecting Lord Eldon. Works*, ed. Sir John Bowring (Edinburgh, 1843), V, 375.
29. Lytton, 1883, II, 249.
30. The fable of the predatory political groups parallels an idea frequently expressed by Bentham. *The Book of Fallacies* had it as follows:

> In plain language, here are two bodies of men, and one individual more powerful than the two bodies put together—say three powers—each pursuing its own interest, each interest a little different from each of the two others, and not only different from, but opposite to, that of the greatest number of the people. Of the substance of the people, each gets to itself and devours as much as it can. (*Works*, II, 447.)

31. *Fraser's Magazine*, I (April 1830), 318–35.
32. *Paul Clifford* (London, 1830), Dedicatory Epistle, I, xviii–xix.
33. Most notably in a review of his *Devereux*, July 15, 1829, pp. 433–34, although he was mentioned unfavorably several times before.
34. Sadleir, *Bulwer*, pp. 209–11.
35. Lytton, 1883, II, 248.
36. *Blackwood's Magazine*, XXVI (October 1829), 562. The mutual dislike between Bulwer and Lockhart is described in Sadleir's *Bulwer*, pp. 180–85.
37. Miriam M. H. Thrall, *Rebellious Fraser's* (New York, 1934), p. 164.
38. Thrall, pp. 178–83; Sadleir, *Bulwer*, p. 224.
39. R. H. Horne, *A New Spirit of the Age* (Oxford, 1907), p. 388.
40. "Mr. Edward Lytton Bulwer's Novels; and Remarks on Novel-Writing," *Fraser's Magazine*, I (June 1830), 526.
41. Sadleir, *Bulwer*, pp. 245–51, 422–26; Thrall, pp. 217–28. In Miss Thrall's note, "Two Articles Attributed to Carlyle," *Modern Language Notes*, XLVI (May 1931), 316–21, the opinion that MacGrawler was based upon Maginn is expressed almost incidentally. It does not appear in *Rebellious Fraser's*, published three years later.
42. *Fraser's*, XXII (January 1840), 22.
43. *Athenaeum*, May 15, 1830, pp. 289–91.
44. *Fraser's Magazine*, I (June 1830), 530.
45. *Examiner*, June 20, 1830, p. 387. *Spectator*, May 15, 1830, pp. 311, 312.
46. "Noctes Ambrosianae," No. 58, *Blackwood's Magazine*, XXX (September 1831), 532.
47. "Recent Novels," *Monthly Review*, CXXII (June 1830), 260.
48. *Edinburgh Review*, LV (April 1832), 212.
49. "*Zohrab the Hostage*, by the author of Hajji Baba," *Quarterly Review*, XLVIII (December 1832), 395.

50. A list of such materials is to be seen in Eric R. Watson, *Eugene Aram: His Life and Trial* (Edinburgh, 1913), Appendix VI (F), p. 219.
51. Rayner Heppenstall, "The Children of Gomer," *Times Literary Supplement,* October 17, 1958, p. 600.
52. Lytton, 1913, I, 386–87.
53. Thomas Hood, *Poetical Works* (Oxford, 1911), pp. 209–11. Its long life must amaze any reader who has not developed a fondness for it in youth. One finds it remembered by Percy A. Scholes (*The Great Dr. Burney* [Oxford, 1948], I, 64); V. S. Pritchett says it contains "the most frightening dramatic lines in English narrative verse" (*The Living Novel* [New York, 1947], p. 73).
54. Sadleir, *Bulwer*, pp. 244, 251–52.
55. Such as those by the Yorkshire lawyer and antiquary, Norrisson Scatcherd: *Memoirs of the Celebrated Eugene Aram* (London, 1832) and *"Gleanings" after Eugene Aram, at Knaresborough* (London, 1836).
56. Watson, p. 2.
57. *Eugene Aram* (London, 1832), I, 66.
58. *Eugene Aram*, II, 62–63.
59. *Eugene Aram*, I, 249–50.
60. By an odd coincidence, one of the well-known pamphlets about Aram, which Bulwer very possibly read, suggested that Aram had committed incest with one of his daughters. Watson, p. 40.
61. *Bulwer*, p. 287.
62. *Eugene Aram*, II, 180.
63. Watson, pp. 44, 85. There were also accounts (pp. 122, 125) of how Aram's wife and children visited his gibbet; these Bulwer could not use.
64. Watson, p. 119. There were both private readers and reviewers who thought the motive which Bulwer provided was inadequate. Young Thackeray said so in his diary. *The Letters and Private Papers of William Makepeace Thackeray*, ed. Gordon N. Ray (Cambridge, Mass., 1945), I, 198.

 John Forster thought the jealousy motive would have been more plausible, as he said in a friendly letter dated January 4, 1832. Sadleir, *Bulwer*, p. 249.
65. *Eugene Aram*, III, 251–52.
66. *Eugene Aram*, III, 262.
67. *Eugene Aram*, III, 272–73.
68. *Eugene Aram*, III, 249, 256–57.
69. William Godwin, who had also thought of the subject, would have made that his message. According to his notes, he would have proposed that a man should not be punished who was found to have spent ten years after a crime "blamelessly, and in labours conducive to the welfare of mankind"; and that "No man shall die respecting whom it can reasonably be concluded that if his life were spared, it would be spent blamelessly, honourably, and usefully." Kegan Paul, *William Godwin* (Boston, 1876), II, 304–5.

 After the publication of *Eugene Aram*, Godwin told Bulwer that he had himself considered using the story. In the Preface to the edition of 1840, Bulwer gracefully deprecated himself and praised Godwin, but mentioned no obligation. It seems unnecessary to follow Kegan Paul in believing that Godwin had given "his subject and his material to his younger and more vigorous friend."

70. Sadleir, *Bulwer*, p. 245.
71. Sadleir, *Bulwer*, p. 219. Perhaps a half-century later, Molly Bloom also read it when she was a young miss. James Joyce, *Ulysses* (New York, 1942), p. 741.
72. Lytton, 1913, I, 389.
73. *Athenaeum*, January 7, 1832, pp. 3–5; *Edinburgh Review*, LV (April 1832), 208–19; *Spectator*, January 7, 1832, p. 17; *Monthly Review*, CXXVII [I, n.s.] (February 1832), 302–7.
    Mr. Sadleir scans the reviews, noting favorable ones in the *Literary Gazette* and the *Court Journal* and unfavorable ones in a variety of magazines.
74. The review was unsigned, but the historian of *Fraser's* lists it as probably by Maginn. Thrall, p. 304.
75. *Fraser's Magazine*, V (February 1832), 110.
76. *Fraser's Magazine*, V (February 1832), 112.
77. For example, *Edinburgh Review*, XL (March 1824), 201.
78. *Eugene Aram*, New Knebworth Ed. (London, 1895), p. 11.
79. *Eugene Aram*, New Knebworth Ed., p. 17.
80. Nicoll, II, 304, 407, 507.
81. Nicoll, II, 349, 447.
82. *Fraser's Magazine*, VI (August 1832), 67–88; VI (September 1832), 131–48.
    Reprinted in *Sultan Stork and Other Stories and Sketches by William Makepeace Thackeray*, ed. R. H. Shepherd (London, 1887), pp. 114–92.
83. Thrall, p. 64. Thackeray's authorship was accepted by Michael Sadleir; but it had already been denied by Thackeray's earlier biographer, Lewis Melville, and Gordon N. Ray does not find it necessary to discuss the matter in his *Thackeray* (2 vols.; New York, 1955–58). Thackeray's authorship was accepted by Ernest Boll, in "The Author of 'Elizabeth Brownrigge': A Review of Thackeray's Techniques," *Studies in Philology*, XXIX (January 1942), 79–101, who argued from stylistic and other internal evidence. The article pointed out interesting parallels. Curiously, it made no reference to Miss Thrall's book.
84. *Poetry of the Anti-Jacobin*, ed. Charles Edmonds, 3rd ed. (New York, 1890), pp. 16–17.
85. *Fraser's Magazine*, VI (August 1832), 68.
86. *Fraser's Magazine*, VI (September 1832), 144.
87. *New Monthly Magazine*, XXVII (January 1833), 82–87.
88. Sadleir, *Bulwer*, 258–59.
89. *Rookwood*, Everyman's Library (London, 1931), p. 3.
90. The borrowing is pointed out by E. A. Baker, in his *History of the English Novel*, Vol. VII: *The Age of Dickens and Thackeray* (London, 1936), p. 94.
91. *The Complete Newgate Calendar*, ed. G. T. Crook (London, 1926), III, 88–97. A very full account is given in Arty Ash and Julius Day, *Immortal Turpin* (London, 1948).
    Turpin has also made a twentieth-century appearance in a poem by Alfred Noyes, "Dick Turpin's Ride," *Collected Poems* (Philadelphia and New York, 1939), pp. 384–88.
92. *Rookwood*, Preface, pp. 6–7.
93. S. M. Ellis, *William Harrison Ainsworth and His Friends* (London, 1911), I, 237–46.
94. *Rookwood*, pp. 67–68.

95. *Rookwood*, p. 196.
96. *Rookwood*, p. 304.
97. "Gallery of Literary Characters, No. L: William Harrison Ainsworth," *Fraser's Magazine*, X (July 1834), 48.
98. Ellis, I, 280.
99. *Rookwood*, p. 242.
100. *Rookwood*, pp. 210–11.
101. Ellis, I, 254. Quoted from *The World*, March 28, 1878.
102. Ellis, I, 247–49.
103. *Rookwood*, Preface, p. 7.
104. Ellis, II, 357–59.
105. Ellis, I, 258.
106. Edward S. Turner, *Boys Will Be Boys*, rev. ed. (London, 1957), p. 46.
107. Ellis, I, 247.
108. Ellis, I, 258.
109. Nicoll, II, 363.
110. Nicoll, II, 536. Ainsworth, getting revenue from this production, asked the favor of Lady Blessington's patronage. (Ellis, I, 267–68. Letter of May 31, 1834.)
111. Maurice Willson Disher, *Blood and Thunder: Mid-Victorian Melodrama and Its Origins* (London, 1949), p. 120.
112. Ellis, I, 285.
113. Ellis, I, 286.
114. *Examiner*, May 18, 1834, p. 308. Presumably the reviewer was Forster; he became literary critic of the paper in 1833.
115. *Athenaeum*, May 3, 1834, p. 323.
116. Ellis, I, 229.
117. "Hints for a History of Highwaymen," *Fraser's Magazine*, IX (March 1834), 279.
118. With some justification, the review has been attributed to Thackeray by several students; for a discussion of this opinion, see Thrall, *Rebellious Fraser's* pp. 254–56.

But Thackeray cannot have written the whole of it. The political portion, in which Whigs are compared unfavorably with Newgate characters, might have taken its inspiration from the editor of *Fraser's*. And there is a passage in which the reviewer recalls the boyish excitement of a first visit to London, when his father pointed out the scenes of highwaymen's exploits along the great North Road; besides being impossible for Thackeray, this forms a close parallel in tone and substance to Ainsworth's remarks about his father's tales. Since all is speculation, Ainsworth may as well be proposed as an author of this review. It would have been most natural for Maginn to ask him to do Whitehead's book.
119. *Fraser's Magazine*, IX (June 1834), 724–28. According to Ainsworth, written by John Churchill (Ellis, I, 294).
120. *Fraser's Magazine*, X (July 1834), 48.
121. "Another Caw from the Rookwood—Turpin Out Again," *Fraser's Magazine*, XIII (April 1836), 488–96.
122. *Quarterly Review*, LI (June 1834), 483.
123. *Edinburgh Review*, LXV (April 1837), 195.

124. *Fraser's* II, (September 1830), 185; *Westminster Review*, XIII (July 1830), 39–44.
125. Horace Smith, *Gale Middleton* (London 1833), III, 128. The novel deserves to be better known as a document of the period. I have failed to find reviews in the most prominent weekly periodicals.
126. The mixed reception of the book is noticed by Whitehead's biographer, H. T. Mackenzie Bell, in *A Forgotten Genius: Charles Whitehead* (London, 1884), p. 14.

CHAPTER V

1. John Forster, *The Life of Charles Dickens*, ed. J. W. T. Ley (New York, 1928), p. 111. Further citations of this title will be shortened to Forster, *Dickens*.
2. Edgar Johnson, *Charles Dickens: His Tragedy and Triumph* (New York, 1952), I, 188, 221. Further citations of this title will be shortened to Johnson, *Dickens*.
3. The only revisions of substantial interest, made later, were those by means of which Dickens de-emphasized Fagin's label of Jew. These have been noticed more than once, most recently by Harry Stone, in "Dickens and the Jews," *Victorian Studies*, II (March 1959), 223–53. At the time *Oliver Twist* was first published, there was no public objection to the presentation of Fagin as a Jew; the matter did not enter into the Newgate controversy.
4. A search for information is indicated in a letter written, it appears, during the early months of *Oliver Twist*. *The Letters of Charles Dickens*, ed. Walter Dexter (Bloomsbury, 1938), I, 116–17. Further citations of this work will be shortened to *Letters*.
5. This account follows that in Camden Pelham's *Chronicles of Crime, or the New Newgate Calendar* (London, 1887), II, 235–41. (First edition, 1841.)
6. "*The Condemned Cells*, from the Note-book of the Ordinary," *Fraser's Magazine*, XXIV (December 1841), 664.
7. Johnson, *Dickens*, I, 61.
8. Johnson, *Dickens*, I, 93, 179–80; Forster, *Dickens*, 59, 67n.; 78, 83n.
9. See above, pp. 24–25.
10. *Bentley's Miscellany*, II, (July 1837), 2–3. *Oliver Twist*, Oxford Illustrated Dickens (Oxford, 1949), p. 59. Further citations refer to this edition except where another is designated.
11. Johnson, *Dickens*, I, 29–30.
12. Forster, *Dickens*, p. 76.
13. The editor of the *Morning Chronicle* helped to arrange his admission to the prison. He visited it probably in the early part of November 1835, and completed the sketch by November 20. Dickens, *Letters*, I, 47, 53, 56.
14. "The Hospital Patient," *Sketches by Boz* (Oxford, 1957), p. 243. First published August 6, 1836.
15. A letter shows that a sketch on "Hospitals" was among those already projected before October 27, 1835. Dickens, *Letters*, I, 47.
16. *Oliver Twist*, p. 306.
17. Edmund Wilson, *The Wound and the Bow* (Boston, 1941), pp. 10–14;

Lionel Trilling, *The Opposing Self* (New York, 1955), p. 53. See also Johnson, *Dickens*, I, 163–65, 177.

18. E. A. Baker, VII, 104, 106.

19. Johnson, *Dickens*, I, 109.

20. Letter to James Martin, February 8, 1843. *Letters of Elizabeth Barrett Browning*, ed. Frederic G. Kenyon (London, 1897), I, 124. To R. H. Horne she objected that he had omitted Hugo in discussing Dickens in *A New Spirit of the Age*. *Letters of Elizabeth Barrett Browning addressed to Richard Hengist Horne*, with preface and memoir by R. H. Stoddard (New York, 1877), pp. 190–91.

21. See below, p. 181, for the same thing in *Barnaby Rudge*.

22. Ellis, I, 273–74; Forster, *Dickens*, p. 84; Johnson, *Dickens*, I, 103–4, 186.

23. Dickens, *Letters*, I, 132, 138–39, 145, 151, 154; Johnson, *Dickens*, I, 192, 198, 215; Ellis, I, 332.

24. Una Pope-Hennessy, *Charles Dickens* (New York, 1946), p. 85.

25. Johnson, *Dickens*, I, 258–59; Ellis, I, 386–89. In one detail, Johnson is surely in error when he says (p. 259) that Ainsworth may have felt aggrieved, in March, because of Forster's treatment of *Jack Sheppard;* Forster's review appeared in the *Examiner* the following November.

26. Johnson, *Dickens*, I, 210; Lytton, 1913, II, 74.

27. The name Fagin comes from Dickens' childhood. Bob Fagin, an older boy, befriended him at the blacking warehouse. Johnson, *Dickens*, I, 41. No one tells whether Bob Fagin was still living in 1837. Jack Lindsay speculates that though Dickens was "aware of the ingratitude," the name stood in his mind for "the level of wretched toil into which he had feared himself sinking, the proletarian pit yawning under the petty-bourgeois feet. . . ." *Charles Dickens* (London, 1950), pp. 170–71.

28. Here Dickens made a recognizable portrait of an obnoxious magistrate who sat in Hatton Garden; the book was instrumental in his removal. Forster, *Dickens*, p. 549.

29. "The First of May," *Sketches by Boz*, p. 171.

30. George Gissing, *Charles Dickens* (New York, 1898), p. 54.

31. *Oliver Twist*, Preface to the third edition. See Dickens' *Works* (New York, 1911), III, ix.

32. *The Dickens World*, p. 217.

33. Johnson, *Dickens*, I, *passim*.

34. Forster, *Dickens*, p. 199.

35. He wrote to Forster in August 1838: "Nancy is no more. I showed what I have done to Kate last night, who was in an unspeakable 'state': from which and my own impression I augur well. When I have sent Sikes to the devil, I must have yours. . . ." Dickens, *Letters*, I, 172.

36. *Oliver Twist*, p. 363.

37. Wilson, *The Wound and the Bow*, pp. 16–17.

38. Johnson, *Dickens*, II, 1104.

39. Dickens, *Letters*, I, 179.

40. Nicoll, II, 504.

41. As quoted in S. J. Adair Fitzgerald, *Dickens and the Drama* (New York, 1910), p. 106.

42. W. S. Macready, *Diaries*, ed. William Toynbee (London, 1912), I, 475.

43. Nicoll, II, 243; Fitzgerald, *Dickens and the Drama*, playbill opposite p. 102; Forster, *Dickens*, p. 125.

44. Nicoll, II, 311, 396. But see also F. Dubrez Fawcett, *Dickens the Dramatist* (London, 1952), pp. 53–57, 234–35.

45. George Ford is led to remark concerning the reception of *Oliver Twist* that "the extraordinary relationship between Dickens and his public was a more tempestuous affair than is always recognized." *Dickens and His Readers* (Princeton, 1955), p. 42.

46. *Westminster Review*, XXVII (July 1837), 214–15; *Quarterly Review*, LIX (October 1837), 518.

47. *Edinburgh Review*, LXVIII (October 1838), 77–78.

48. *Monthly Review*, CXLVIII (January 1839), 29–41; *Athenaeum*, November 17, 1838, pp. 824–25; *Examiner*, November 18, 1838, p. 723, and November 25, pp. 740–41; *Spectator*, December 1, 1838, pp. 1114–16.

49. *Quarterly Review*, LIV (June 1839), 87–88.

50. "Charles Dickens and His Works," *Fraser's Magazine*, XXI (April 1840), 381–400. Much of what *Fraser's Magazine* had to say about Dickens will be included in the account of Thackeray's *Catherine*, where Dickens is bracketed with Ainsworth and Bulwer.

51. *Cambridge History of English Literature*, XIII, 351.

52. Thackeray, *Works*, Biographical Ed. (London, 1898), III, 642–43. Reprinted from *Fraser's Magazine*, August 1840.

53. Dickens, *Letters*, I, 240. Horne's proposal, which drew this reply, is not clear.

54. *Oliver Twist* (New York, 1911), pp. v–vi.

55. *Oliver Twist* (New York, 1911), p. x.

56. R. H. Horne, *A New Spirit of the Age*, p. 25.

57. Horace Bleackley, *Jack Sheppard*; with an Epilogue on Jack Sheppard in Literature and Drama, a Bibliography, a Note on Jonathan Wild, and a Memoir of Horace Bleackley, by S. M. Ellis (Edinburgh, 1933). This work is cited hereafter as Bleackley and Ellis, *Jack Sheppard*.

For a more recent and more "popular" account, there is also Christopher Hibbert, *The Road to Tyburn, the Story of Jack Sheppard and the Eighteenth-Century London Underworld* (Cleveland, O., 1957). It includes some details not to be found in Bleackley.

58. Hibbert, p. 157.

59. "The History of the Remarkable Life of John Sheppard," London, 1724; "A Narrative of All the Robberies, Escapes, &c. . . . of John Sheppard," London, 1724. Bleackley and Ellis, *Jack Sheppard*, Bibliography, pp. 127–28. This extensive bibliography includes both eighteenth-century and later items, pp. 127–36.

60. Bleackley and Ellis, *Jack Sheppard*, pp. 71–74.

61. Bleackley and Ellis, *Jack Sheppard*, p. 68.

62. Letter of May 29, 1837, in Ellis, I, 328.

63. Lauriat Lane, Jr., "Dickens' Archetypal Jew," *PMLA*, LXXIII (March 1958), 95.

64. W. H. Ainsworth, *Jack Sheppard*, Windsor Ed. (London, 1902), I, 173.

65. *Jack Sheppard*, I, 55.

66. *Jack Sheppard*, II, 89, 183.

67. *Jack Sheppard*, II, 183.

68. Ellis, I, 352–53; Bleackley and Ellis, *Jack Sheppard*, pp. 89–90; Harold Locke, A *Bibliographical Catalogue of the Published Novels and Ballads of William Harrison Ainsworth* (London, 1925), pp. 9–12.

69. Ellis, I, 362–63; Nicoll, II, 312; Bleackley and Ellis, *Jack Sheppard*, pp. 92–94.

    Ellis does not mention the earlier Sheppard play by Moncrieff, but Nicoll (II, 349) records it at the Coburg, as the Victoria was then called, in April 1825.

70. As quoted in Ellis, I, 366.

71. *Letters*, I, 395.

72. *Athenaeum*, October 26, 1839, p. 803.

73. *Standard*, October 29, 1839, p. 1.

74. Ellis, I, 345–61.

75. *Examiner*, November 3, 1839, p. 691.

76. Ellis, I, 358. Malcolm Elwin also suspects Forster of pique because Ainsworth had disregarded his advice. *Victorian Wallflowers* (London, 1934), p. 192.

77. Forster, *Dickens*, p. 95; notes by J. W. T. Ley, pp. 101–2, n. 107; p. 128, n. 130.

78. Ellis, I, 359, 377. Ellis prints Forster's note about the matter but gives no date.

79. *Literary Gazette*, October 19, 1839, pp. 657–58; Ellis, I, 376, gives the *Literary World*; *Spectator*, October 26, 1839, pp. 1020–21.

80. *Tait's Edinburgh Magazine*, VIII n.s. (March 1841), 187; on the *Mirror*, Ellis, I, vi, 370; *Monthly Chronicle*, V (January 1840), 33–38 (March 1840), 219–22.

81. *Examiner*, June 28, 1840, p. 402.

82. *The Times*, July 7, 1840, as quoted in Bleackley and Ellis, *Jack Sheppard*, p. 106.

83. As quoted in Bleackley and Ellis, *Jack Sheppard*, p. 107.

84. *Examiner*, July 12, 1840, p. 434.

85. Camden Pelham, *Chronicles of Crime* (London, 1887), II, 563–83.

86. Ellis, II, 3–33.

87. [Francis Mahony] "The Cruel Murder of Old Father Prout by a Barber's Apprentice. A Legend of Modern Latherature," *Bentley's Miscellany*, XI (May 1842), 467–72.

88. *Fraser's Magazine*, XVIII (October 1838), 500.

89. Thackeray, *Letters*, I, 198. On *Pelham*, see I, 228.

90. As quoted by Ernest Boll, "The Author of Elizabeth Brownrigge," *Studies in Philology*, XXIX (January 1942), 83.

91. Harold S. Gulliver, *Thackeray's Literary Apprenticeship* (Valdosta, Ga., 1934), pp. 195–96. Mr. Gulliver reprints the article because he believes it written by Thackeray. According to Gordon N. Ray, most of the material in the later months of the *National Standard* was by Thackeray or James Hume. *Thackeray* (New York, 1955), I, 160–61. But the possibility remains that such an item as this might have been written by Maginn, who had been paid to do some editorial work for the paper.

92. Some examples: "A Word on the Annuals," *Fraser's Magazine*, XVI (December 1837), 760; review of Ernest Maltravers, XVII (January 1838), 85–89; "Miss Shum's Husband," XVII (January 1838), 39; "Half a Crown's Worth

of Cheap Knowledge," XVII (March 1838), 280; "Mr. Yellowplush's Ajew,"
XVII (August 1838), 195–200; "Passages from the Diary of the Late Dolly
Duster," XVIII (November 1838), 597; "Epistles to the Literati. No. XIII,"
XXI (January 1840), 71–78.

93. *Fraser's Magazine*, XIX (April 1839), 407.
94. *Frazer's Magazine*, XIX (May 1839), 618.
95. Thackeray, *Works*, Biographical Ed. (London, 1898), IV, 519–20. All citations
of Thackeray's works refer to this edition, unless some other is designated.
96. Radzinowicz, I, 212, n. The narrative most easily available is in *The Complete
Newgate Calendar*, III, 30–40.
    Thackeray's reference, near the end of the tale, to the account of the
ordinary, indicates that he used the Rev. John Villette's *Annals of Newgate*
(London, 1776), I, 394–428.
97. As Lionel Stevenson puts it, "His loathing for the Newgate Calendar school
had by now almost reached the stage of fascination." *The Showman of Vanity
Fair* (New York, 1947), p. 82.
98. *Works*, IV, 634–35.
99. *Works*, IV, 581.
100. *Works*, IV, 555–56.
101. Thackeray, *Works* (London, 1869), XXII, 165.
102. *Fraser's Magazine*, XXI (February 1840), 210.
103. *Fraser's Magazine*, XXI (February 1840), 211. *Catherine, etc.*, ed. George
Saintsbury ("The Oxford Thackeray," London, 1908), pp. 185–87. This passage occurs immediately before the last paragraph of the work.
104. "William Ainsworth and Jack Sheppard," *Fraser's*, XXI (February 1840),
227–45. For the attribution to Thackeray, see Thrall, p. 255. It is convincing,
but one or two details do not fit him.
105. "Hints for a History of Highwaymen," *Fraser's*, IX (March 1834), 279–87.
This review has been mentioned in connection with *Rookwood*. See p. 107,
above.
106. Not concerned solely with fiction, Thackeray twice in 1840 spoke vigorously
against capital punishment and public executions. The first utterance was in
"The Case of Peytel," in the *Paris Sketch Book*, published in July. (*Works*,
V, 209–34.) The second, "Going to See a Man Hanged," (*Fraser's*, XXII
[August 1840], 150–58), began thus: "X——, who had voted with Mr.
Ewart for the abolition of the punishment of death, was anxious to see the
effect on the public mind of an execution, and asked me to accompany him
to see Courvoisier killed." Deeply, bitterly impressed by the evil thing he
had seen, Thackeray used the starkest words, and he avoided a pen name. The
article was signed, uniquely, with his own initials, W.M.T. The effort of
William Ewart had been made in March. "X——" was Richard Monckton
Milnes. See Munford, *William Ewart*, pp. 103–4; also James Pope-Hennessy,
Monckton Milnes: The Years of Promise, 1809–1851 (New York, 1955), p.
130. Some eight years later, Thackeray witnessed the execution of the
Mannings in the company of Dickens.
107. "Essay on the Genius of George Cruikshank," *Westminster Review*, XXXIV
(June 1840), 1–60.
108. *The Times*, September 2, 1840. Reprinted in *Complete Works* of W. M.
Thackeray, XXV, *Literary Essays, Essays on Art* (New York, 1904), p. 239.

109. *Works* (New York, 1904), XXV, 233, 234.
110. "Hogarth, Smollett, and Fielding," *English Humorists of the Eighteenth Century, Works*, Biographical Ed., VII, 582.
111. *Fraser's Magazine*, XIX (April 1839), 408.
112. *Letters*, I, 421.
113. *Letters*, I, 432–33.

CHAPTER VI

1. *Spectator*, May 30, 1840, p. 519.
2. Frederick Marryat, *Japhet, in Search of a Father* (London, 1896), p. 303.
3. E. S. Turner, *Boys Will Be Boys*, rev. ed. (London, 1957).
   Margaret Dalziel, *Popular Fiction One Hundred Years Ago* (London, 1957). There are chapters on Salisbury Square fiction and on G. W. M. Reynolds. Richard D. Altick, *The English Common Reader*, pp. 289–93.
   There is also a chapter on "Salisbury Square and the Newgate Novel" in an unpublished work by Alec Lucas, "Studies in the Newgate Novel of Early Victorian England, 1830–1845," Harvard University doctoral dissertation, 1951.
4. Montague Summers, *A Gothic Bibliography* (London, 1941), pp. 146–59. A sample illustration from the *Mysteries* is given and an episode described in George H. Ford, *Dickens and His Readers*, pp. 78–79. Another illustration and circulation figures taken from Henry Mayhew may be seen in John W. Dodds, *The Age of Paradox* (New York, 1952), pp. 124–26.
5. *Examiner*, January 17, 1841, p. 35.
6. *Examiner*, August 30, 1840, p. 550.
7. This and the further extracts immediately after it are from unpublished portions of a letter from Bulwer to John Forster, in the Forster Collection, Victoria and Albert Museum. Bf3145 no. 100. The middle part of the letter, not presented here, was published in Lytton (1913), II, 85–88.
8. *Athenaeum*, January 16, 1841, pp. 45–46.
9. *Tait's Edinburgh Magazine*, VIII, n.s. (March 1841), 191.
10. *Examiner*, November 20, 1841, p. 738.
11. Bon Gaultier, "Illustrations of the Thieves' Literature—No. 1, Flowers of Hemp, or, the Newgate Garland," *Tait's Edinburgh Magazine*, VIII (April 1841), 215–23.
12. The date of 1841 is given for *The Drunkard's Progress* by Joshua Kunitz and Howard Haycraft, *British Authors of the Nineteenth Century* (New York, 1936), p. 519. In the *Cambridge Bibliography of English Literature*, the title is included in an undated list.
13. Coleman O. Parsons, "The Friendship of Theodore Martin and William Harrison Ainsworth," *Notes and Queries*, CLXVI (June 23, 1934), 435–37.
14. Bon Gaultier, "Lays of the Would-be Laureates," *Tait's Edinburgh Magazine*, X (May 1843), 273–76.
15. "A Lucullan Meditation" is included in W. E. Aytoun, *Poems*, ed. F. Page (Oxford, 1921), pp. 261–63.
16. John Butt and Kathleen Tillotson, *Dickens at Work* (London, 1957), p. 78.

Mrs. Tillotson also points out the germ of certain chapters of *Barnaby Rudge* in one of the *Sketches by Boz*.

17. Johnson, *Dickens*, I, 336–37. For the background of the message, see also *Dickens at Work*, pp. 82–84. Much the same material is in Mrs. Tillotson's introduction to *Barnaby Rudge*, New Oxford Illustrated Dickens (Oxford, 1954). Harold F. Holland, in "The Doer and the Deed: Theme and Pattern in *Barnaby Rudge*," *PMLA*, LXXIV (September 1959), 406–17, objects (wrongly, I think) to the "common view" of the social message of the novel but does single out the attitude toward capital punishment; however, the article is primarily an effective analysis of structure.

18. Butt and Tillotson, p. 86.

19. *Barnaby Rudge*, New Oxford Illustrated Dickens, pp. 567–68.

20. *Barnaby Rudge*, p. 584.

21. Johnson, *Dickens*, II, 589–90; 672.

22. Both books are noticed in *Tait's Edinburgh Magazine*, IX (January 1842), 63.

23. Jonathan Curling, *Janus Weathercock* (London, 1938); Charles Norman, *The Genteel Murderer* (New York, 1956).

24. Curling, pp. 258–60.

25. Lytton, 1913, II, 86.

26. Forster, *Dickens*, p. 132. Macready also recorded the incident. June 27, 1837. *Diaries*, I, 401–2. His date, not Forster's, is correct.

27. Curling, pp. 357–65.

28. "Poisoners, Living and Dead.—Arsenic Novels," *Punch*, VIII (January 30, 1845), 68.

29. *Lucretia*, New Knebworth Ed. (London, 1895), Preface to the first edition, p. 10.

30. Lytton, 1913, II, 86–88 n.; Curling, p. 313.

31. Lytton, 1913, II, 86, n. It is true that the *Examiner* (December 5, 1846, p. 773) spoke of the other criminal as a Frenchwoman. But this Frenchwoman is elusive. Such collections of French cases as I have been able to see do not provide a suitable original for Lucretia Clavering within the years Bulwer specified. He might, though, have had a narrative about a case that, like Wainewright's, never came to trial.

Mr. Curling (pp. 373–75) disbelieves the biographer and argues for a second criminal, the Frenchwoman. He takes Bulwer's statements literally, forgetting that there might be a reason for concealment; his evidence comes down to chiefly this, that Mrs. Wainewright, so far as existing documents show, had not the intellect which is ascribed to Lucretia in the novel.

Forster's remark in the *Examiner* cannot be taken to prove the existence of the Frenchwoman. It might be deliberate mythmaking, to assist Bulwer.

In the United States, in 1831–32, there was an alleged poisoner by the name of Lucretia Chapman; the name arouses expectations, but the details of the case destroy them. William Roughead describes it in *The Art of Murder* (New York, 1943), pp. 49–83, mentioning two earlier works which had printed an account of it. For details see *Celebrated Trials of All Countries and Remarkable Cases of Criminal Jurisprudence*, Selected by a Member of the Philadelphia Bar (Philadelphia, 1837), pp. 327–411.

So far as the dates are concerned, Bulwer might have seen this book before writing *Lucretia;* I think it unlikely. Except the name, there is nothing in the trial, nothing in the novel, to link Lucretia Chapman with the fictional Lucretia.

32. W. C. Hazlitt, as quoted in Curling, p. 369.
33. *Lucretia*, New Knebworth Ed., p. 31.
34. *Athenaeum*, December 5, 1846, pp. 1240–42.
35. *Examiner*, December 6, 1846, p. 772.
36. *Literary Gazette*, December 5, 1846, p. 1025.
37. Partially unpublished letter, [December 7, 1846], No. 39, in the volume 1846–50, Forster Collection, Victoria and Albert Museum, South Kensington. Further letters from this volume will be cited by date and number only. Bracketed dates were not in the text but were added, possibly by Forster.

    One paragraph of this letter ("I see it presumed elsewhere . . . the elder Ardworth, etc."), is excerpted and combined with parts of another letter in Lytton, 1913, II, 86–87.
38. Partially unpublished letter [December 9, 1846], No. 40. The published portions are in Lytton, 1913, II, 87–89.
39. *Examiner*, December 12, 1846, pp. 788–89; letter from Bulwer to Forster, [December 14, 1846], No. 41.
40. *Spectator*, December 12, 1846, p. 1190.
41. *The Times*, December 17, 1846, p. 7.
42. [December 18, 1846], letter No. 43. In this and the other letters, the spelling and punctuation are Bulwer's.
43. [December 20, 1846], letter No. 46. See also Lytton, 1913, II, 84–85, 90–91.
44. [December 24, 1846], letter No. 47.
45. *John Bull*, XXVI (December 26, 1846), 824.
46. *Morning Chronicle*, January 1, 1847, p. 6.
47. *Morning Herald*, January 1, 1847, p. 6.
48. [January 1, 1847], letter 51 and 52, single letter with postscript.
49. *Reynolds's Miscellany*, January 2, 1847, p. 141.
50. The neglect by the theatres seems strange, but I have come upon no title in Nicoll that indicates a *Lucretia* play. Equally strange in view of all that had happened, is the fact that Bulwer himself seems to have begun or drafted or made notes for one. In a letter from Forster to Bulwer, November 21, 1848, the following occurs: "Did you think of the Lucretia play when at Knebworth? I wish you would, and let me see it again." (Letter No. 43, Forster to Bulwer volume.)
51. *New Monthly Magazine*, n.s. LXXIX (January 1847), 124–31; *Bentley's Miscellany*, XXI (February 1847), 204–8.
52. *Fraser's Magazine*, XXXV (January 1847), 115.
53. *Fraser's Magazine*, XXXV (January 1847), 123. Thackeray mentions his article in a letter to Mrs. Norton, January 5, 1847. *Letters*, II, 263–64.
54. Labeled January, no day given, letter No. 53.
55. [January 1847], no day given, but probably written on a Tuesday, letter No. 54.
56. [January 28, 1847], letter No. 57.
57. *Athenaeum*, January 30, 1847, pp. 120–21.
58. Letter of February 20, 1847, Lytton, 1913, II, 93–94.
59. *Fraser's Magazine*, XXVII (May 1843), 524–25; XXI (February 1845), 221.

The latter article, on *Anti-Coningsby, or the New Generation Grown Old*, was suggested as perhaps Thackeray's by Harold S. Gulliver, *Thackeray's Literary Apprenticeship*, p. 86.

60. Thackeray had had an article on Laman Blanchard in *Fraser's* in March 1846, which placed him in opposition to Bulwer, Forster, and Dickens on a different matter, the dignity of professional authors; this had no connection with Newgate fiction, but the recurring argument about "the dignity of literature" was evidence of still another opposition of temperament and opinion between Thackeray and the authors of the crime novels. The controversy is described by Gordon Ray, in *Thackeray*, II, 136–38; and more closely examined by K. J. Fielding in "Thackeray and the 'Dignity of Literature,'" *Times Literary Supplement*, September 19 and September 26, 1958, pp. 536, 552.

61. *Punch*, I (August 7, 1841), 39. Ellis attributes the item to Thackeray. *Ainsworth*, I, 361.

62. *Punch*, II (February 12, 1842), 68.

63. *Punch*, II (February 26 and March 5, 1842), 82, 98; VIII (April 13, 1845), 177.

64. *Punch*, VI (January 20, 1844), 43, Thackeray; VI (March 23, 1844), 130, Thackeray; VII (December 14, 1844), 268, not identified; X (February 21, 1846), 94. This last, a trifle not previously identified, I attribute to Thackeray because it makes use of Carus' *Travels in England*, which he reviewed elsewhere (*Contributions to the Morning Chronicle*, ed. Gordon N. Ray [Urbana, Ill., 1955]), pp. 107–13). A week after the last item mentioned, on February 28, 1846, *Punch* printed Tennyson's famous retaliation against Bulwer, "The New Timon and the Poets." In *The New Timon*, a verse narrative, Bulwer had introduced topical satire on various matters, including Tennyson and his government pension and thus brought upon himself a reprisal more violent than the attack. So far as I know, the episode has no connection with the Newgate controversy. Thackeray wrote a neutral review of the *New Timon* for the *Morning Chronicle*, April 21, 1846 (*Contributions to the Morning Chronicle*, pp. 128–34).

65. Ellis, *Ainsworth*, II, 115–18; *Punch*, IX (July 5, 1845), 14.

66. Ray, *Thackeray*, I, 389.

67. *Vanity Fair*, No. II, February 1847, pp. 43–44.

68. *Vanity Fair*, No. II, February 1847, pp. 45–46.
The manuscript in the Pierpont Morgan Library contains two forms of Chapter VI, one in the earlier slanting hand, the other in the later upright hand but utilizing some bits of printed proof. (The bits of proof, incidentally, do not tally perfectly with the slant-hand manuscript; there must have been an intermediate version of this chapter.) Gordon Ray assigns "half a dozen chapters or more" in the earlier slanting hand to February–March 1845. *Thackeray* I, 384.

The passage quoted here exists in the later form of the chapter in manuscript. A slightly longer passage, different but making the same point, exists in the slant-hand version of the chapter, dating therefore from early 1845. The burlesques of styles, with minor variations, exist in both manuscript forms of the chapter.

69. Ray, *Thackeray*, I, 496, n. 3.

70. *Vanity Fair*, No. II, February 1847, p. 64.

71. *Vanity Fair*, No. III, March 1847, p. 72.
72. Ray, *Thackeray*, I, 386.
73. Ray, *Thackeray*, I, 391–92. One cannot agree with Mr. Ray that Aram's murder "was not merely palliated by Bulwer but actually justified." To say this is to go somewhat beyond Thackeray. Bad as the book was, it was not bad in that way.
74. Geoffrey Tillotson argues, rightly enough, that moral commentary was no new thing in Thackeray's work. *Thackeray the Novelist* (Cambridge, 1954), pp. 211–15. The stance of the commentator does indeed seem natural to him, and his observation of the flaws of the Newgate novels probably influenced him, from the time he began to notice them, in a direction he was inclined to by temperament. Nevertheless, the circumstances detailed here point to renewed attention on Thackeray's part at a crucial time and to a consequent emphasis on commentary in *Vanity Fair*.
75. Ray, *Thackeray*, I, 398, 497, n. 31.
76. *Vanity Fair*, No. III, March 1847, p. 76.
77. *Letters*, II, 270–71. The letter concludes with a postscript which indicates that Thackeray had delicately suggested that his name might be put up by Hallam at the Athenaeum, and that Fonblanque had thereupon offered to recommend him also.
78. Ray, *Thackeray*, I, 243.
79. Thackeray had been anticipated, perhaps not surprisingly, by some Cambridge undergraduate in 1836. Archibald Shepperson, *The Novel in Motley* (Cambridge, Mass., 1936), Appendix, p. 253.
80. Ray, *Thackeray*, I, 393. But *A Word to the Public*, whose appearance Ray attributes to the same cause, had preceded the parody.
81. The quarrel and the reconciliation dinner must surely be the reason for the omission of Dickens from *Punch's Prize Novelists*. Dickens, Forster's intermediary, stated his low opinion of the parodies in the course of the conferences, and gave the dinner on June 21. After all this, Thackeray could not include the man with whom he had had his legs *sub iisdem trabibus*. This seems a more likely explanation than those suggested by Edgar Johnson, *Dickens*, II, 615.
82. The letters in which the quarrel may be followed are in Thackeray, *Letters*, II, 294–304. Both Edgar Johnson (*Dickens*, II, 314–15) and Gordon Ray (*Thackeray*, I, 288; II, 135–36), not knowing of Bulwer's unsent challenge, make less of "George de Barnwell" and more of some caricatures Thackeray had made. More is made of them, indeed, than the letters seem to justify. Forster himself writes that the report of the caricatures came to him long ago, though he mentions them now, as a stick to beat Thackeray with. Forster, who cannot remember saying the offending words, thinks caricatures may have been talked about, apparently; and the others take it up from him. Then Taylor completes the comedy by telling Forster that he has been thinking about the wrong conversation altogether—Forster said "false as hell" at an earlier time, when they were on the way to dinner at Macready's. The caricatures, therefore, though brought into the quarrel, were not the beginning of it.
83. Thackeray, *Letters*, II, 308–9.
84. Ray, *Thackeray*, I, 243–44; Thackeray, *Letters*, III, 278.
85. "The Thieves' Literature of France," as it was later called, appeared in the

Foreign Quarterly Review, XXI (July 1843), 231–50. In this review of the first six volumes of Sue's *Mysteries*, published in Paris, Thackeray repeated his objections against vice and crime made palatable. Oddly enough, at an earlier time he had thought of translating Sue's book (*Letters*, II, 139, 159). The cartoon mentioning Sue and Dumas: "Literature at a Stand," *Punch*, XII (March 13, 1847), 113. Thackeray had done an article on cheap publications, "Half a Crown's Worth of Cheap Knowledge," *Fraser's*, XVII (March 1838), 27–90, but this was before Reynolds' lurid serials began.

86. Stevenson, *The Showman of Vanity Fair*, p. 63. Thackeray's newspaper report of a meeting at which Reynolds spoke was neutral in tone, but a later allusion to it was satirical. *Thackeray's Contributions to the Morning Chronicle*, pp. 192–98, 194, n.

87. Dalziel, pp. 47–50.

88. As quoted in the *Examiner*, November 6, 1847, p. 709.

89. *Examiner*, October 30, 1847, p. 691. This was the first issue of the paper to appear under the editorship of Forster; but since Fonblanque was to contribute something each week, one is inclined to attribute this remark to him. Forster became editor on October 27, 1847, according to Richard Renton, *John Forster and His Friendships* (London, 1912), p. 145.

90. *London Labour and the London Poor*, Extra Volume (London, 1864), p. 221. The two following quotations are from pp. 302 and 347, respectively.

91. *Report* from the Select Committee of the House of Commons on Criminal and Destitute Juveniles . . . Ordered by the House of Commons to be printed, 24 June, 1852, Appendix 3 C, pp. 435–37.

92. *Report*, 1852, Appendix No. 2, "Juvenile Delinquency, Liverpool," pp. 408–24.

93. The potentialities were sometimes denied. John Stuart Mill could write in the thirties, Richard Stang reminds us, that fiction was "an inferior genre because it could depict *only* outward things and not the inner man." *The Theory of the Novel in England, 1850–1870* (New York, 1959), p. 9. Mr. Stang goes on (pp. 11–14) to praise Bulwer's ambitious view of the novel and his essay of 1838, "Art in Fiction."

BIBLIOGRAPHY

I NOVELS

Ainsworth, William Harrison. *Jack Sheppard*, Windsor Ed. London, 1902.
———. *Rookwood*, Everyman's Library. London, 1931.
Borrow, George. *Lavengro: The Scholar, the Gypsy, the Priest*, Everyman's Library. London, 1906.
———. *The Romany Rye*, Everyman's Library. London, 1931.
Bulwer, Edward Lytton. *The Disowned*, Library Ed. 2 vols. Edinburgh, 1863.
———. *Eugene Aram*. 3 vols. London, 1832.
———. *Eugene Aram*, New Knebworth Ed. London, 1895.
———. *Lucretia, or the Children of Night*. 3 vols. London, 1846.
———. *Lucretia, or the Children of Night*, New Knebworth Ed. London, 1895.
———. *Night and Morning*, New Knebworth Ed. London, 1895.
———. *Paul Clifford*. 3 vols. London, 1830.
———. *Paul Clifford*, in *Works*, Knebworth Ed. London, 1874.
———. *Pelham*, New Knebworth Ed. London, 1895.
Bulwer, Mrs. Rosina. *Chevely, or the Man of Honour*. 3 vols. London, 1838.
Burke, Thomas. *Murder at Elstree, or Mr. Thurtell and His Gig*. London, 1936.
Clive, Caroline. *Paul Ferroll: A Tale*. London, 1929.
Crowe, Catherine. *Susan Hopley, or Circumstantial Evidence*. Edinburgh, 1842.
Dickens, Charles. *Barnaby Rudge*, New Oxford Illustrated Dickens. Oxford, 1954.
———. *Martin Chuzzlewit*, New Oxford Illustrated Dickens. Oxford, 1951.
———. *Oliver Twist*, Oxford Illustrated Dickens. Oxford, 1949.
———. *Oliver Twist*. Vol. III, *Works*, 36 vols. New York, 1911.
———. *Pickwick Papers*, New Oxford Illustrated Dickens. Oxford, 1949.
Gaspey, Thomas. *The History of George Godfrey*. 3 vols. London, 1828.
———. *Richmond, or Scenes in the Life of a Bow Street Officer, Drawn up from His Private Memoranda*. 3 vols. London, 1827.
Godwin, William. *Caleb Williams*. New York, 1926.
———. *Fleetwood, or the New Man of Feeling*. London, 1832.
Holcroft, Thomas. *Memoirs of Bryan Perdue*. 3 vols. London, 1805.
Hook, Theodore. *Gilbert Gurney*. London, 1850.
———. *Sayings and Doings: A Series of Sketches from Life*. 3 vols. London, 1824.
Hugo, Victor. *Bug Jargal, Le Dernier jour d'un condamné, Claude Gueux. Oeuvres Complètes*. 27 vols. Paris: Nelson, n. d.
Joyce, James. *Ulysses*. New York, 1942.
Lister, T. H. *Arlington*. 3 vols. London, 1832.
Lytton, Edward George Earle Lytton Bulwer, first Baron Lytton of Knebworth, 1803–73. His works are listed under BULWER.
Marryat, Frederick. *Japhet in Search of a Father*. Vol. VIII, *Works*, 24 vols. London, 1895–96.
———. *Joseph Rushbrook, or the Poacher*. Vol. XV, *Works*, 24 vols. London, 1895–96.
———. *Snarleyyow, or the Dog Fiend*. Vol. IX, *Works*, 24 vols. London, 1895–96.

257

Mudford, William. *Stephen Dugard.* 3 vols. London, 1840.

Peacock, Thomas Love. *Crotchet Castle.* Vol. IV, *Works,* ed. M. F. B. Brett-Smith and C. E. Jones, Halliford Ed. 10 vols. London, 1924–34.

Sherwood, Mary Martha. *History of the Fairchild Family,* in Vol. II, *Works,* Harpers' Stereotype Ed. 16 vols. New York, 1834–58.

Smith, Horace. *Gale Middleton, a Story of the Present Day.* 3 vols. London, 1833.

Surr, Thomas Skinner. *The Magic of Wealth.* 2 vols. Philadelphia, 1815.

————. *Russell, or the Reign of Fashion.* 3 vols. London, 1830.

————. *A Winter in London, or Sketches of Fashion,* 2nd ed. 3 vols. London, 1806.

Thackeray, William Makepeace. *Catherine, etc.,* ed. with intro. George Saintsbury. London, 1908. ("The Oxford Thackeray.")

————. *Sultan Stork and Other Stories and Sketches by William Makepeace Thackeray,* ed. R. H. Shepherd. London, 1887.

————. *Works,* with biographical introductions by his daughter, Anne Ritchie. 13 vols. London, 1898–99.

————. *Works,* ed. W. P. Trent and J. B. Henneman. 14 vols. New York, 1904.

Trollope, Frances. *Michael Armstrong, the Factory Boy.* London, 1840.

Whitehead, Charles. *Autobiography of a Notorious Legal Functionary,* 4th ed. London: Charles Daly, n.d.

————. *Richard Savage, a Romance of Real Life.* 3 vols. London, 1842.

II WORKS OTHER THAN FICTION

Altick, Richard D. *The English Common Reader: A Social History of the Mass Reading Public, 1800–1900.* Chicago, 1957.

Ash, Arty, and Julius Day. *Immortal Turpin.* London, 1948.

Aytoun, William E. *Poems,* ed. F. Page. Oxford, 1921.

Ballantine, William. *Some Experiences of a Barrister's Life.* New York, 1882.

Barham, R. H. *Ingoldsby Legends.* Oxford, 1921.

Bell, H. T. Mackenzie. *A Forgotten Genius: Charles Whitehead.* London, 1884.

Bentham, Jeremy. *Works,* ed. John Bowring. 11 vols. Edinburgh, 1843–59.

Bleackley, Horace. *Jack Sheppard,* with an Epilogue on Jack Sheppard in Literature and Drama, a Bibliography, a Note on Jonathan Wild, and a Memoir of Horace Bleackley, by S. M. Ellis. Edinburgh, 1933. ("Notable British Trials.")

————. *The Trial of Henry Fauntleroy and Other Famous Trials for Forgery.* Edinburgh, 1924. ("Notable British Trials.")

Block, Andrew. *The English Novel, 1740–1850, a Bibliography.* London, 1939.

Borrow, George. *Celebrated Trials and Remarkable Cases of Criminal Jurisprudence from the Earliest Records to the Year, 1825,* ed. Edward Hale Bierstadt. London, 1928.

————. *The Zincali, an Account of the Gypsies of Spain.* London, 1907.

Boswell, James. *The Hypochondriack,* ed. Margery Bailey. 2 vols. Stanford, Cal., 1928.

————. *Life of Samuel Johnson,* ed. G. B. Hill, rev. L. F. Powell. 6 vols. Oxford, 1934.

————. *Private Papers of James Boswell from Malahide Castle,* ed. Geoffrey Scott. 18 vols. Mt. Vernon, N. Y., 1928–34.

Bridie, James. *A Sleeping Clergyman, and Other Plays.* London, 1934.

Brightfield, Myron S. *Theodore Hook and His Novels*. Cambridge, Mass., 1928.

Browning, Elizabeth Barrett. *Letters of Elizabeth Barrett Browning*, ed. Frederic G. Kenyon. London, 1897.

——. *Letters of Elizabeth Barrett Browning addressed to Richard Hengist Horne*. Preface and memoir by R. H. Stoddard. New York, 1877.

Bulwer, Edward Lytton. *England and the English*, in *Works*, Knebworth Ed. London, 1874.

——. Letters of 1841, 1844, 1846, and 1847 to John Forster, unpublished. Forster Collection, Victoria and Albert Museum, South Kensington.

——. *A Word to the Public*, included with *Lucretia*, Library Ed. Edinburgh, 1863.

Butt, John and Kathleen Tillotson. *Dickens at Work*. London, 1957.

Carter, John. *New Paths in Book Collecting*. London, 1934.

Celebrated Trials of All Countries and Remarkable Cases of Criminal Jurisprudence, Selected by a Member of the Philadelphia Bar. Philadelphia, 1837.

Chandler, Frank W. *The Literature of Roguery*. 2 vols. Boston, 1907.

Chitty, Joseph. *Practical Treatise on the Criminal Law*, 3rd American ed., from the 2nd and last London ed. 3 vols. Springfield, Mass., 1836.

Colquhoun, Patrick. *Treatise on the Police of the Metropolis*, 6th ed. London, 1800.

Complete Newgate Calendar, ed. G. T. Crook. 5 vols. London, 1926.

Curling, Jonathan. *Janus Weathercock*. London, 1938.

Curtis, James. *The Murder of Maria Marten*, ed. Jeanne and Norman Mackenzie. New York, 1948.

Dalziel, Margaret. *Popular Fiction One Hundred Years Ago*. London, 1957.

Debrett's Baronetage of England, rev. and cont. G. W. Collen. London, 1840.

DeQuincey, Thomas. *Collected Writings*, ed. David Masson. 14 vols. London, 1896–97.

Dickens, Charles. *The Letters of Charles Dickens*, ed. Walter Dexter. 3 vols. Bloomsbury, 1938.

——. *Sketches by Boz*, New Oxford Illustrated Dickens. Oxford, 1957.

Disher, Maurice Willson. *Blood and Thunder; Mid-Victorian Melodrama and Its Origins*. London, 1949.

Dixon, Hepworth. *John Howard and the Prison World of Europe*. New York, 1850.

Dodds, John W. *The Age of Paradox, a Biography of England, 1841–1851*. New York, 1952.

Eaton, Horace A. *Thomas DeQuincey*. New York, 1936.

Ellis, S. M. *William Harrison Ainsworth and His Friends*. 2 vols. London, 1911.

Elwin, Malcolm. *Victorian Wallflowers*. London, 1954.

Farmer, J. S. *Slang and its Analogues*. 7 vols. London, 1890.

Fawcett, F. Dubrez. *Dickens the Dramatist*. London, 1952.

Fitzgerald, S. J. Adair. *Dickens and the Drama*. New York, 1910.

Fonblanque, Albany. *England under Seven Administrations*. 3 vols. London, 1837.

Ford, George H. *Dickens and His Readers*. Princeton, 1955.

Forster, John. *Life of Charles Dickens*, ed. J. W. T. Ley. New York, 1928.

——. Letter to Bulwer, November 21, 1848, unpublished. Forster Collection, Victoria and Albert Museum, South Kensington.

Gagey, Edmond M. *Ballad Opera*. New York, 1937.

Gay, John. *Poetical Works*, ed. G. C. Faber. Oxford, 1926.

Goddard, Henry. *Memoirs of a Bow Street Runner*, intro. Patrick Pringle. London, 1956.

Godwin, William. *An Enquiry Concerning Political Justice*, ed. Raymond A. Preston. 2 vols. New York, 1926.

Grant, James. *The Great Metropolis*, 2nd ser. 2 vols. London, 1837.

Griffiths, Arthur. *Chronicles of Newgate*. 2 vols. London, 1884.

Gulliver, Harold S. *Thackeray's Literary Apprenticeship*. Valdosta, Ga., 1934.

Haycraft, Howard. *Murder for Pleasure*. New York, 1941.

Hazlitt, William. *Works*, ed. P. P. Howe, after the ed. of A. R. Waller and Arnold Glover. 21 vols. London, 1930–32.

Hibbert, Christopher. *The Road to Tyburn: The Story of Jack Sheppard and the Eighteenth Century London Underworld*. Cleveland, 1957.

Holdsworth, Sir William. *A History of English Law*. 13 vols. London, 1920–52.

Hood, Thomas. *Poetical Works*. Oxford, 1911.

Hooker, Kenneth W. *The Fortunes of Victor Hugo in England*. New York, 1938.

Hooper, W. Eden. *A History of Newgate and the Old Bailey*. London, 1935.

Horne, R. H. *A New Spirit of the Age*. Oxford, 1907. ("World's Classics.")

House, Humphry. *The Dickens World*. Oxford, 1941.

Jerdan, William. *Autobiography of William Jerdan*. 4 vols. London, 1853.

Jerrold, Blanchard. *Life of George Cruikshank*. London, 1883.

Johnson, Edgar. *Charles Dickens, His Tragedy and Triumph*. 2 vols. New York, 1952.

Knapp, William I. *Life, Writings, and Correspondence of George Borrow*. 2 vols. New York, 1899.

Lamb, Charles, and Mary Lamb. *Letters*, ed. E. V. Lucas. 2 vols. London, 1912.

Lindsay, Jack. *Charles Dickens, a Biographical and Critical Study*. London, 1950.

Locke, Harold. *A Bibliographical Catalogue of the Published Novels and Ballads of William Harrison Ainsworth*. London, 1925.

Lucas, Alec. "Studies in the Newgate Novel of Early Victorian England, 1830–1845." Unpublished doctoral dissertation, Harvard University, Cambridge, Mass., 1951.

Lytton, Edward George Earle Lytton Bulwer, first Baron Lytton of Knebworth, 1803–73. His works are listed under BULWER.

Lytton, Edward Robert Bulwer, first Earl of Lytton, 1831–91. *The Life, Letters, and Literary Remains of Edward Bulwer, Lord Lytton, by His Son*. 2 vols. London, 1883.

Lytton, Victor Alexander George Robert, second Earl of Lytton, 1876–1947. *Life of Edward Bulwer, First Lord Lytton*. 2 vols. London, 1913.

Maccoby, Simon. *English Radicalism, 1832–1852*. London, 1935.

Macready, W. C. *The Diaries of William Macready*, ed. William Toynbee. 2 vols. London, 1912.

Madan, Martin. *Thoughts on Executive Justice*, 2nd ed. London, 1785.

Martineau, Harriet. *A History of England during the Thirty Years' Peace, 1816–1846*. 4 vols. London, 1877.

Mayhew, Henry. *London Labour and the London Poor*. 3 vols. and "Extra" vol. London, 1864.

Messac, Regis. *Le Detective novel et l'influence de la pensée scientifique*. Paris, 1929.

Milbanke, Ralph, Earl of Lovelace. *Astarte*, ed. Mary, Countess of Lovelace. New York, 1921.

Munford, W. A. *William Ewart, M.P., 1798–1869: Portrait of a Radical*. London, 1960.

Murch, A. E. *Development of the Detective Novel*. New York, 1958.

Nicoll, Allardyce. *A History of Nineteenth Century Drama, 1800–1850*. 2 vols. Cambridge, 1930.

Norman, Charles. *The Genteel Murderer*. New York, 1956.

Old Bailey Experience. By the Author of *A Schoolmaster's Experience in Newgate*. London, 1833.

Paul, G. Kegan. *William Godwin, His Friends and Contemporaries*. Boston, 1876.

Payn, James. *Some Literary Recollections*. New York, 1884.

Pelham, Camden [pseud.] *Chronicles of Crime, or the New Newgate Calendar*. 2 vols. London, 1887.

Phillips, Walter C. *Dickens, Reade, and Collins, Sensation Novelists*. New York, 1919.

Poetry of "The Anti-Jacobin," ed. Charles Edmonds, 3rd ed. New York, 1890.

Pope-Hennessy, James. *Monckton Milnes: The Years of Promise, 1809–1851*. New York, 1955.

Pope-Hennessy, Una. *Charles Dickens*. New York, 1946.

Porter, G. R. *The Progress of the Nation in Its Various Social and Economical Relations from the Beginning of the Nineteenth Century to the Present Time*. 4 vols. London, 1843.

Pritchett, V. S. *The Living Novel*. New York, 1947.

Punch's Real History, ill. George Cruikshank. 3rd ed. London, 1844.

Radzinowicz, Leon. *A History of the English Criminal Law and Its Administration from 1750*. 3 vols. New York, 1948–57.

Ray, Gordon N. *Thackeray*. 2 vols. New York, 1955–58.

Renton, Richard. *John Forster and His Friendships*. London, 1912.

Reynolds, G. W. M. *Mysteries of the Court of London*. 20 vols. Boston: ptd. for the Oxford Society, n.d.

Romilly, Samuel. *Memoirs of the Life of Sir Samuel Romilly*, written by himself, with a selection from his correspondence edited by his sons. 3 vols. London, 1840.

Roughead, William. *The Art of Murder*. New York, 1943.

———. *The Trial of Burke and Hare*. 3rd ed. Edinburgh, 1948. ("Notable British Trials.")

Rousseau, Jean-Jacques. *Oeuvres complètes*, édition de Ch. Lahure. 8 vols. Paris, 1856–58.

Sadleir, Michael. *Bulwer, a Panorama. I. Edward and Rosina, 1803–1836*. Boston, 1931.

———. *Nineteenth Century Fiction, a Bibliographical Record Based on His Own Collection*. 2 vols. London, 1951.

Scatcherd, Norrisson. *Memoirs of the Celebrated Eugene Aram*. London, 1832.

———. *"Gleanings" after Eugene Aram, at Knaresborough*. London, 1836.

Scholes, Percy A. *The Great Dr. Burney*. 2 vols. Oxford, 1948.

Schultz, William E. *Gay's "Beggar's Opera": Its Content, History, and Influence*. New Haven, 1923.

Select Committee of the House of Commons on Capital Punishment, 1929–1930. *Report*. London, 1931.

Select Committee of the House of Commons on Criminal and Destitute Juveniles, 1852. *Report*. London, 1852.

Shepperson, Archibald. *The Novel in Motley*. Cambridge, Mass., 1936.

Shorter, Clement K. *George Borrow and His Circle*. London, 1919.

Smith, John Thomas. *A Book for a Rainy Day: Recollections of the Events of the Years 1766–1833*, ed. Wilfred Whitten. London, 1905.

Spaeth, Sigmund. *Read 'em and Weep, the Songs You Forgot to Remember*. New York, 1935.

Stang, Richard. *The Theory of the Novel in England, 1850–1870*. New York, 1959.

Stephen, Sir James Fitzjames. *A History of the Criminal Law of England*. 3 vols. London, 1883.

Stevenson, Lionel. *The Showman of Vanity Fair*. New York, 1947.

Summers, Montague. *A Gothic Bibliography*. London, 1941.

Swift, Jonathan. *Poems*, ed. Harold Williams. Oxford, 1937.

Thackeray, W. M. *Contributions to the "Morning Chronicle,"* ed. Gordon N. Ray. Urbana, Ill., 1955.

————. *Letters and Private Papers of William Makepeace Thackeray*, ed. Gordon N. Ray. 4 vols. Cambridge, Mass., 1945–46.

Thrall, Miriam M. H. *Rebellious "Fraser's": Nol Yorke's Magazine in the Days of Maginn, Thackeray, and Carlyle*. New York, 1934.

Tillotson, Geoffrey. *Thackeray the Novelist*. Cambridge, 1954.

Tillotson, Kathleen. See BUTT, JOHN.

Trilling, Lionel. *The Opposing Self*. New York, 1955.

Turner, Edward S. *Boys Will Be Boys*, rev. ed. London, 1957.

Vidocq, Eugene François. *Les Vrais mémoires de Vidocq*, ed. Jean Savant. Paris, 1950.

————. *Memoirs of Vidocq, Principal Agent of the French Police until 1827, and Now Proprietor of the Paper Manufactory at St. Mandé*. 4 vols. London, 1828–29.

Villette, John. *Annals of Newgate, or Malefactors' Register*. 4 vols. London, 1776.

Watson, Eric R. *Eugene Aram: His Life and Trial*. Philadelphia, 1913. ("Notable English [sic] Trials.")

————. *The Trial of Thurtell and Hunt*. Edinburgh, 1920. ("Notable British Trials.")

Wilson, Edmund. *The Wound and the Bow*. Boston, 1941.

Wölchken, Fritz. *Der Literarische Mord: Eine Untersuchung über die englische und amerikanische Detektivliteratur*. Nürnberg, 1953.

Wordsworth, William, and Dorothy Wordsworth. *Letters of William and Dorothy Wordsworth: The Later Years*, ed. Ernest de Selincourt. 3 vols. Oxford, 1939.

Yates, Edmund. *Memoirs of a Man of the World*. New York, 1885.

INDEX

This manuscript was edited by Barbara Woodward. The book was designed by S. R. Tenenbaum. Photographs of illustrations were made by Joseph Klima, Jr. The typeface for the text is Mergenthaler Linotype Electra designed by W. A. Dwiggins, in 1939. Garamond, the display face, was cut by American Type Founders in 1917.

The book is printed on S. D. Warren Paper Company's Olde Style Antique and bound in Joanna Mills, Parchment cloth. Manufactured in the United States of America.